THE COAST ROAD

The Coast Road – A 3,000-Mile Journey Round the Edge of England is Paul Gogarty's second English travelogue. The first, *The Water Road – A Narrowboat Odyssey Through England,* was published by Robson Books in 2002.

Praise for The Water Road

Gogarty has a sharp eye for character and his warm-hearted book proves a triumph of the romantic spirit, a labour of love among the slow-moving, quick-witted narrow-boaters of England. This world is evoked with wit and a wealth of lively anecdotage by a writer who is always good company.' Roger Deakin, the *Daily Telegraph*

Paul Gogarty manages brilliantly to convey a boatman's total euphoria in his delightful account of a four-month narrowboat idyll spent pootling along the 900 miles of central England's inland waterways known as the Cut . . . his enthusiasm bounces off every page and I was completely mesmerised.'
Val Hennessy, Critic's Choice in the *Daily Mail*

'. . . entertaining, informative and thought-provoking . . .
The book is a classic.'
Margaret Cornish, *Waterways World*

'His tale is a compelling contrast of light and shade populated by a peculiar cast of characters of almost Dickensian eccentricity.'
Morgan Falconer, *Ham & High*

'Since Rolt, it would be reasonably true to say that there has been no one who has written a successful account of a voyage round canals which has captured their essence, recorded the lives of those on the Cut and Bank and seized the popular imagination. But all this could change with the publication of Paul Gogarty's *The Water Road* . . . It is Gogarty's ability to write intimately – with no holds barred – about all he sees and meets that makes the book a fascinating read.'
Tim Coghlan, *Canal & Riverboat*

THE COAST ROAD

A 3,000 mile journey round

the edge of England

PAUL GOGARTY

ROBSON BOOKS

First published in Great Britain in 2004 by Robson Books, The Chrysalis Building, Bramley Road, London, W10 6SP

An imprint of Chrysalis Books Group plc

British Library Cataloguing in Publication Data
A catalogue record for this title is available from the British Library.

ISBN 1 86105 726 1

Typeset by SX composing DTP, Rayleigh, Essex
Printed and bound in Great Britain by
Creative Print & Design (Wales), Ebbw Vale

Contents

To my parents – Pat and Joan Gogarty –
and to my sister Lynn and brother Patrick.

Acknowledgements

I'm grateful to all the characters that appear in the book and made the journey what it was. Thanks too to Swift for providing me with my most reliable steed, the Sundance G306. Visitengland and the British Holiday & Home Parks Association provided me with invaluable assistance during the trip, as did many local councils, tourist boards and tourist information centres. Penny Johns at South Hams, Mike Chadwick in Blackpool, Joan Turnbull in Northumberland and Peter Joyner in North Norfolk are deserving of particularly large drinks in this respect. Thanks to my agent Laura Susijn and to both Susanna Abse and Nick Crane for reading the manuscript and offering sound advice.

The list of other individuals I'm indebted to is long, and no doubt should be longer (to those missing I can only plead senility as defence): Trudi Dunlop, Emily Grubb and Helen Coop at Bronwyn Gold Blyth and Associates; Helen Morley of the White Agency; Andy Pietrasik at the *Guardian*; Nigel Richardson of the *Daily Telegraph*; Jo Roberts for Margate Voices; Roy and Tina Dunlop at Hyde; Phil Wyburne Browne, Senior Custodian at Dover Castle; Mel Wrigley of White Cliffs Countryside Project; Simon Ovenden at White Cliffs National Trust; Julian Browne at *Reader's Digest* for the copy of the irreplaceable, sadly out of print, *Illustrated Guide to Britain's Coast*; Nick Ewbank at Folkestone's Metropole Gallery; Art Hewitt and Simon Bolton at Strange Cargo; Owen Leyshon at Romney Marsh Countryside Project; the Walpole Bay Hotel; Julie Larner at Migrant Helpline; Glenda Clarke of Brighton Walks; Richard Baker at Brighton's Grand Hotel; Mick McCorley at the Salvation Army in Gosport and Alan Smith for finding my camera; George Malcolmson at Gosport Royal Navy Submarine Museum; Shaun Garner at Russell-Cotes Museum, Bournemouth;

Louise Night at The Imperial, Torquay and Peter Gibbs the hotel's PR; Malcolm Darch of the Salcombe Maritime Museum; Frank Smith, ex-Salcombe coxswain; Deborah Clarke and Tony Orchard of Burgh Island; Colin Richards at Gara Rock Hotel; Lesley Brunning at the Ship Inn, Mayo; Brian Dudley Stamp at Bude; Sarah Durnford May at Blackpool Pleasure Beach; Charles Crane for his overview of Maryport; Peter Ward and the Echoes of Art Deco trail in Morecambe; Derek Sharman, Berwick-upon-Tweed guide; Barry Mead at the Woodhorn Colliery; Ken Proud at Bempton Cliffs RSPB Nature Reserve; Andrew Fox at Grimsby's National Fishing Heritage Centre; Chris Baron at Butlin's Skegness; Tim Lidstone-Scott of Peddars Way; Steve Rowland at Titchfield RSPB; Glenn Ogilvie at Thorpeness; Doreen Raynor, Felixstowe historian; Andy Russer of the Harwich Preservation Society; and Mike Baird at Clacton Pier.

'The Gods do not subtract from the allotted span of men's lives the
hours spent in fishing.'
Sign in Lyme Regis harbour

'The strangest country I ever visited was England: but I visited it at a
very early age and so became a little queer myself.'
GK Chesterton, *Autobiography* (1936)

'England is the paradise of individuality, eccentricity, heresy,
anomalies, hobbies and humours.'
George Santayana, *Soliloquies in England* (1922)

'The only real voyage of discovery consists not in seeking new
landscapes, but in having new eyes.'
Marcel Proust

A low rumble of thunder
a leviathan stirring fathoms deep.

6 a.m. dawn trips on a storm
blowing in from the Atlantic and scurries
back in its cave
leaving night to pick over the day.

Above the hieroglyphs of fishermen
the neat mnemonic of a skylark
following its songline, singing
its *laus perennis* to the English coast.

Introduction

The highest temperature ever experienced in Britain was recorded the summer I drove 2,800 miles round the edge of England. Things were changing and everyone knew it. Sure, locals continued to be concerned about coastal erosion, the demise of fishing and their villages becoming London's un-gated retirement home. But there was something else in the air. We had arrived at the beginning of the end. Within our children's lifetime, if not our own, the British coastline, and our way of life, would change for ever.

After two thousand years of land reclamation, we have finally accepted the inevitable and embarked on a programme of managed retreats, allowing the sea to take back swathes of coast. Rising water levels and bigger storm surges are just two of the sentences wreaked upon us by the gods for ripping open the ozone layer and treating our home planet like bad house guests. In the galaxy of global-warming doomsday scenarios currently occupying our scientists, the one gathering ever more support sees the gods upping the stakes further and switching off the conveyor belt of the Gulf Stream. As a result, in ten, twenty or a hundred years, Britain may well plunge into the kind of Arctic conditions our latitude deserves – three months of snow annually, ice floes off the coast and no Punch and Judy on Weymouth Beach.

The coast has always felt the wind of change first: Christianity, slaves, Romans, Normans and asylum seekers in the Southeast; American-imported 45s and albums in the Liverpool docks. We live between America and the Continent, not quite possessing either the easy mobility of the former nor the rootedness of the latter. The demographics of our restless island have changed in the past thirty years as never before and now we are about to see unprecedented physical change.

My summer journey round the English littoral in that quintessential 21st-century charabanc, the motorhome, was to be both a celebration of Englishness and an inventory before irrevocable change. Its Dickensian cast includes a druid high priest with Stonehenge in his garden, Somalian asylum seekers, a family-planning pioneer with a predilection for nude sunbathing, a centenarian white-knuckle rider, the Wild Man of Bowls (isn't that an oxymoron?), Dracula, a man who spends three months a year holidaying at Butlin's Skegness, a professor of Punch and Judy, a Jewish bookie who once knocked out Oswald Mosley, and fifty George Formbys who gallop through more innuendo in two minutes than Benny Hill managed in a lifetime.

Paint a picture of your own seaside . . . a kissing-gate, perhaps leading from a field edged with red poppies? High cliffs, crowned with mustard gorse or delicate pink thrift, making a swallow dive to the sea. No? A thatched village beside a stream leading to a harbour perfumed with kelp and brine? Five miles of empty sands flanked by mosaic marshland?

As an island race, we are all suckled by the sea, and whatever the particulars of the image seared on our memory, inside each of us there is a seaside all of our own. We carry it with us like the buckets of sand we once used to build doomed castles. Caught in the massive acceleration of lifestyles and increasingly itinerant lives, we relocate ever more frequently. But still that seaside marks us. The childhood day trip or week-long holiday captured in a photograph becomes an Avalon in adulthood. For the English, the Balearics and the Caribbean are distractions. The real beach is the one on our home shore.

My own snapshot is of a man, circa late 1950s, weaving a lobster pot on the beach at Mevagissey. Dressed in a ribbed crew-neck sweater, lips pursed with concentration beneath a woollen pom-pom, he is using his thumb to spring the cane. Two kids watch intently, drinking in learning. One boy, hands in pockets, secretly mimics the man's every move. The other, younger, boy sits open-mouthed on a finished pot that bears testimony to the resilience and strength of the man's handiwork. Short-back-and-sides children, scuffed-knee children, out-and-about adventuring children. My brother and I on holiday on a beach somewhere in England.

The sea shapes us, separates us, defines us. An island race. A race of islanders against the rest.

'This fortress built by Nature for herself
Against infection and the hand of war,
This happy breed of men, this little world,
This precious stone set in the silver sea,
Which serves it in the office of a wall
Or as a moat defensive to a house,
Against the envy of less happier lands . . .'

William Shakespeare, *Richard II*

'Brighton . . . is still very gay and full of balls.'
Samuel Rogers letter to Thomas Moore (29 January 1829)

'Dover and Calais. What mean, amorphous entrance portals to great
kingdoms! Mere grimy untended back-doors!'
Arnold Bennett, *Journal* (23 October 1897)

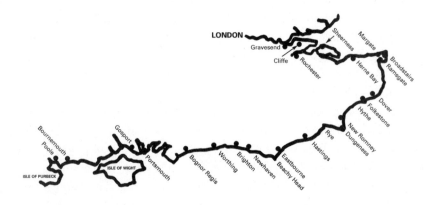

Chapter One: The Southeast

Coastal Defences

The Eastern Docks at Dover doesn't offer the most promising benediction to an English journey. Cold tarmac, concrete hulks, tailgating cars, dead skies. There are no mellifluous notes of Vera Lynn cascading over the car park and the 'Welcome to Dover' sign is more an introduction to English humour than an actual greeting.

I park beside the ferry terminal and cross a busy road to the East Cliff area, where I've been told most of the port's asylum seekers are temporarily housed. I'm in luck. Ali Jamac and Hassan Abdullah Ali are returning to the slatternly Gordon House Hotel, after a walk. I thrust out my hand and smile, a greeting that has worked pretty well for me around the globe. Ali looks suspicious but takes the hand and half returns the smile. We then move on to exchanging names, like gifts. Then I'm stumped. The easy bit's over. As I thrash around for a way to take things forward, I grin inanely and mouth something overly familiar and ridiculous – 'Where have you been?'.

'I don't know. We just walked,' Hassan replies vaguely, seemingly not having taken umbrage at my adopting the inappropriate register of an old friend. Ali, on the other hand, has already drawn back and is scanning the horizon for an escape route. He pulls at Hassan's sleeve and speaks in Somali. His companion, however, is a more trusting soul and starts firing

1

off questions of his own. He wants to know why I'm talking to him and what I'm doing here. I tell him about my journey around the English coast and the book I'm writing. Hassan translates for Ali, who has virtually no English. A briefer pause ensues while Hassan then translates Ali's response, an eminently sensible but incredulous, 'Why?'

I begin to enumerate reasons: 'The changing face of England . . . the coast is where things are felt most keenly and where communities and geography adapts first . . .' My voice trails off as I catch the incomprehension in Hassan's eyes.

'Are you married?' he asks.

'Yes.'

'Do you have children?'

'Yes.'

I notice Ali is again tugging at Hassan's T-shirt suggesting with some urgency that they be on their way. To leave your family for two months when you don't need to must indeed sound like the act of a madman. Fortunately Hassan is a trusting, friendly soul and keen to meet English people. He tells me his friend wants to be an author too and to write the story of their journey once they get settled. Ali mimes studying books. 'He wants to go to school and learn and work, work, work.' Ali nods his head enthusiastically.

Ali's mime reminds me of the children I used to teach in a London comprehensive – how recent arrivals would mostly have to resort to Ali's communication technique while the easy slang of second-generation kids was totally indistinguishable from that of the rest of the class. The English language did not seep into the land with melting icecaps. It arrived 1,500 years ago, a guttural Germanic dialect brought by tribes who arrived on the east coast after the Romans packed for home. Today two billion people understand and speak our language and it has even been spoken on the moon. Hassan is clearly already on his way to mastery. He asks if he can contact me when they are safe and I give him my phone number.

In return, I ask for their full names but Hassan is cagey. So far they have been in the country fifteen days and they don't want to do anything that will prejudice their chance of being granted asylum. Ali rubs his stomach, feigning hunger, and suggesting they really should be on their way. I push my luck further by asking if I can take a photograph. Ali refuses. Hassan kindly poses by the 'Welcome to Dover' sign. As I snap away, I ask him how he reached England.

'I came by aeroplane.'

'Do you still have family back home?'

'Yes, brothers, sisters and my mother. But my father was killed by the army. They tried to kill me too.' Hassan points to the skeleton of a knife wound running about three inches down his neck. 'The soldiers did it with a bayonet in 2002. They thought I was dead but I survived.'

Suddenly Ali joins in animatedly. 'Very dangerous, very dangerous, Somali.' Hassan expands on his theme, 'It *is* very dangerous. We would be killed if we went back. Even staying here is better.' He indicates the ugly barracks of Gordon House that is his temporary home. After his father's death, his uncle gave his home to an agent as payment for smuggling his nephew out of the country. The agent brought him to England and then vanished.

The dream of a new start that has brought Ali and Hassan to England is the same one my great-grandmother had when swapping Dublin for London and my wife's Jewish great-grandparents had when they quit Poland for the Welsh Valleys.

Ali finally gets his way and persuades Hassan to head off for lunch. I watch them walking down the street, two new waves washing up on the beach of England beneath the white unscalable cliffs.

Five weeks before my encounter with Ali and Hassan, I'd stood on Market Road in Holloway, eyeing second- or fifteenth-hand vans, trying to sniff out whether vehicles were reliable or on their last legs. It had been a fantastic spring – long unbroken sunshine, T-shirts, bird calls and wolf whistles – but now summer was just round the corner and I still hadn't the wheels for my journey.

Across the busy street, kids hollered and showed off feints and keepy-uppies on an Astroturf pitch. Three hooded teenagers overtook me, bragging about a wallet one had squeezed out of someone's back pocket while riding a lift the night before.

'Mornin'.' A large bear of a man in baseball cap, blue T-shirt and generous jeans greeted me from the open door of a camper van. Clearly he'd noticed me scanning the handwritten CV of his white Bedford van plastered to the rear window. He opened his sales pitch: 'Very good runner. Had £2,400 spent on her last year and she's still got eleven months' MOT. Fridge, cooker, shower, double bed – it's like a bloody country hotel inside!' I peered inside. Not bad. But it did have 120,000 miles on the clock and its owner, Phil, wanted £4,750, which was considerably more than I intended spending. My plan was to travel several thousand miles, have absolutely no mechanical problems and then flog the beast in the autumn for the same amount I paid for it, preferably here on Market Road.

On my last English pilgrimage, a four-month, 900-mile (620-lock) journey through England's inland waterways, the choice of vehicle had been straightforward: a narrowboat or a narrowboat. This time, though, at various stages in the planning, I'd considered a bicycle, a sixties Lambretta like the one I rode in my teens, a large motorbike like the one I'd owned between Mod-dom and middle age, and a reliable VW camper van – unlike the unreliable clapped-out one I used when teaching in an Algerian mountain village in the mid-1970s. A caravan was definitely out of the question. But I had started considering the possibility of a small motorhome. The anorak world of narrowboats had been a challenge; making the pebbledash world of motorhoming fashionable, however, could well be beyond me.

I'd been told that the place to look for vans was Market Road in the wastelands between Holloway and King's Cross. It was here, apparently, that impecunious itinerant Aussies tried to resell vans after European tours before heading home. A little further down the street, a pop-up-top Bedford camper had its doors thrown wide like a Tuscan villa letting in the sun. Stan was particularly proud of the 75p lock he'd fitted to the inside doors so no one could get in at night. 'And even if they do, I've got a second line of defence.' Stan nodded his head in the direction of an axe lying on top of a cupboard.

Ultimately, buying an old banger comes down to good fortune. I could take Stan's ugly clapped-out van and it might last me the whole 3,000-mile trip. On the other hand, the engine could – and most likely would – expire on me before I reached the coast.

As I was about to give up and leave, a motorhome pulled up. Two men, one decidedly the worse for wear, sat silently inside munching sausage butties. Reluctantly, the elder one wound down the window and in an

Irish brogue undiminished by twenty years in Bethnal Green admitted, 'Bit of a night last night. You won't mind if I don't get out for a minute?'

I duly inspected the outside while Tom continued his rehab. A little rust, but nothing that was likely to collapse under me. It was, however, a motorhome and there was no ducking the issue. A box on wheels. The ugliest denominator in motorised transport, without a single concession to aesthetics. Tom claimed a new engine had recently been fitted that had just 3,300 miles on the clock and the van also had a new shower and electrics. He claimed the only reason his uncle (he looked too old to have an uncle) was selling was that he'd just been banned. 'Drink driving. I have all the MOTs and history. He wants £3,000 and won't go below £2,500.'

'How many miles to the gallon?' I asked, but Tom worked on a different system.

'A tenner usually gets me 100 miles.'

I took the van for a short spin along Caledonian Road and Brewery Road. It was like driving a tank, but I said I'd think about it and give him a ring. Early the next morning I duly rang to tell him I'd take it.

'Sorry pal, someone paid cash for it as soon as you left.'

I took it as an omen and switched to Plan B, firing off emails in all directions trying to blag a van. Most drew blanks. Autosleeper offered a reduced rental that was still more than I'd consider paying to actually own one. Eventually, however, I got a reply from Swift, which was willing to loan me a motorhome in exchange for publicity. 'Unfortunately we only have a six-berth, which might be a bit big. Does it matter?' It did. I wanted a compact two-berth. But it mattered even more that it was free and would almost certainly be reliable. I took it. The only other snag, apart from size, was that it would not be available until three weeks after my planned departure.

Impatient to be off, I decided to pick up the motorhome en route and stashed everything I'd need in the boot of my old Nissan Primera.

'Kent' – the oldest recorded place name in Britain – is the major spiritual and commercial gateway between London and the Continent. Predictably, therefore, it has seen more military action than the rest of the 5,496km of English coastline put together. There are more castles in Kent than in any other county, as well as 74 Martello towers and a

28-mile royal canal dug in the early 19th century to act as a deterrent to Napoleon. Hitler, like Bonaparte, intended using the Southeast as his baulkhead. Julius Caesar landed here in 55 BC, followed by St Augustin, the Jutes, Saxons, Vikings and Normans. It therefore seemed altogether appropriate to be starting my coastal journey where the English story began and continued to be played out.

So a month after my visit to the Holloway Road, on a dull Monday in early summer, I slipped on to the capital's M25 shirt tail, sailing over the Queen Elizabeth II Bridge, surprisingly whimsical and airy in its prosaic endless load-bearing drudgery. Beneath me, industrial doll's houses, aluminium carcasses and smoking towers hunkered, the confused detritus of new millennium commerce. On the southern bank a parked truck named Albion (Albion Chemical Distribution) had been abandoned as if its driver had suddenly become bored of the life, parked obliquely and walked off across the tarmac Nasca Lines.

London's A–Z spaghetti gave way to the obese Bluewater Shopping Centre, London-in-miniature, gagging on its 330 shops and restaurants. The largest shopping mall in Europe had queued at the exchange counter and traded community for superslick shopping efficiency. A few miles further east, I took a slip road (the wrong one) that followed a trail of retail parks and light industrial complexes through Gravesend's hinterland. It was a hot day but not as hot as it would get a couple of months later, on 10 August, when the temperature in Gravesend hit 37.6 degrees, the highest ever recorded in Britain. On a factory wall, in large hurried letters, 'Dave's sorry' had been scrawled. A piece of paper was clearly not big enough for Dave's sense of guilt.

Recently the Government announced that the unseemly brown tea spill left by expired heavy industry in Gravesend is to be carpeted with thousands of new homes as part of a plan to transform 40 miles of the Essex and Kent coast (and a swathe of Bedfordshire) into a seamless London dormitory. One day, perhaps before the century's out, someone will repeat my journey and be able to travel clockwise right round the English coast from Gravesend to Southend without ever leaving a suburb.

Equally recently, in August 2003 a survey by the Royal Institute of Chartered Surveyors discovered that 42 per cent of Britain's population now live in suburbs but only a quarter of them actually want to. The dream of the manufactured middle-class suburb, born on the wheels of the motorcar, is over: surburbanites have discovered their vehicles are as much a prison as their Barratt-land closes and their dreams have now turned to coastal cottages in the Southwest and carless walks with their liberated pooches along the cliffs.

In Gravesend I briefly pop in to pay my respects to Pocohontas, an Indian maid I've carried a torch for since childhood. I find her – in life-sized bronze form anyway – in the garden of St George's church, dressed in the clothes of her native Algonquin tribe, her hands open, just as they were to the first white men she encountered in her native Virginia. At the age of 21, she was brought to England to be paraded like a circus act to raise money for the Virginia Company's settlement. A year later, finally granted leave to return home, she became gravely ill (possibly from the plague), died and was buried in St George's graveyard.

As I move down the pedestrianised cobbled high street from the church, the estuary beyond the pier is suddenly eclipsed by a vast Maersk container ship sliding silently past, a giant ghostly funeral barge heading for the vanished island of Thanet. According to Derek Williams in *Romans and Barbarians*, it was traditionally believed on the Continent that England 'was the abode of the dead and that souls were rowed in unmanned boats, which left the coast of Gaul at nightfall and returned before dawn'. Williams suggests the legend was spawned by an earlier Roman belief that the dead were transported to the island of Thanet (which historically wasn't then part of the mainland). I'd like to throw in my own twopennyworth here by noting that although 'Thanet' may be geographically a long way from southern Europe, it's actually only a few letters removed from the Greek 'thanatos', meaning 'death'.

I continue down the high street towards the ghost ship, but by the time I reach the bottom of the hill it has vanished and light has returned like the resurrected dawn. The ship's place in my curiosity is replaced by a newly installed ceremonial gate that prevents anyone parking next to the pier and shopping at the handful of businesses still managing to operate. The gate is the latest folly of the English heritage industry, which is in danger of mothballing the entire country.

A small dapper barber, dressed in a thin blue cotton jacket that's flecked with customers' hair, is standing outside Continental Gents Hairdressing kicking his heels, looking for clients. Tom McGuire has hardly missed a day in the 39 years he has worked here. He tells me that when he opened the shop in the 1960s, 'You could walk the river from Tilbury to Gravesend across the barges, it were that busy. Five thousand people a day passed my shop. There were fourteen ferries an hour and eight thousand dockers and lightermen working the port and across at Tilbury it was the same.' Now no ferries call in and his regular customers have trouble parking because of the new gates. Tom, on his little island, has literally been left behind.

Across the grazing pastures flanking the Isle of Grain peninsula (its name deriving from the Old English *greon*, meaning 'sand' or 'gravel'), a pea-souper is rolling in as in the old days, stealing the cattle like rustlers. Spidery lanes lead me through a landscape as remote as the Trough of Bowland and yet I'm still only 30 miles from the capital. Opposite the 13th-century flint-and-ragstone St James's church on the shoulder of the village of Cooling, workers are picking tomatoes inside a clear-plastic tent. In the graveyard, as the fog lifts, I find thirteen lozenge-shaped miniature tombs, each no more than 3ft in length, that are the graves of children from two families who all died of marsh fever (malaria) in the 19th century. Their inscriptions have been erased by time but their occupants are immortalised in the opening of Dickens' *Great Expectations* when Pip is assailed by the convict Magwitch in the graveyard with 'the dark flat wilderness beyond the churchyard, intersected with dykes and mounds and gates, with scattered cattle feeding on it'. Pip had strayed on to the marshland and quickly realised that 'the low leaden line beyond, was the river; and that the distant savage lair from which the wind was rushing, was the sea'.

Looking out today from the raised cemetery across the meadows, it's easy to imagine manacled convicts like Magwitch fleeing the prison at Egypt Bay, running humpbacked through the rushes. Today, instead of guards on prison sentry duty, however, a heron perches on the church wall surveying its estate, looking for frogs on the move rather than escaping prisoners.

The next island-that-is-not-an-island eastwards has far greater personal resonance for me, for it was on the Isle of Sheppey that my own story began before I was even born. It was at a dancehall in Sheerness in 1941 that my father first met my mother when he was stationed with the Coastal Gunnery Royal Artillery, manning the anti-aircraft guns that provided London's defence against the Luftwaffe. Mum was a Sheerness girl and was sitting, like the rest of the local girls, on hard wooden chairs that lined the walls of the dancehall. Dad, reading the female semaphore, asked her to dance and they've been dancing round their living room ever since – legs, bones and general decrepitude permitting.

During the war there was a large naval dockyard on the island (Samuel Pepys supervised its construction in 1665 while employed as Secretary to the Admiralty during Charles II's reign) and, according to Dad, 'More pubs than Soft Mick'. Sailors frequented one pub, the 'Brylcreem Boys' (air force recruits) another, and the army had the rest. Occasionally, at closing time, they all met out on the street for a ruck.

As I walk the streets of the two-storey town just a whisper from the sea, lives flicker behind marbled curtains. It's clear there are still more pubs than Soft Mick. The dancehall, however, is proving less easy to locate. At Stead and Simpson I crane my neck for any clues on the floor above but the place is locked and has a 'To Let' sign up. I cross off a carpet warehouse, department store, the 99p Store and Delboy's Tasty Food café. It is a Delboy town, as far removed from young romance as it's possible to get. The high brick wall of the Sheerness Dockyard may originally have been built to protect locals from seeing the ugliness of the port but now those travelling on the car ferry or container ships must be equally grateful to it for shielding them from the awfulness of the town.

The dancehall is nowhere to be found in this hunchbacked, arthritic, sausage-and-chips town. In an estate agent's window, a terraced flat is for sale at £45,000. My suggestion is that the Government make the Isle of Sheppey the new building epicentre instead of Gravesend and that they keep erecting homes on the island until it sinks.

Beyond the open paddling pool and leisure centre, a sea wall buffers the muddied estuary as it snakes its way past a pebbled beach from which kids are skipping stones across the water towards the longest pier in the world projecting from the Essex coastline at Southend. A cell of black-headed gulls in their priests' cowls meditates on the sea wall. A teenager with a pierced belly button and dressed in bra and shorts scares them off by noisily jimmying off the top of a Beck's bottle on a yellow 'No Parking' sign.

At the Heritage Centre I explain my mission to the woman behind
the desk and tell her my father thought the dance hall was above a
department store – possibly Burton's. Initially I think she's ignoring
me but she's simply cogitating, dusting off her own history, gathering
thoughts. 'Well, it can't be Burton's because I used to work there.'
Gaynor ponders a little more. 'My bet is it's the old Wheatsheaf Hall
above the Co-Op. Unfortunately it's been knocked down and an
Iceland has replaced it.'

At the supermarket, instead of a plaque commemorating my parents'
first dance, there's a special offer on fish fingers. The only dancehall
equivalent I come across is the gaudy Top Club, where a special-
offer Double Vodka and Red Bull offers instant foreplay instead of
romance at £5 a hit.

As I continue on the A299 along the Thanet coast, the mouth of the
Thames estuary gapes ever wider. Come autumn it will be filled with
the crackling call of brent geese, dressed in Siberian coats, settling on
the mud flats. The estuary is earmarked (like other shallow sea zones
such as the Wash) for vast windfarms. Aeolus, the god of wind, has
been generous in providing our land with five times greater potential
for turbines than that of any other European country. In a green vision
of the future, it's hoped one day windfarms will replace nuclear power
plants and provide all the clean, renewable energy the country needs.

Today, however, it is not wind but lashing rain that I'm having to deal
with. A radio forecast has warned that last night's storms were a mere
curtain raiser to today's 'severe weather in Kent'. The rain hammers and
the windscreen wiper develops an irritating tic. Large tracts of Kent
appear to have been cling-filmed by Christo, keeping the new breed of
farm workers perfectly dry in their bubbling plasticulture world. The tic
grows more pronounced. The world is opaque, the chalk weald's gentle
glides, broad valleys, sweeps and swells made even softer by the dreadful
weather. The sound of the wipers are all I hear as the storm rages outside.
The landscape slides past as if it were a 35mm home movie with the
celluloid clicking through spool gates providing the soundtrack.

Up on the high lawns of Herne Bay – which isn't a bay at all – men
in carcoats and women in their own hairdo-protective wraps are

walking waggy-tailed dogs. The rain has almost stopped and by the time I'm parked, the heavens have closed. Beneath the 80ft clock tower, built the year Victoria came to the throne, a beach cleaner dressed in municipal yellow is collecting rubbish from the beach. Marooned offshore is the end of a pier that was orphaned when the rest was swept away in a storm.

'Nineteen sixty-four, I believe,' the municipal bag man informs me. 'At least, I'm reasonably confident it was 1964.' He pauses, seemingly concerned his date may be less than accurate (in fact the 3,920ft pier vanished in 1978). 'And they replaced it with the ugliest building I've had the misfortune to behold.' He indicates a grey boxed building on the seafront. The man speaks as if he's 70 but looks about 25; his register is that of either someone who started life at a more elevated station or someone with elevated aspirations. The beach-cleaning aesthete has a tic of the eye like my Nissan. The day before, he'd cleared five bin-bags' worth of rubbish from the beach and another seven from the car park. 'And I have those to clean those too . . .' – aesthete bin man points to a Himalayan dog dump – 'even though they're prohibited.' He shakes his head despairingly. 'That must have been left by a Great Dane . . . minimum.'

Sedate and sedentary, Herne slumbers through the dank morning. In Macari's Ice Cream Parlour, locals peer over newspapers through the wrap-round plate-glass window. I shun the seductive invitations of knickerbocker glories, butterscotch sundaes and peach melbas, and order instead a sausage sandwich in white bread with brown sauce. Encased on the walls is the black-and-white record of Herne Bay – its fires and storms, the arrival of gas lamps and the penny-farthing, and the eclipse of the old-fashioned windmill. There are also ice-cream diplomas and two identical plaques commemorating Herne Bay being the western terminus of a 3km course that HJ Wilson sped down at 606mph in a 'Gloster Meteor Aeroplane Britannia' on 7 November 1945, breaking the world air-speed record. Glory days that Herne is thankfully at the back of, enjoying its long retirement.

Which is where I find nearby Margate too, the first of a triumvirate of resorts on the Thanet headland. Dismissed as 'the catflap at the end of the A28' in a recent newspaper feature, the town has certainly known better days but today is singing a new psalm from the battered hymn book of regeneration.

At the lifeboat station up on the hill, more hairy adventures in the HJ Wilson mould have been enjoyed or endured by the 12m Mersey Class (1991) lifeboat, *Leonard Kent*. Outside the station, a volunteer is leaning up against one of the doors dressed in cut-off Levi's and a black vest brought back from a holiday in Mauritius, beneath the left sleeve of which is the tattoo of a luscious wriggling lady. The man kicks at a stone, misses, turns on his heels and walks inside. I follow him, remembering to pop a coin into the donations box.

Trevor Lamb is second coxswain and, like every member of the crew apart from the coxswain, an unpaid volunteer. He is, however, the only one who actually earns a living at sea. The rest are a ragbag of bus drivers, engineers and removal people. Yesterday Trevor had been out rescuing a yacht 10 miles offshore. Today, so far, it's been quiet.

Each day Trevor takes his small trawler (virtually the only one still working daily from Margate) out to the territorial limit, seeking cod in winter and Dover sole in summer. And each year he gets squeezed a little more by quota restrictions. 'If they left us alone, we'd make a living, but we're down from working three-handed to two and although there's more cod out there this year than I can ever remember, they still impose cod quotas on us.'

Changes in global weather have brought about further complications. 'Summer fish hang on longer and the cod season gets shorter. In the West Country they've got all kinds of exotic tropical fish turning up.' Whatever Trevor catches, he sells at his wet-fish stall in the harbour and the shop he has in Market Place. Both are called Mannings and they're run by his wife and mother-in-law.

I am transported down to the harbour on the heady aroma of kelp. Below me, in the sand, a 40-ft heart has been drawn and inside it, the words 'I LOVE YOU'. I believe it to be a message to someone specific, otherwise surely the author would have used the current texting generic 'I LUV U'. The sea kisses its cheeks and then scurries back flatly to a sky now cleared of rain clouds. At the harbour I call in for cockles at Trevor's stall, where his mother-in-law manages to transcend even her familial stereotype for frostiness.

Adjacent is the handsome Georgian old customs house, Droit House, inside which the barometer has swung to 'fine' and the welcome is altogether warmer. Until the ambitious £11.5 million Turner Centre opens in 2007 on the stone jetty, Droit House is temporary home to both an exhibition on Turner's life (1775–1851) and contemporary shows. The very young Ashley Penrose, who's manning the desk today, claims preposterously that Margate was the biggest influence on Turner's career. 'He painted more works with the town as a backdrop than any other place. One hundred of his paintings, including thirty big canvasses, were executed in or around the town.' I'm not sure if my jaw was hanging or whether I had a disbelieving smirk lurking but Ashley was unabashed, going on further to claim outrageously that Margate's fiery skies and seascapes were probably what nudged Turner, and the world, towards Impressionism. I smile indulgently and move on, concluding that young Ashley is simply barking. Much later I read in John Ruskin's *Praeterita* (1885–9), 'I have only known too late . . . the absolutely literal truth of Turner's saying, that the most beautiful skies in the world known to him were those of the Isle of Thanet.'

In a second room I discover there are others touched by Ashley's dementia. A video by contemporary artists, led by local girl Tracey Emin, similarly extols Turner's pioneering work with light and points to the artist as embodying the crucial turning point when intensity and mood replaced literal representation as art's holy grail. Emin is equally evangelical about Margate and its sunsets. Her own history is pretty much that of the resorts: she grew up here, was raped here and even tried to commit suicide from the harbour wall (very close to where the new Turner Centre will stand). Sandwiched historically between Turner and Emin, Sickert lived and lectured in Margate for four years and Van Gogh taught at the William Stokes school in nearby Ramsgate.

Turner himself attended Thomas Coleman's school in Love Lane and returned to the resort frequently as an adult, attracted as much by his widowed landlady, Sophia Booth, as he was by the memorable sunsets seen from her lodgings on Cold Harbour. Unlike Constable, who moth-balled the feudal landscape, Turner attempted to capture the elemental forces at work on land and at sea. In 1841, at the age of 66 (and still in love with Mrs Booth), he even had himself lashed to a mast on the steamship *Ariel* to enable him to experience a snowstorm at sea.

Everyone prays that the new Turner Centre will be groundbreaking and staggering, the catalyst for regeneration that Margate urgently needs, the Big Idea that does for Kent what Tate St Ives has done for Cornwall.

To withstand the sea its three floors, shaped like a sail, will be made of dam-construction concrete and clad in timber.

The view of the bay through the window of Droit House today is very different from how Turner would remember it. In the 18th century, 80,000 arrived annually on paddle steamers from London; today the sweeping bay that once teemed with boats has just a handful of fishing boats canted in the mud. There is a cigarette burn from a recent fire in the cream Regency terracing; the sixties tower block Arlington Tower is hideous (however much Emin loves it); and the 1930s Dreamland amusement park now dreams only of the relief that death will bring.

As I sit at a table and stare out of the window, I listen to interviews with locals recorded by contemporary artist Jo Roberts ('A mass exploration of the Isle of Thanet'). Like ghosts, voices drift in and out of consciousness through the headphones. A town shopkeeper complains of a big shopping centre at Westwood stealing all her business; a disabled resident bemoans the lack of discipline in the able bodied; others seek a daily market or the resurrection of dilapidated buildings. All speak, like Tracey Emin, with a passion for the place, anger at the years of neglect and hope for a better future. One elderly voice, cracking with emotion, underscores her sense of belonging. 'My home is a wonderful place. My house is safe and sound.'

The tightly arched bay may be relatively quiet today but the dankness has gone and the sun is breaking through, drawing everyone out of their warrens to feed off Turner's light. The fact that Margate is surrounded by water on three sides means that despite sitting on the east coast, residents can enjoy a west-facing sunset from the pier as they watch men prospecting for lugworms on the beach beneath their golden shower.

Emin's belief is that Margate, pre the Turner Centre, already has plenty of gems right under the nose. This is definitely the case of the Shell Grotto, which hides down a precipitous side street from KFC (above which Emin's mum used to have a flat). The grotto was discovered by chance in 1835 by Mr James Newlove when he lowered his young son Joshua into a hole that had suddenly appeared while he was digging a duckpond in his garden. What the boy discovered, as I do today, is an underground maze lined with 2,000 sq ft of mosaic decorated with 4.6 million shells. Crawling on his belly, in the darkness, he must have taken some time to realise the extent and miracle of the discovery. Walking upright today with the panels bathed in natural and artificial light, I make out mosaics evoking Indian fertility symbols and Cretan corn goddesses.

The grotto is a great enigma. The vaulted ceiling and altar suggest devotional practice rather than a mere secular folly, and a similar temple discovered in Sardinia has been dated back two millennia. Unfortunately English Heritage, when attempting carbon dating, concluded that the site 'defied analysis' (the carbon from Victorian gas lamps used when Newlove opened it as an attraction confused the dating process). Was the Shell Grotto built by Cretans or Romans? Was it, as some believe, merely a prototype Victorian folly or one of Dashwood's Hell Fire Club orgy hangouts? The jury's still out but one thing's for sure: 2,000 sq ft of shell mosaic would need several decades and a formidable army of slaves to complete (and how come there's no written record or local hand-me-down tales about the enormous chalk spill and the arrival of 4.6 million shells?).

Back inside the grotto shop at ground level, I find the owner, Sarah Vickery, arranging shell jewellery and other gifts. Dressed in a black lacy top, black skirt and black shoes, with raven-black shoulder-length hair, Sarah has the stylish hallmarks of the transplanted London fashion journalist. Her family regularly holidayed in Margate when she was a young girl and the Shell Grotto was where she always liked to hang out. When she returned to the resort a couple of years ago, she found the grotto was for sale and made a spur-of-the-moment decision. She gave up her job, sold her one-bedroom flat in Blackheath for £140,000 and with the proceeds bought the grotto, two houses and the shop.

Sarah, naturally, has inveigled her way into the local art scene ('It's very vibrant here') and sits on various committees. Her current pre-occupation, however, is neither with art nor with her own shell dreamland, but with the Dreamland down the road.

'Jimmy Godden, who owns amusement parks up and down the coast, has been trying to get planning permission so he can close the park and sell it for development. We've managed to get the Scenic Railway – did you know it's the oldest roller coaster in the country? – given a Grade II listing by English Heritage so at least that *has to* stay now whatever else happens.'

A French amusement park group is currently interested in creating a new park, based around the Scenic Railway. 'Their plan is to recreate the fantasy park that you *thought* existed in your childhood. We're all for it. We don't need more apartment blocks or car parks. What we do need is another Dreamland.'

Down on the prom, alongside the 'Dreamland' sign, are the screaming words 'Cash' and 'Bingo' and that's what owner Jimmy Godden is clearly more interested in than in fantasy. The site is probably worth around £5 million but if he gets planning permission he could get closer to £20 million by selling it off to a residential and business developer.

The park has been at the heart of Margate tourism for 83 years but seems to have suffered a stroke. Half its rides aren't operating. Even the oldest roller coaster in the country (the plans were brought over from Coney Island in 1920) is idle and its carved lions sleeping. I'm hugely disappointed. I'd been dying to ride it ever since seeing Lindsay Anderson's 1953 short cult classic *O Dreamland*. If Anderson were to re-shoot the documentary today it would be simply depressing rather than powerfully bleak. The park, I'm told, only ever comes alive on summer weekends when the topless, down-heeled Cockney resort sparkles with lights that race each other along the seafront, through the screaming arcades and on to the rides.

I move on to my base for the night, the Walpole Bay Hotel, where Tracey Emin stays when she's in town. Inside the suitably battered and eccentric lobby there's a trellis-gated lift installed in 1927, guest ledgers dating back to the same year and comfy sofas for browsing them on. The corridors are littered with Singer sewing machines, tasselled lamps, golliwogs, skittles and a Bakelite radio. Eventually I find my bedroom, which instead of central heating has an electric fire and a heated towel rail.

I stare out of the window to the bowling green across the street where two old timers are slapping high-fives after one successfully knocks the other's ball into the gutter. Rapt gulls applaud. The luminous gold of the shoreline drains to a sunless sea whose greyness is broken only by the early lights of a passing tanker. On the horizon clouds gather in pale mauve ruffles topped by a scarlet peacock feather that would not be out of place gracing the downstairs lobby. A sliver of new moon is rising. For some, the Thanet coast is all about donkey rides and amusement arcades;

for others, it is art and shell grottos; but the real dreamland is down by the sea with the sun rising and setting, the ocean breathing, the gulls calling, and an ineffable light washing over the resort.

The following morning I set off early to meet Margate's more sophisticated sisters, Broadstairs and Ramsgate. In the backstreets of the latter, a senior citizens' 50th anniversary Coronation party (part of the Jubilee celebrations) is in full swing and an MC in a Union Jack suit leads a chorus of 'Ain't She Sweet' while swinging bunting expansively as if he were Morrissey. When the song ends, and false teeth return to the sandwich triangles and fairy cakes, the MC asks if anyone has any Coronation memories from half a century earlier. 'The Queen of Tonga and the pouring rain,' one large woman shouts. MC Union Jack smiles and announces 'Jelly's on its way.'

Ramsgate has been slowly chugging upmarket in recent years, pedestrianising a street here, adding an alfresco café there. It has adopted a continental swagger and converted the generously endowed man-made harbour from a simple safe haven for fishing boats to a whacking great marina where yachts and cruisers gently buck, their jockeys all ensconced in seafront bars.

Broadstairs, on the other hand, has always had an elevated sense of its station, preferring to market itself as Dickensville (he spent his summers here and called it 'one of the freshest, freest watering places in the world') rather than Mr Nouveau Gin-Palaceville. Down at the Pavilion an organist is playing a foxtrot while couples dance their way through the late afternoon, as they always have on holiday. Outside, on the terrace, those taking a break sit over halves of lager, staring out to a fishing boat returning to port with an ensign of gulls trailing behind.

High above the crescent bay, I stop for a sundae in a Deco heaven with a 6ft ice-cream cone at its door and red lettering above it, spelling out 'Morelli's Cappuccino Bar and Ice Cream Parlour'. Sinking into one of the Lloyd Loom chairs, I study the row of illuminated sundaes. Just as you can become a connoisseur of wine, so too you can become a connoisseur of ice cream and, immodestly, I would like to declare myself to be one. The major constituent of a sundae, of course, is the vanilla ice cream, and the stuff here, made with double cream, sugar, eggs, milk and natural flavouring, is second to none. Mind you, it should be good – Morelli's has been practising for seventy years.

Marino Morelli tells me that the family concern has expanded to 25 parlours, a sandwich factory and a bakery in recent years. He is a typically dapper Italian but, bizarrely, speaks with a slight Scottish burr despite never having visited the country. 'It's the influence of my mother, who was born there,' he explains.

Three generations back, in 1907, Marino's great-grandfather fled the grinding poverty of his Italian home near Monte Cassino and with five hundred others walked across Europe seeking a better life. En route they shared what they had, got what work they could, and eventually made their way to Dover before dispersing.

'All the resorts at the time had ice-cream parlours and simple catering restaurants – usually fish and chips – run by Italians. Like all immigrants, the first generation cannot communicate well and try to protect their culture. As their children become less noticeable, differences vanish even more and there is less resentment on all sides.'

Recently, according to Marino, illegal immigrants and asylum seekers (the two tend to merge in the newspapers) in Dover had apparently featured luridly in the local press. 'The trouble is there are hundreds of immigrants wandering the streets waiting to be granted permission to stay or be sent home. It's not a good system. Of course there's resentment. They're forced to wait months or years before they're allowed to work and therefore have to be supported financially. That's when you get the stories of them being given cars and flats.' Flats become palaces, old bangers Aston Martins.

Marino's grandfather was interned on the Isle of Wight during World War II. He knows things can get whipped up quickly. He wipes a corner of the ice cream from the bowl and pushes the sundae across to me. 'Our Italian community here is totally integrated, like the Greek Cypriots. There was also a large Jewish community here too but they've moved on.'

Marino has an Albanian working behind the counter who's embarking on his own English story. Rightly we give Great-Grandfather Morelli's epic journey from Italy the respect it deserves and applaud his desire to provide a better life for his family. Curiously, however, it seems that epic journeys such as the one Hassan and Ali have made lead only to accusations that they are out to milk the system. Is the Morelli migration palatable to people today because it happened so long ago, or is it simply that some people find the Somalis more threatening because of their colour?

At Dover I have my encounter with Hassan and Ali down on East Cliff and then stroll back to the ferry terminal, deep in thought. In the car park bikes are being taken off roof racks and car boots are being rearranged. Soon their owners will slip across the Channel as freely as they drove into Dover. Inside the ferry terminal building, people buy tickets and exchange money with the easy confidence that comes with belonging. I ask a policeman hovering at the door what happens to those who present themselves at port as asylum seekers. Apparently they're given a provisional screening by immigration officers and are then either sent packing or passed on to Migrant Helpline. The policeman points me in the direction of the outfit's HQ, a hundred yards away across the car park.

Inside the swish new offices, a smartly dressed man of Middle Eastern appearance is sitting in a chair being questioned by a female immigration officer standing over him. The asylum seeker had appeared in the office, unaccompanied, an hour earlier, claiming he had come straight from the ferry. The officer clearly doesn't buy it and asks why he isn't in a more dishevelled state if he was a stowaway less than an hour ago. She then asks where he slept the night before and then tries to catch him out by asking how long he's been in the country. I cannot understand for the life of me why it should matter whether he arrived an hour, a day or a week ago.

I have inadvertently stumbled into the Kafkaesque web spun by Section 55 of the Immigration and Asylum Act introduced on 8 January 2003. In the past, those found wandering the M20 or M6, or those who declared themselves as asylum seekers at a seaport or airport, were all treated the same way and granted emergency support while their request for asylum was processed. Now, however, those seeking temporary accommodation and financial support who didn't request asylum immediately at the point of arrival must convince authorities at a special National Asylum Support Service (NASS) interview that they applied 'as soon as was reasonably practicable'.

Until that interview, for which they may have to wait six months, Migrant Helpline can assist with temporary accommodation and financial support. If, however, they are unsuccessful at their hearing (and it's estimated that 75 per cent are), they are made destitute despite still having a legal right to remain in the country while awaiting their full asylum interview. Their only option in such cases is stealing or begging as a means of support while they wait.

Rather than fast-tracking the asylum procedure, the introduction of Section 55 has resulted in two queues instead of one. The number of homeless living on the streets in Dover has escalated, exacerbating local grievances. In Croydon, where all the cases are heard, charity soup kitchens such as Nightwatch have also seen a big increase in those seeking free meals.

While Migrant Helpline was seeing forty people a day two years ago, today the number is down to fifteen and yet its hostels are still full to bursting, as around 66 per cent of those housed are awaiting NASS decisions (as are 97 per cent of those currently housed in Croydon). The net effect is that fewer new arrivals are likely to apply for asylum through legal channels. This might, of course, be exactly what the Government intends in its quest to massage figures and assuage racist voters. The UK receives around one per cent of the world refugee population and comes seventh in the European league of refugee placements and yet the anti-asylum hysteria in the British media would be laughable if it wasn't so shameful.

The Media Officer for Migrant Helpline, Julie Larner, tells me that four asylum seekers whose NASS applications for support have been successful are about to have their 'Dispersal Briefing' over the road before they are rehoused in Southampton to await their full asylum interviews. I ask if I might sit in on the session and am surprised to have my request granted.

Julie sends me across to the Cliffe Court Hotel where the briefing is to take place in a small room overlooking the busy main road into the port. Gerry Bearman, who used to run a care home and has been delivering induction briefings for Migrant Helpline for two years now, leads me into the anonymous room. The four asylum seekers are already seated round a long melamine table, staring mutely into their futures. Four blue folders, bulging with forms and bureaucracy, lie in front of them.

Borhan, the Arabic translator, who had fled from Iraq two years earlier, arrives and sits next to me. Abdul Raziq Adam Suliman from Chad, Youcef Marouf from Algeria, Abdelaziz Aliadam Ghandima and Ibrahim Adam, both from the Sudan, are praying they too will be granted permanent asylum soon.

The briefing swings into action, Gerry providing information about tickets and emergency payments, appointment times and schedules, before pausing for Borhan's translation. I find the information and instructions totally bewildering despite my low anxiety level and familiarity with the language. What I do keep catching every few sentences from Gerry, however, is warnings about racial harassment. At the end of the briefing, I bring the subject up. Gerry explains that harassment is almost certain. 'Local feeling runs high. Often the hostels are in estate areas with high unemployment and poverty.'

Through Borhan I ask the four men on the other side of the table whether Britain is considered a tolerant and welcoming society in their own country or one that is heavily racist. All four claim it has a good image. I then ask, in view of Gerry's warnings, whether they are concerned about the kind of reception they might get in their new home. Youcef smiles. Borhan translates for him, providing a wonderfully idiomatic reply: 'Small potatoes.' I guess after enduring the persecution that goes with running a cinema showing western films in Algeria, anything we can throw at him will indeed be a breeze. His companions – a shepherd, a miner and a farmer – are similarly escaping terrorism, persecution, civil war and/or political harassment. I ask what their priorities are. All four say to get permission to stay and then to learn the language. I shake their hands, wish them well and emerge back into daylight.

To clear my head, I drive up on to the White Cliffs where the National Trust has introduced migrant grazing Exmoor ponies to the downland, as they have along other coastal stretches. The animals do not seem to be suffering persecution from those there before them and their presence is allowing the flora and fauna that died out with chemical pesticides and intensive farming to establish themselves once more. Pretty much what Oliver Letwin, of Russian parentage, and Michael Howard, of Romanian immigrants, are reputedly doing for the Conservative party.

It is a spectacular high cliff walk with resident kittiwakes and fulmars and eight or nine leapers per year. When someone does make the leap here, it is not a cry for help like Ali's and Hassan's, and they have definitely given up believing in a better life. There's no way back when you step off this cliff; you've reached the end of your tether. This was literally the case with one recent leaper found dangling from a 20ft rope tied to a tree. Clearly he hadn't wanted to endure the entire 300ft plummet. Either that or he preferred strangulation to the sensation of feeling his body breaking into a hundred pieces.

A short walk away is Dover Castle, the best known of all the county's fortifications, but where the fighting these days is confined to medieval reenactments by out-of-work actors. The castle is no crumbling fey relic. It is the real McCoy – a concentric stone hulk on a crag dwarfing everything on land and sea. And so it should be, as the defender of the town closest to the perfidious French (21 miles away at this point). The 3,000-year-old rings of defence on its headland record the history of England and beyond; what we are today and where we came from. From the remains of an Iron Age hill fort to the Roman stone lighthouse – at 95ft the tallest Roman building standing outside Italy and built in AD 70 by legionaries who just conceivably might have witnessed the Crucifixion – the place screams defiance and defence.

I climb to the top of the 12th-century keep – the last great rectangular keep built in Britain – and stare out to sea from its rooftop eyrie. Below me ferries are shuttling backwards and forwards and the defence of the realm is now the responsibility of a handful of customs officials. Somewhere across the still waters in the haze, Boulogne hovers at around one o'clock, Calais is at ten or eleven and Dunkirk at eight. On a clear day they can feel *almost* like neighbours. It reminds me that this English bastion was actually built by a Frenchman – Maurice the Mason – for a Frenchman, Henry Plantaganet (Henry II) at a time when we were speaking French. Today, coincidentally, there's a swarm of French school kids sweeping through rooms once occupied by Richard the Lionheart and Henry V.

Two hundred yards away, I find an entrance to an underground warren and burrow into a 4-mile, 100-ft deep maze of caves and tunnels that served as a 13th-century defensive system, a Napoleonic barracks, a World War I hospital and a World War II War Room. It was in the latter, in May 1940, that Vice-Admiral Sir Bertram Ramsay orchestrated the miracle of the Dunkirk evacuation, when 339,000 soldiers were rescued by a flotilla of 693 fishing and pleasure boats in Operation Dynamo. The hospital and War Room have been recreated but the final floor, 60ft closer to hell, is closed to the public. Known as 'Dumpy', it was to be the regional seat of Government in the event of a nuclear war. The bunker was last used actively during the 1962 Cuban missile crisis when 'Dumpy' was prepared for the arrival of the Cabinet before the first Big Bang (at nearby Manston, Vulcan Bombers stood loaded on the runway with engines running).

The emblematic White Cliffs are synonymous with Fortress Britain but the irony is not so much that they're retreating at an average rate of 2–5cm a year but that they're so riddled with tunnels that should a ship crash on to them in a particularly vigorous storm, the whole edifice would probably crumble like a meringue.

Back at ground level, and blinded by the light, I put on my sunglasses and squint across the valley southwards to Shakespeare Point where Gloucester is warned from inadvertently going the way of the leapers by Edgar in *King Lear* (Shakespeare is believed to have visited Dover with his theatre company in 1605):

> . . . here's the place; stand still.
> How fearful
> And dizzy 'tis, to cast one's eyes so low!
> The crows and choughs that wing the midway air
> Show scarce so gross as beetles. Half way down
> Hangs one that gathers sampire, dreadful trade!
> Methinks he seems no bigger than his head.

The samphire gatherers no longer hang suicidally on ropes as they did a century ago, collecting the bitter-tasting plant to sell as a pickled delicacy in Covent Garden. People do, however, still gather the plant from the seashore at spots such as Samphire Hoe, and it is here, to the south of the port, where I continue my afternoon stroll.

When the owners of the Channel Tunnel donated spoil to create this new 80-acre nature reserve in 1997, a carpet of sea lavender, thrift and sea arrowgrass quickly colonised it (also sharing the coastal garden today are kidney vetch, sea kale, wild cabbage and sea beet). Increasingly French migrants are found too, seeded by the wind crossing the Channel. Among the indigenous and foreign guests calling Samphire Hoe home are more than 4,000 spider orchids, dragonflies, stonechats, black redstarts, meadow pipits and skylarks. As I stroll this newest piece of England, 300ft above me a solitary man plays a penny whistle on the cliff edge – whether to the wind, to God or to the French, only he knows.

Skirting the nature reserve, the path of the Saxon Shore Way continues on its journey to Folkestone. The Saxons first migrated here during a change in the climate pattern that resulted in their home lowlands flooding. Now our own vulnerable eastern seaboard is being eaten away, and at an accelerated rate, thanks to global warming. The White Cliffs themselves are made up of millions of sea creatures from the bottom of a long-vanished tropical ocean: the English people are similarly made up of migrants, such as Saxons, blown on the wind of fortune to our shores.

In Hythe, later that evening, I meet a former fishmonger enjoying his retirement, strolling the beach with his pooch, as the sea crackles around him. He tells me that four years earlier he was still working an eighty- or ninety-hour week in a business that had been in his family since 1847.

'I was the seventh generation, and at the age of 53 I just stopped. Gave it up. I'd had enough.' Geoff Griggs sold up and retired. 'It was the best thing I ever did. People say to me, "Don't you miss it?"' Geoff's eyes roll dramatically as if he is shocked by the ludicrousness of the question, before he quickly answers it with a long, 'Nooooooo. I'm enjoying life. I never had time before.'

Every day of his working life, Geoff had risen at 2.30 a.m. and set off either for Billingsgate Market or across to France. His halcyon working years had come late. 'When the Channel Tunnel was being built, I suddenly found I had a queue of French workers down at my wet-fish stall here on the beach. They felt at home because I had it laid out like at French markets with wicker baskets and stainless-steel containers filled with ice. The locals started noticing the French were buying from me and so they decided it must be good, and suddenly my shop in the town and our beach stall went mad. I used to go mushrooming in the hills with one of the French workers and we're still in touch. One thing hasn't changed with retirement, though . . . having spent my life getting up early means

I do the gardening at 4 a.m.! The advantage is weeds come out easier with dew on them.'

The Channel Tunnel changed many lives in the Southeast. To the rest of the world, the Continent of Europe extends beyond the Shetland Isles but to the English it has always ended at Calais. Returning from the Normandy trenches or aboard booze cruises, the English have always known they were safely back to the Continent of England when the bone-white escarpment came into view. But how can we know these days when to sigh with relief, when burrowing beneath the Channel?

The town of Folkestone felt the change more than most. Down at the harbour a beached yacht, apocryphally named *Ghost,* sits in the mud. Beside it is the dock that became moribund on 6 May 1994 when the ferry service to Boulogne became surplus to requirements. When the Tunnel opened, the Continent crept closer (today Calais is just a 35-minute train-shunt away). Locals always knew that alongside escalating house prices there would be other grim realities, and their fears were confirmed when road signs in Kent substituted Folkestone for the new route beneath the water. Now drivers still know the way to Canterbury and Dover but Folkestone has slipped off the map.

Up on the mile-long Leas, the most handsome of all leafy English promenades, the town's current epidemic of drug addiction, crime and reputedly the second-highest teenage pregnancy figures in Europe seems a very long way off. In its heyday 'the finest marine promenade in the world' even had its own resident bobby to check that ladies and gentlemen were booted and suited.

The city's current pathology is a direct result of its parlous, ferryless, fishingless, holidaymakerless state. The Southeast may be viewed as London's prosperous hinterland but while inland towns and cities have seen plenty of regeneration money, the littoral has been largely ignored. Now, finally, Folkestone, Margate and other forgotten resorts are seeing a little of the cash drip and attempting to reinvent themselves. And, like Margate, Folkestone is going for an arty makeover.

Chameleonlike, the Metropole, one of the grandest buildings along the Leas, has taken on all the town's historic guises. Opening with much ostentatious pomp in 1897 as a grand hotel, it foundered from the outset owing to more commercially minded local competition. Daniel Baker, a local builder, irritated at failing to get the Metropole contract, built his own state-of-the-art building next door. The full-bearded Prince of Wales would often sit in a window seat in the Grand with his similarly bearded inner circle awaiting a visit from his intimate friend Alice Keppel (grandmother of Camilla Parker Bowles) from nearby Hythe. Folklore has it that the group looked so much like monkeys in a cage that this is where the term 'monkey business' was first coined.

The Metropole struggled, and in World War I, when Folkestone was the main point of embarkation for the trenches, the hotel was requisitioned as the officers' quarters (Wilfred Owen in one of his letters talks of 'the mud of Flanders as thick as the carpets of the Metropole'). After the war the Metropole became derelict and was left to grumble to itself as it crumbled quietly in a corner. Now, once more, it's risen: one half health club and the other half contemporary art gallery. The Metropole Gallery is owned by the Creative Foundation, a charity that is buying up derelict properties in run-down areas and transforming them into cheap rental spaces for artists, gallery owners, web designers and media-linked enterprises.

Strange Cargo, on the corner of the old town's High Street, is a loose collective of artists that first got together in 1994 when the Tunnel opened and has been running events and exhibitions, promoting local artists and organising the annual carnival ever since. The two streets it sits at the corner of typify the Janus-faced nature of the town: boarded buildings and shameless run-down 'dole-on-sea' rental properties rub shoulders with Strange Cargo murals and refitted traditional shop fronts (Sew Simple, a joke shop, a rock shop, a new craft gallery, a health clinic and a tattoo parlour). The old forgotten corner of town has become fashionable and expectantly awaits the arrival of art-safari weekenders from London when the new high-speed rail link cuts travelling time from King's Cross to just 48 minutes.

It's all-change in Folkestone. A seven-bedroomed house currently sells for around £200,000. But not for long. The buckets and spades have been stashed and old photographs are being dusted off as Folkestone is rebranded. Instead of 1950s family fun, the arty makeover – 'Folkestone: on the edge, by the sea' – will soon no doubt shine like a lighthouse on forgotten luminaries and events. One-time resident author Joseph Conrad will be at the forefront, his regular meetings with nearby Rye resident Henry James immortalised, the place of Folkestone in the ending of *The Secret Agent* underscored. Perhaps too a play will be written about the fabled supper at HG Wells' home in Sandgate (twinned with Sangatte) when the author, Winston Churchill and GB Shaw reputedly invented the tank.

People used to say that Brighton was to the Continent what Folkestone was to the incontinent. Saga (the fifties-and-over tour operator which is active in the regeneration programme) has its HQ here. Interestingly, the De Haan family who own Saga arrived in Folkestone fleeing persecution in Holland (just as the family of Conservative leader and local MP Michael Howard came to Britain to escape Jewish persecution in Romania). Give them a few more years and Margate, Broadstairs, Ramsgate and Folkestone may do for Kent what Aldeburgh, Walberswick and Southwold have done for Suffolk.

Four resorts in just as many days has left me in need of the open road and open vistas and so I quit town, passing a squat Martello tower at Dymchurch. The arrow-straight road gallops alongside the sea, growing progressively skinnier. It ends, and so does England, at Dungeness – the largest shingle formation (along with Cape Canaveral) in the world. The reclaimed land is a blazing white pebbled garden decorated with blooms of white sea kale, a sub-Saharan hallucination beside the sea.

Derek Jarman, a former resident, believed Dungeness to have been singly blessed, claiming it has 'the strongest sunlight, the lowest rainfall, and two less weeks of frost than the rest of the UK'.

A couple of lighthouses rise up from the ness and behind them stand the steaming fumeroles of two nuclear power stations that are both up for decommissioning by 2016 (core-wrapped and abandoned like the four monkeys – see-no-evil, hear-no-evil, speak-no-evil, and hopefully-do-no-evil). Surreally, a miniature 15in-gauge steam train – reputedly the world's smallest public railway when it opened in 1927 – trundles across the desolate backdrop. Scattered around it are homes made of wood shingles, black tarred weatherboard and even requisitioned railway carriages. All that's missing is Ry Cooder's bottleneck guitar, drifting across the blasted landscape like tumbleweed.

By the water's edge an elderly woman in a straw hat is sitting on a shingle bank reading *Middlemarch*; but today is the middle of June and the spartan landscape is at its most bountiful. Outside a wood-tiled cottage called 'Caithness', a vertical raft of jumbled found objects stands festooned with jellies, fins, goggles, shoes and buoys. The doll's house is both home, work studio and gallery to photographer Chris Shore and his artist wife Helen. Displayed inside are dramatic and moody framed black-and-white photographs that record Chris's twenty years on the ness. I try to find out more about the pair but he is unresponsive and decidedly frosty. It's a fine line he treads, having chosen to live misanthropically at the world's end but needing tourists to support that lifestyle. What he definitely doesn't need is another author writing a book, or another film crew. Chris therefore gives monosyllabic responses to my questions and, as he continues framing another photograph in the sanctuary of his workshop, never once looks up at me nor at his young daughter wandering the shop floor trailing her comfort blanket behind her.

To make matters worse for Chris and others like him, fiercely protective of their unfenced privacy, an increasing number of pilgrims have been making their way to the promontory over recent years. The object of their obeisance is cult film-maker Derek Jarman, whose black varnished home with its brilliant yellow window frames has become a shrine since his death. Ask Betty at the old lighthouse (open to visitors) to direct you to Jarman's garden and she'll probably send you back to Greatstone. Geraldine Thomas, a member of one of the oldest fishing families, has the misfortune of having her home located next to Jarman's and has to endure eyes beaming like flashlights regularly through her windows.

It was in Prospect Cottage that Jarman spent much of his later life. On 19 February 1994, however, he died of AIDS. Through the window today, resting on a well-worn bench, I can see his paint brushes protruding from an old can, as if awaiting their owner's return. Jarman's paintings adorn the walls, his sculptures decorate tables and alcoves. But it is the shipwrecked coastal garden outside that is the real memorial: Jarman's bit of heaven among the desert of shingle and kale. Here a tide line of beachcombed *objets trouvés* has been arranged with an artist's eye amid poppies, marigolds, dog roses, cornflowers and beds of gorse and sage. On the far side of the tar-black wooden cottage, the words of a John

Donne poem, 'The Sunne Rising', have shrivelled like old mushrooms to provide the ultimate obituary.

Since the 11th century the Southeast has been transformed through painstaking land requisition, the drift of shingle, the rise in sea level and Scotland's insistence on tilting England's bottom-right-hand corner towards Davy Jones' locker (the result of the Scottish mountains' continued rise since the last ice age). Owing to accretion, many communities like New Romney (and Old Romney before it) found their port stranded inland and had to relocate or find new ways to survive. Other towns, meanwhile, were snatched by the sea.

The lighthouses at Dungeness are typical examples of the dynamic. The original lighthouse, a pear-shaped pensioner now stranded 500 yards inland, was replaced in the 1960s by a trim minaretlike lighthouse close to shore. It too is starting its march inland. Each year shingle is manually transferred from the eastern flank, of the power station to the western flank, only for it to be transported back by the sea (before the power stations arrived and had to be protected, the spit was adding a metre a year as it crept its way back to France). Dungeness is my introduction to the Sisyphean task of coastal communities attempting to defy nature.

At nearby Greatstone, William Clough Ellis' Romney Bay House calls to me like a siren. Built in the 1920s as a holiday home for the American actress and journalist Hedda Hopper, the whitewashed hotel has only a handful of rooms and unfortunately they're all fully booked. I sit in the sun-drenched garden with a cream tea, taking it in turns to watch the relative progress of a gardener zipping about seated on a lawnmower, and then that of a dredger regurgitating shingle from the Hastings beds on to the beach. The latter is part of a multi-million-pound project to strengthen the coastal defences. The sea, meanwhile, continues to rise whatever defence we put up and this process will accelerate considerably this century unless we attack global warming more effectively than we have the movement of shingle.

The nightmare of global warming is accepted by just about everyone apart from George W Bush, even if our only attempt to deal with it appears to be gallows humour. Although there are a number of potential futures, none of them is one you'd have on your Christmas wish list. The most likely imminent change for Britain is that our generous, mild climate will soon be relegated to folklore. Daily, enough fresh water is melting on the northern ice cap to service London for several months. Only it's not coming to London – instead, it heads for where the Gulf Stream becomes so saline heavy that it sinks beneath the waves and returns south. Because of the huge quantities of fresh water reducing this salinity, the conveyor belt of the Gulf Stream has already had its power radically reduced over the past decade and in twenty, fifty or a hundred years, it's likely to stop altogether. It is the Gulf Stream currents that keep our land cosy and our seas warm enough for mad Englishmen to swim in. It is highly probable that during our children's lifetime, if not our own, the country will be enduring the arctic winters that our latitude rightly deserves: three annual months of snow, ice floes off the coast and no Punch and Judy on Weymouth Beach. The climate of Iceland but without the hot geysers.

In the meantime, following two thousand years of land creation through reclamation, we are now entering a period of far more rapid 'managed retreat'. DEFRA, in consultation with English Nature and the Environment Agency, has already allowed certain areas that have long battled the sea to revert to marshland. The largest deliberate breach of Britain's sea defences happened at Freiston Shore near Boston when 66 hectares were flooded to become an RSPB nature reserve. Another recent breach was carried out at the Essex Wildlife Trust Abbotts Hall on the Blackwater Estuary in Essex.

Latest research from the Government's Climate Change Scenarios (UKCIPO2, April 2002) warns that the frequency of extreme weather, which exacerbates the dangers of a rising sea, will increase enormously this century. It's predicted that ferocious storms that traditionally hit the North Sea coast every 120 years may be calling in every seven years in the near future and intense rainstorms will become ten times more common. In the Atlantic waves are already reported to be 10 per cent higher than they were a decade ago.

The RSPB is all in favour of the managed retreats as a method of rebalancing the loss of intertidal habitats to rising sea levels. The North Kent Marshes, North Norfolk and sparsely populated areas of the Severn are all examples of areas that have traditionally been defended at enormous financial cost.

The National Trust, Britain's largest private landowner (and the world's biggest independent conservation charity) has also abandoned the Canute position, taking an unpublished decision to allow properties at more than fifty sites to be taken by the sea. Rob Jarman, head of sustainability at the Trust, was recently quoted as saying, 'It is impossible to tell exactly how long it will take for them to be eroded, but if we have similar storms to those that hit the east coast in 1953, it could happen overnight.'

The Trust owns half of the worst-hit Cornish coast. Soon, perhaps, the Cornish fishing village of Porthleven (and St Mullion and St Michael's Mount?) may be told to give up the ghost, to roll over and concede defeat in its historic battle against the prevailing south-westerlies. On the eastern coast Lindisfarne's ancient causeway may also be soon submerged for ever. The Trust – which owns 650 miles of British coastline – is now buying up thousands of acres inland before it becomes the new coastal frontier.

By 9 p.m. I'm checked into White Horses Cottage (built in the 1920s, largely from the spoils of a 17th-century Sussex home) and ensconced on a balcony, staring out across the shingle and rocklike blooms of kale. The tide has peeled back, revealing a rumpled bed of mud and shallows. Thoughts turn to my children and what kind of English coastline they will show their children (and whether that will include anything at all of East Anglia, come the Great Flood). I drift off to sleep dreaming of glacial bungalows calving into the sea.

On Romney Marsh sheep are grazing and terns wheeling above sun-splashed ponds as a sign welcomes me to Sussex – which Hilaire Belloc, in *Hills and the Sea* (1906), bizarrely called 'that part of England which is very properly called her Eden, that centre of all good things and home of happy men'. The South Downs rise up and I turn westward for the first time. Beyond Camber the mean slits of pillboxes squint from behind generous eyelashes of marram grass. The road winds, rises and plummets, the Roman straightness of the east coast flatlands already consigned to memory. In around thirty miles I've swapped the chalk cliffs of Dover for Romney Marsh's coastal shingle fringe and patchwork of dykes, and I am now rising into the flame-red sandstone outcrop at

Fairlight Cliffs, close to where the weald of Kent and the weald of Sussex meet. I disappear into a vaulted forest that occasionally unclasps supplicating fingers to reveal views over the rolling Wold.

Eventually I descend the cramped Bourne Valley into Old Town Hastings, where half a millennium of architectural fashions has been emptied on to the streets. Medieval mansions that once breathed expansively on their vast-acred estates now suffer the indignity of having neighbours encroaching up to their gabled ends. The interconnecting 'twittens' (alleys) even have to duck beneath overhanging floors.

Old Hastings is a wonderful hodgepodge of architectural styles and infinitely more attractive than the urban jungle of the adjacent new town with its bland high street shops, swirling traffic, beggars, junkies and drunks. Any pebble on Hastings beach will spin you a tale of an earthquake or a lazy yarn of balmy days beneath a tropical sea. For such a small island, we possess an extraordinary geology, a coloured-in schoolbook that is a rainbow of sandstone, chalk, granite, basalt, schist and flint. The vernacular architecture of the best towns, like Old Hastings, are similarly expressive, their walls whispering similar local tales, unless the original home owner happened to have been wealthy enough to import foreign slates, granite lintels and a marble column or two.

Despite its quaintness, the old town resists being smug but neither is there any of the raciness here of neighbouring Brighton. In short, it is the first town I've visited on the journey so far that I can imagine living in. Hastings' fifteen minutes of fame arrived not in the 11th century as many believe (the Battle of Hastings doesn't count, as it was fought six miles inland at Battle), but in 1925 when John Logie Baird made the world's first TV transmission over a distance of three yards in his rooms on Queens Avenue.

I start my tour at the top of town on West Hill and the as-good-as-gone Hastings Castle, the location of William the Conqueror's first garrison after the defeat of Harold. The ruins now guard civilised Old Hastings from the fast-food culture, drug problems and steeply rising unemployment of the new town.

In the local newspaper, the *Hastings & St Leonards Observer*, I read the glad tidings that an art college has been approved for the town. While they await their first glut of art students, local lads practise by beating up foreign-language students. A £400 million regeneration programme is also about to kick in, which will probably lift Hastings' image a notch or two, along with house prices (at present they're half what you'd pay in Brighton). The local rag, however, is dominated by bad news rather than good. The front-page headline is 'Street Fight Murder Trial'. Page two follows up with 'Thousands stolen in half-term burglary rampage'. Page three cheerily proclaims, 'Tax credit fiasco puts hundreds on breadline', while page four bemoans the weather – 'From scorcher to floods in 24 hours'. And so it goes on.

Crime has always been high on the list of preferred career options in Hastings. 'Smugglers Adventure', also located on West Hill, provides testimony to this fact. With commentaries in French, Dutch and German (and the fact that admission can be paid for in euros or sterling) it's also a reminder of the proximity of the Continent. Today, however, this old maze of tunnels no longer stores booty but instead fleeces tourists, re-telling, in sublimely tacky style, Hastings' epic smuggling tales.

In 1820 Joseph Golding, a 34-year-old greengrocer, discovered the tunnel network by chance (for several decades it had been boarded up and abandoned on the orders of a puritanical mayor outraged by couples using it for sex). Golding bought the site and augmented the network, digging by hand the 45m candlelit Monk's Walk as well as a spacious ballroom. During World War II it became an air-raid shelter and after the war, it was a venue for jazz evenings and dances. But these were just footnotes to the real history and the Southeast's leading role in tax evasion long before the days of cross-Channel booze cruises and lorries smuggling fags.

When import taxes were introduced, a thousand years ago, the south coast took to smuggling with gusto and never looked back – except to check that no one was following. John Wesley swung through Hastings in 1773 and wrote, 'I found an abundance of people willing to hear the good word . . . but they will not part from that accursed thing, smuggling, so I fear with regard to these, our labour will be in vain.' He wasn't wrong: at that time a tunnel ran from the Stag public house into the crypt of All Saints church where liquor was stored with the vicar's blessing.

The contraband boom years occurred between 1700 and 1830. In 1782 a quarter of all Britain's smuggling vessels were landed in Kent and Sussex. It probably helped that those being paid to stop the trade were invariably relatives of the smugglers and also on their payrolls. The nearby Bo-Peep Martello tower, which served as the HQ for the Preventive Service officers, soon became fabled in nursery rhyme:

> Little Bo-Peep *(Preventive Service officers)*
> Has lost her sheep *(smugglers)*
> And doesn't know where to find them;
> Leave them alone
> And they'll come home
> Dragging their tails *(tubs of neat alcohol)* behind them.

As taxes became more punitive and smuggling rewards therefore greater, larger out-of-town gangs muscled in and became increasingly audacious. One incident involved sixty members of the Hawkhurst Gang breaking into Poole customs house to reclaim their booty.

As profits grew, deterrents became harsher. 'One of my ancestors, Caleb, was hung for smuggling around 1820,' a man with cropped hair, a warm smile and eyes that appear to have been starved of light is telling a small group taking notes. The party is on an educational trip and Kevin Boorman has been asked to escort them because of his local knowledge. I tag along but the group appear to be in a hurry and pass through the present-day simulated customs check, ignoring the looping request and interrogation, 'Do you mind stepping over here please . . . What country have you just come from? . . . Do you mind stepping over here please . . . What country have you come from?' They hurriedly shake Kevin's hand and rush off to another meeting. Kevin stands in the sunlight and squints. I snare him with a couple of dumb questions, both of which he answers graciously. The first I can't remember but the second is to do with other local families whose ancestors were smugglers.

'Apart from Moon – that's the family name on my mother's side – I can think of Noakes, Adams and White that are still common local names from old fishing families that may well have been involved in smuggling in the past.' Kevin smiles and shuffles his feet, seemingly uncertain whether to turn on his heels and return to the Old Town or politely wait to see if I have more questions. I resolve his dilemma by accompanying him across the rolling lawns to a path winding down the hillside. As we stroll, I try another social lubricant, the one that's always the first to be used on the Indian subcontinent. 'Do you have children of your own?' It opens up another saga. 'Yes, and they go to All Saints, the same school that I attended, and that my mother and Nan did before me . . . the only difference was Nan had to write her answers on a slate with chalk!'

Soon we are breathing in, descending cat creeps and squeezing through twittens that link to larger roads flanked by an architectural miscellany of half-timbered homes, shingle walls, weatherboarding, brick and stone, and even leaded cupolas. Obese gulls squawk and crap all over the place. 'We still get letters in the newspaper from incomers complaining about them and asking why the council can't do something about them.' Kevin chuckles. In the front garden of the diminutive Sinnock Square, a pair of boots stand as memorial to the house's gardener, who died at the age of 92.

The twitten feeds into a larger road where Nat King Cole takes up pride of window space in the record shop and in the bookshop Robert Carrier cookbooks outsell Jamie Oliver. In Old Hastings cobblers still exist and local butchers flourish alongside resident artists and galleries.

'That's where my mum was born.' Kevin points to a building on Croft Road. 'It's Elizabethan. The 5ft 4in doors are the giveaway. They were midgets in Tudor times.' Before I can estimate the particular size of the house he's indicating, Kevin has already moved on to a cannonball embedded in St Clement's church wall. 'A Portuguese man-of-war did that . . .' Kevin is a man clearly proud of his patch and in no way coy in singing its praises: 'As one of the original Cinque Ports, we've had our own fleet here since the early 11th century at least. And our fishing fleet – despite shrinking every year – is still the largest land-based fleet in Europe.'

'How come the fleet is land based?' I ask as we round another corner.

'The harbour was never completed. The original section was lost in the great storm of 1287.' Kevin makes it sound like yesterday. 'There was a Victorian harbour wall but that was destroyed by the Luftwaffe. After the bombing raid Lord Haw-Haw announced that the Germans had destroyed Hastings submarine base! Never was one here but all we're left with now is that little snub of wall.' I follow Kevin's pointing finger to a dark curl of stone like an ammonite jutting into the sea.

Down on the foreshore we pass the Fishermen's Co-Op, which sells nets, waders and other fishing gear: 'My cousin Maggie Moon runs it but now she's married into the Starr family so she's gone from being a Moon to a Starr!' We detour round Johnny Swann's chalkboard advertising

Dover sole, conger eel and fresh coley ('Johnny was in my class at school') and tiptoe through the shingle detritus of floats, buoys, chains, trammel nets, generators and brightly coloured beached trawlers. Nowadays they use tractors to get the boats in and out of the water, but twenty years back it was still done with sweat.

Many of those working the boats also grew up with Kevin. One regularly fell asleep on his desk because he'd been out with his dad fishing from two in the morning. 'It's still a very close, tight community. Even if they privately slag each other off, woe betide any outsider that tries – and by outsider that means anyone who hasn't been fishing several generations.'

Before disappearing, Kevin points me to the Fishermen's Museum, which is housed in the mid-19th-century Fishermen's church. Most of the chapel is taken up by the 29ft-long *Enterprise*, the last sail-driven fishing lugger built at Hastings (in 1912) and from the deck of which the vicar still leads the Christmas carol concert. Along the cramped corridor between ship and walls, old maritime tomes, winches and a champion plaice (20lb 10oz, caught in Rye in 1994) jockey for space.

Among the collection of black-and-white photographs of lifeboatmen and old fishermen is one of a man whose nose is a continent and whose pugilist's face is lined with a thousand breaking waves. Biddy the Tubman was born in 1879, the fifth child in a family of eight boys, and by his early teens was already a fully fledged fisherman. In 1904 he was awarded the RNLI silver medal for bravery as a lifeboat man by Edward VII (by the end of his life, he had saved 46 people in total), and he and his boat, *The Unity*, were part of the fleet that sailed the Channel to evacuate troops from Dunkirk during World War II. All this, however, is just a precursor to his real fame.

The clue in the photograph is the blue fisherman's sweater he's wearing, on which is emblazoned 'Champion Tub Man of Europe'. To prove the point he is balancing in the ocean on the rim of a large wooden barrel with a couple of women cowering beneath his legs. Biddy the Tubman is propelling the barrel to spin like a dervish by smashing the water with a short oar. When and how he discovered his particular gift is not recorded, though it is known that he continued his aquatic trick well into his seventies (and pushed his fish cart through the streets into his eighties). He died, aged 85, in 1964. Fittingly, the framed photograph stands upon the gunnels of his old battered tub next to his oar.

Outside the museum there are a number of tarred wafer-thin four-storey net huts and a fish market where a dawn Dutch auction is held daily (at a Dutch auction prices come down instead of rising and the first bid secures the catch). Unfortunately the place is empty. The doors of a final container truck, shrouded in dry ice, yawn as it gobbles the last of its breakfast. I stroll the foreshore in search of fishermen. A shopowner on the high street had earlier told me that they are the most militant and bloody-minded fishing fleet on the globe. 'Call a spade a spade or talk shit, depending on how you look at it,' he summed up.

Upstairs in the Fishmarket Café, I am doubly disappointed to discover breakfasts aren't being served and that I'm the only customer. I console myself with tea and a view out to sea over the beached fishing boats. Maggie Banfield, in striped-cotton baggy pantaloons and a grey Tommy Hilfiger sweatshirt, apologises for the lack of breakfast. 'I gave up doing them when the hawker vans left. They were my main customers. Now there's just one or two and as fishermen don't have breakfast, I just do teas in the morning.'

Maggie has seen the fleet slowly dwindle along with the hawker vans. Each year someone else gives up. Boats are expensive to maintain and the quota restrictions mean no one makes enough to live on. 'Trouble is, there's no work in town either. My own husband gave up three years ago and has been working as a labourer in Ireland ever since.'

I thought it was meant to be the other way around – Irish labourers building our roads and homes over here.

'Things change.' Maggie stops looking me in the eye and stares out of the window. 'He gave up when his 23-year-old son disappeared overboard and was never found.' There is a long pause, my own stunned silence seeming the only appropriate response. 'He couldn't face going back to the sea.'

'I'm sorry.' I manage to dredge up some useless words.

'I wasn't his real mum,' Maggie almost apologises before her eyes fill and I'm left with the certainty that this is simply not the truth, blood or no blood. She looks away again and then walks out of the door on some invented errand. I return to staring out of the window. The colour has drained from the beached fleet and all I can see is blackness – the black flags on the marker buoys, the black tarred net shops, the dark unforgiving sea.

Maggie returns having regathered herself and has clearly decided to switch to safer, less personal and painful subjects. 'There were around 44 boats operating in the fleet six years back; now there's 15.' The sun catches the jar of Sarson's vinegar on the plastic checked tablecloth, transforming it into a kaleidoscope of swirling colour.

'What do they do for work when they leave the fleet?'

'Nothing. They're unemployed. But they're still better off because they don't have the cost of boat maintenance.'

'I suppose that explains why I haven't been able to find any fishermen to talk to.'

Maggie points out of the window to a man in a red baseball cap walking the beach. 'That's Peter White. He was a fisherman. Until three months back. He was the last to give up.'

Old habits die hard. Peter White is pacing the shore, looking to sea one moment, down at his feet the next, and then across to the small beached, red fishing smack, RX 87, that he owned for most of his working life. Peter doesn't seem to know quite what to do with himself.

I make my way painstakingly across the beach. With every step I take, the shingle falls away and drags me down like quicksand. I introduce myself and ask Peter why he gave up trawling.

'It wasn't easy.' He shakes his head and then quickly sidesteps sentimentality. 'I don't regret it, mind. It had to happen, even though there's been fishermen in my family as far back as the early 1800s when one died in the Great Storm.'

For an hour Peter, with nothing else to fill the ocean of his days, holds me spellbound. Remarkably open and honest, he displays a passion for the sea that those who rule it with their laws and quotas can have no grasp of. 'To the Government, we're just a disposable industry. It just doesn't mean anything to them.' Peter shakes his head once again. He may have quit the sea several months back but it is still coursing through his veins.

'Most of all I miss the early mornings, like today, when you can smell the salt on the air.' Together we stroll aimlessly through the graveyard of boats. In the years leading up to his quitting the sea, Peter was making around £8,000 a year before outgoings on the boats and nets. He couldn't carry on and sold his trawler for £12,000.

'Last year six gave up and went to London but they're back now and unemployed. I was the last to go, three months back. I'm just grateful I've got two daughters so I'll have no sons going into a dying business.'

In another decade, Peter believes, 'the largest land-based fleet in Europe' will be extinct. 'At least then we'll have no fishermen dying at sea,' he throws in a bitter crumb of comfort. Dressed in blue overalls left open to the waist, Peter recounts the roll-of-honour that confirms a fisherman's lot as the most dangerous there is.

'Usually it's silly accidents, not storms. The public mostly don't hear about them – one fisherman dying at sea isn't newsworthy. In 1972 I remember Tom Adams died trapped in the winch. He was working single-handed the same way I had to because we couldn't afford to pay wages. In 1974 my dad was one of the crew that brought two dead home from the RX 90 *The Valiant*, which got run down by a cargo ship. George Mitchell – Gammy – he died back on shore – can't remember when that was. In October 1987 a hurricane ripped the roof off a shed and it killed Jim Reed. In 1988 Maggie's young lad – well, stepson – Darren Fox, he was lost overboard. And in 1999 another young lad, Russell, was killed under a tractor.'

Working from the shore always increases the risks. 'You sail out of a harbour and you're in control from the off. Launching from the shore, though, it's the waves that do the controlling; going in arse-first and then trying to turn her round to get out over the breaking waves, the old wooden boats get a right mauling.'

Peter tells me that the fleet isn't going out today because the sea's too rough. 'Last year, in a five-week spring period, there were just three days' fishing because of bad weather and heavy seas. It's global warming, I don't care what anyone else says. In this business you can only keep financially afloat if you're fishing and too many times these days we can't trawl, particularly if you're sailing a boat with a wooden hull. The bigger steel boats can do more – scalloping and beam trawling – but it's impossible for the small wooden boats. Even when they do get out at the moment, the spider crabs are ripping up the nets.'

'Do you miss it?'

'Fishing?'

I nod my head. Peter's eyes mist. Passion rises like a marker buoy as a net sinks. 'I've been going to sea thirty years. Every day since I left school in 1974. Well, until three months back. My whole working life. And I never had a day's illness. The lovely sunny early mornings. The

salt air. Now it's over. Of course I miss it. I tell you, it breaks my
heart. Sometimes I'd be out there on my own and there would be
dolphins and porpoises swimming beside me or a cruise liner off
somewhere exotic. One day a tall ship loomed up in front of me out of
the mist. It's a wonderful life.' He shakes his head one last time and
heads off for the Angling Club along the beach where he helps out a few
hours a day. 'It's pocket money really.' But pocket money is better than
running at a loss.

From Hastings I cross the mangy Downs to Brighton's pinched drapes,
cardsharp fanlights, hangover canopies and laceless sash windows that
reveal Bacchanalian revellers romping across ceilings. Continental England.
Where the English go to have affairs. Racy, rakish, bohemian Brighton.

Little did Richard Russell realise, when he published his *Dissertation
on the Use of Sea Water in Diseases of the Glands* in 1750, that he was
inventing the seaside holiday. Seemingly overnight, London's high
society abandoned the capital, seeking the good doctor's 'oceanic fluid
cure' – a nasty concoction containing crabs' eyes and vipers' flesh.

The waters are down to Russell; thanks for the town's raciness, however, has to go to the Prince Regent, or Prinny, as he was affectionately
known. In Brighton the young prince enjoyed a raffish freedom away
from his father's shackles; that is, once he'd trimmed two miles off the
Brighton-London road to bring it inside the 50-mile radius of the capital
his father insisted he remain within. Prinny's favourite pastimes away
from the corset of the court were racing his entourage through the
twittens, or burrowing through a network of underground passages to
visit one of his bevy of paramours in town.

Legend also surrounds other royals. A disguised Edward VII
apparently liked to melt into the crowds on the prom. Queen Mary, on
the other hand, preferred strolling the Lanes, pointing to antiques she
fancied and then conveniently forgetting to pay for them. Queen
Victoria, predictably, cared not a jot for Brighton's excesses and foreign
ways. When she finally sold off Prinny's cursed Pavilion, she shipped 143
van-loads of furniture back to Buckingham Palace (including the dining-
room carpet, which was cut into pieces for the servants' rooms).

The Pavilion survived and this evening John Nash's onion-shaped cupolas and finger-thin minarets look as youthful and fantastical as ever in the dusk: a Moghul palace rising from the plains of Rajasthan or a schoolboy's ultimate sandcastle, depending on your age and perspective. When Prinny grew into the 24-stone, virtually immobile George IV, he substituted romps through the town for four-hour dinner parties beneath the one-ton, 30ft winged-dragon gasolier. According to menus still displayed in the palace, a gathering of twenty would typically require 36 entrees and one hundred main courses.

A few minutes' walk from the cornucopia of oriental treasures, I order a more modest risotto in Quod, the newest and hottest restaurant in town. Instead of the dripping chinoiserie of the Pavilion, Quod provides dining distractions in the form of performing chefs in the open-plan kitchen, original contemporary art dripping from the bare-brick walls, and Brighton's coolest denizens garnishing neighbouring tables.

Fantasy, excess and romance remain the staples of the Queen of English resorts. One friend who lives here once told me, 'Bournemouth is where couples who've been together too long go on holiday and Brighton is where they come for their illicit affairs.' Everybody, it seems, has their romantic tale to tell. Mine occurred in 1967, aged seventeen, during my late pimples period when I came down from London for the day and phoned the office the following morning to tell them I wouldn't be going back. My seductress was a gorgeous, gamine sixteen-year-old Swedish language student called Helen. Each night she and I would sit in the Cricketers in Black Lion Street staring into each other's eyes, then we'd walk the Prom and, when it was quiet enough, entangle sweaty limbs on the uncomfortable pebbles beneath the pier. Life doesn't get much sweeter.

After the summer Helen returned to Sweden and I to London, but whenever I visited Brighton subsequently, I still dropped into the Cricketers to stir the memory. Winnie Sexton, the landlady who ran the place for decades, has unfortunately now gone. She was a fund of stories about the razor gangs immortalised in Graham Greene's *Brighton Rock*. Greene himself had been a regular. 'Lovely man,' Winnie once told me, 'Mentioned our pub in *Travels with my Aunt*.' Over the years, she got to know Greene pretty well. 'As a boy, he'd been very sickly and used to get bundled off down to the seaside to take the air. Brighton became a kind of drug to him.' Dicky Attenborough apparently also propped up the bar with his gang in the film version of Greene's *Brighton Rock*. 'John

Gielgud used to come in too, dearie,' – Winnie called everyone dearie –
'but he'd always sit in a corner on his own.'

The fabled Lanes the Cricketers sits at the edge of has also seen plenty
of changes. A century ago fishermen hung their nets to dry between the
diminutive cottages. Now drunks hang themselves out to dry and the place
is packed with out-of-towners from both sides of the Channel. As I sail
across night-time Brighton, its bars and eras commingle in magnificent
confusion: Regency squares, Victorian villas, Edwardian hotels, three-
penny deck chairs, black-and-white-check mobster suits, spotty fried-
eggs-make-me-sick-first-thing-in-the-morning Mods, *On The Waterfront*
greasers. And above it all the Volks Electric Railway trundles oblivious to
the hullabaloo, and the fizz of waves continue surfing to Rottingdean.

By 10 p.m. I am in a slightly inebriated state and mistake a drunk
slumped against a railing for the elephant I posed on for a family
photograph, aged six. I sit on the pier listening to 'Da-Doo-Ron-Ron'
and 'And Then He Kissed Me'. In 2030, I wonder, will my kids, who will
then be in their forties, similarly ensconced and swamped with alcohol
and nostalgia, have a similar religious experience on hearing Mary J
Blige's 'No More Pain' over fish and chips?

Down below me on the beach are human outposts: legs pulled up,
heads resting on knees, eyes staring blankly at the noisy union of land and
sea where grating pebbles are a pneumatic drill on hangovers.

With a fat head of my own the next morning, I burrow back into town.
North Laine continues to dispense alternativeness like blessings in kite
and comic shops, veggie cafés, ethnic handicrafts, 'ultimate ionisers',
tomes on reflexology, and drop-in classes on Buddhist homeopathy, Jung
and juggling. My own particular favourite, however, is Jump The Gun
on Grosvenor Street, a shop selling everything an original or retro Mod
could wish to own.

Within seconds of entering I'm deep in conversation with Dizzy
(Stevie Marriott hair, white Fred Perry shirt and Tonic trousers). 'Have
you been to Brighton Museum yet?' he asks and doesn't wait for a reply.
'Seen the Ben Sherman exhibition?' I shake my head. 'If you had, you'd
have seen my rhubarb-and-custard 1971 classic. Well, it's not really
mine, it was my brother's but I wore it to the opening and then gave it
them for display.' Dizzy's brother apparently gave up being a Mod in the
eighties and passed the priceless heirloom on to his younger sibling. 'He

kept all his records though, the git, and I've yet to come across a better collection.'

On the cramped walls of the shop, half concealed by rows of clothes, are black-and-white photographs of the Whitsun Bank Holiday Mods and Rockers clashes immortalised in *Quadrophenia*. Dizzy follows my stare and puts the record straight on recent history. 'It had nothing to do with Rockers really. The Mods from East London – a bunch of criminals if you take away the clothes – bossed the whole scene and the West, North and South London packs wanted to have rucks to try to take over. They hated each other. So they were rucking and the Rockers got pushed out the way and didn't object but when a couple of their motorbikes went over, that was different. It was a "You can do anything but lay off of my bike" thing.' They bundled in too and that's what became the big story.'

Dizzy's tale reminds me of an LA lawyer on a Harley Electra Glide I once met in Big Sur who told me that he'd recently been divorced and his wife had got the house, the kids, the holiday home and most of his salary. He then smiled and added victoriously, 'But I got the Harley.'

My mental diversion has to be quick as Dizzy is off galloping again. 'Did you know Ben Sherman had his first factory in Brighton?' I shake my head. 'They go on about Anita Roddick's first Body Shop here, and Branson's first Virgin outlet – but who cares? Hippy capitalists! Ben Sherman? Now that's something . . . But they've stopped doing the Sixties cut on the shirts now. Did you know that? Outrageous. Same as Fred Perry.' Dizzy shakes his head in disbelief at the betrayal. 'I've complained and we're not ordering more until they change their policy.'

For half an hour Dizzy and I chat about Smoothies and Suede Heads, the Skatalites, Two-Tone, fishtail parkas, and crombies with silk hankies in the top pocket (we both wore Chelsea blue). Dizzy grows a little misty-eyed. 'We get really old geezers in their fifties calling in here still, like the Odd Mod Squad with their parkas and scooters.' Dizzy is like a religious zealot after a visit from the Pope. I keep my advanced 53 years to myself and leave him sorting a new consignment of Lonsdale bags.

Brighton's Mod history is one layer of the onion. The Grand Hotel is another. Unforgettable images of the building crashed like a house of cards were splashed across the world's newspapers on 12 October 1984, when it was bombed one night during the Conservative party conference and two people died. The Grand Dame today – the hotel, not Thatcher

– is back wearing her best frock on the Prom. The waterfront too is looking better than ever – a Santa Monica at the tip of England with outdoor pool, pick-up basketball, skate hire and a necklace of artisans, fresh shellfish and alfresco cafés. All that's missing is a Muscle Beach, and that will surely come. Next to the Grand stands the city's carbuncle, the Brighton Conference Centre, where 'FETAL ORIGINS OF ADULT DISEASE, 7–10 JUNE 2003' is advertised in stark upper-case lettering. A little further along is the new Kiss Wall with images of people snogging: an elderly couple, a son and mother, two gays and two lesbians. Well, it is Brighton.

It is my second afternoon in town and I have arranged to meet a friend, Phil Magnus, up at the Brighton racetrack. Phil arrives in a pinstriped suit as if he's off to the office. Which in a way he is; it's just that his office happens to be the racetrack. Based at Romford Dogs, Phil is a second-generation bookmaker who lives a couple of streets from me in north London and shares the same gym. He's kindly agreed to a busman's holiday by joining me for the day at Brighton's track. When we meet high on the Downs in the stadium car park, Phil takes one look at me and suggests a change of clothes. 'It's tradition to dress up for the track. Decorum.' I rummage in the boot of the car for a tie and pair of trousers that aren't as crinkled as everything else.

Before Graham Greene made Brighton's underbelly fashionable, Brighton racecourse was already known for its tearaways. Smartly dressed conmen, pickpockets and cardsharps would fleece half the passengers on the train down from London before they even got to the track. Hence the saying, 'The only thing good to come out of Brighton is the London Road.' I think it was Greene too who also wrote something about Brighton being a town helping the police with its enquiries. As I'm executing the difficult changing manoeuvre in the rear seat, I catch Phil grinning in the rear-view mirror from the front seat. He tells me he once knew a bookie called Graham Greene. 'He was a Brummie and whenever anyone asked him whether he wrote books, he replied, "No, I make them!"'

The chill wind is whipping across the exposed Downs as we make our way into the stadium. Beneath its galloping green the town hunkers and the Channel shivers. There is a choice of three entrances. 'Just like the class system,' Phil comments drily. 'Toffs up one end, workers at the other, and the middle classes keeping the two apart.'

Inside the stadium there is a disappointing lack of spivs. No tweed titfers nor Gladstone bags stuffed with £50 notes. There's a new stand, a new owner and the track competes with everyone else for the anodyne leisure business. Where Goodwood and Ascot provide glamour and aesthetics, Brighton offers the everyday for the betting man. Known on the circuit as a gaff, it's a lower-division track providing low-grade racing with poor prize money and second-rate horses. 'The track is a bit of a switchback with cambers in the wrong places and so horses often go over,' according to Phil. 'And it's a particularly hard track for bookmakers to make money at. Fancied horses win – and if there's a plot, it's always here.'

A 'plot', I discover, is when a lot of money suddenly goes on a particular horse and when the fancied horse predictably gallops past the winning post with everything else a furlong behind, it hits bookies particularly hard because more money has to be paid out on early bets taken at punishing long odds.

'Basically it's a hard track to get a skinner.'

'A skinner?'

'A chicken dinner . . . A winner. Where the bookies pay out nothing.'

Phil knows a fair number of the bookies. The majority of those he's close to are Jewish bookmakers who have been connected with his family since way back. Phil's grandfather had a sweet stall in Watney Street Market in Whitechapel and, like those in the schmutter business, would close early on race days to visit the dogs or horses. Often he and his pals would head down to Brighton. 'They'd give directions by the pubs and drive with no licence, no tax and no insurance. To make matters worse, Grandad, who usually drove, was virtually blind.'

The first race has just five runners and very little is happening trackside. Michael Mendoza, whose broken nose sits comfortably in a face that looks as though it's done several rounds with Frank Bruno, is setting up his electronic board along the rails. He is dressed in tracksuit bottoms and no socks (his lack of style much frowned upon by the more conservative horseracing fraternity). Phil has already warned me that Michael, like the rest of the Mendozas, is scared of nobody. The hod (the bag carrying his money) is casually parked at his feet while he adjusts odds on the board.

Michael, I quickly discover, has a feud running with one of his neighbouring bookies. 'The shit said the only mistake Hitler made was wasting gas on Jews. I had him round the neck but got pulled off. I even prosecuted him but didn't get a result with that either.'

When Michael was a lad of thirteen, out walking a pregnant friend along the Hove seafront, he came upon a Black Shirts rally. 'That's the first time I discovered there were racists,' he tells me. 'I was carrying several lemonade bottles I'd collected from the beach, which I planned trading for coppers at a nearby shop. The Black Shirts were coming out with their nasty crap and the pregnant girl, who was also Jewish, started having a go back at them. They grabbed her and started kicking her on the floor. She was pregnant, for God's sake. I smashed one round the face with a bottle.

'What I didn't know, because I was in jail, was that ten minutes later, as Mosley arrived and stepped out of his Daimler to be surrounded by all his thugs, my dad was just coming up from the beach. He walked up to Mosley through the crowd and punched him straight in the face. He was a boxer. Knocked him spark out.'

Final bets are being laid on the race and Michael can't trust his assistants taking bets any longer. He returns to his board, adjusts the odds and takes a final flurry of bets. Suddenly a grey two-year-old gallops past us shaking the world; its rider, in Newcastle black-and-white stripes, stands crouching out of the saddle. None of the bookies even bothers turning his head as the horses clatter down to the start.

'Great story,' I warmly applaud Michael's tale to Phil.

'He's a dying breed. One of the last characters at the track.' Phil then recites a litany of others he's known: Jimmy the One, Micky Fingers, Sideways Charlie, Peanuts, Johnny Lights, Mack the Knife, Micky the Asparagus Kid. Track bookies are an anachronism – self-employed, dealing in cash, living by their wits, visiting a different track each day; a travelling circus inhabiting the race track at society's margins.

After the next race (we both pick donkeys), we wander to the paddock. When the rainbow of jockeys appears, shivering in the cold wind, I'm shocked at just how small they are. In the paddock they are heroes; outside it young children no doubt jeer at their diminutive appearance.

In the paddock we bump into Phil's favourite bookie, Michael Mendoza's Uncle Lulu. As Lulu has retired from bookmaking and he's had enough of the cold and bad luck, he suggests we return for drinks to his home, five minutes' drive away. Lulu doesn't conform to the bookie stereotype, having been schooled at Ovingdean Hall Prep. His wife (also from a second-generation bookmaking family) attended Harrogate Ladies College, and their son, Paul, went to Sandhurst ('He made a fortune and lost one too; his trouble is he can never resist a bet and so he'll always be a punter'). There is an air of the dandy about Lulu, of aristocracy. It comes with the dressing up and a lifetime brushing up against the toffs.

In their maisonette he introduces me to his pretty wife Judy, and opens a bottle of white wine. Having already met one pugilist in the Mendoza family, I'm not in the least surprised to discover that the very urbane Lulu is a direct descendent of the 1760 World Bareknuckle Champion boxer Daniel Mendoza. 'He was only five foot seven,' Lulu says, underscoring the achievement.

Judy's father, Lew Prince, on the other hand, was a bit of an all-rounder. At the age of 88, just a year before he died, he wrote an unpublished autobiography. I ask if I might take a look at it. Judy will only allow me to see the bits she's happy with. 'He wrote too many personal and intimate things about the family,' she explains. One section I am permitted to see concerns the infamous Brighton Trunk Murder. 'Have you heard about it?' Judy asks.

'Wasn't it something to do with a prostitute found in a trunk?'

'Her torso, yes. The man accused of the murder, Henry Mancini, was acquitted, though he did serve four years for other offences. Dad told me his friend Phil Goldberg used to regularly play rummy in Mancini's flat and always sat on the trunk the prostitute was found in. Dad was one of the first to create a form book and he had a cure for rheumatism too; he fancied himself as a bit of an inventor.'

Judy and Lulu rake through the coals with Phil. Late nights, late bets, legendary wins, insufferable losses, friends still here and those departed. Finally it's time for Phil to be heading home to London.

Back in town a mist is settling on Palace Pier as it steps gingerly into the Channel on its stork legs to drink. Pawnbroker lights along the prom fight the fog above a nomadic encampment of inebriated youth. In the murk more Graham Greene *Brighton Rock* dirty deeds no doubt go unseen. The bellies of wheeling gulls are picked out by the Grand's upward illuminations and inside the hotel a quartet competes with the irregular percussion of diners' cutlery. As time ratchets, so the mist slowly lifts like a curtain rising on the party town's nightly pageant. The lights at the end of Palace Pier find their way back to land. A man and a woman, holding on to each other, are tottering past the skeleton of a chained and raped bike. Cars stream by oblivious to the goings-on.

On the pier people come and go in various stages of excitement, inebriation and illumination. One couple skip, another couple dance. A senior citizen, his face mush, sits on a bench staring longingly at everybody. The Troggs' 'Wild Thing' plays, amusement-arcade machines chatter, boys queue for Daytona virtual rides. The tea dance has been replaced by karaoke and the sea is pale and insipid under the barrage of lights. I look back to the five-tier cake that is Brighton: beach, arches, prom, guesthouses, topped by towering apartment blocks. Brighton may have only recently been designated a city but in reality it has always been a city-by-the-sea rather than a mere resort. London-by-Sea. The weekend rake break. Party town. Shopping town. Foody town. Bursting-at-the-seams town. Fallen-down-pier town. Brighton is where England is simultaneously most English, most continental and, increasingly, fledgling Californian.

I quit Brighton while it's having its Sunday-morning lie-in, and cruise past the bowling greens and tennis courts of Hove, the cockle collectors of Shoreham and the colourful beach huts of Wareham. Around lunchtime I arrive in Littlehampton and park beside a Blue Flag proudly fluttering over the stooped shoulders of pitch and putters. On the prom a trolley train passes laden with daytrippers, and beyond it a silver surfer is flying off a wave at the end of a parachute. I notice that smart new signs have gone up since I was last in the resort and there's a massive redevelopment in progress alongside the harbour. The place seems more prosperous than I remember it, apart from the drab, dispiriting shops – Somerfields, Woolworths, Help the Aged.

In the 1970s and 1980s, when I was still teaching, I used to bring school parties down on long-weekend outings to Arundel youth hostel and the kids would always squeeze in a day crocodiling through the funfair, one hand balancing a ghettoblaster on a shoulder and the other glued to dribbly 99s.

Today, instead of Grandmaster Flash's 'The Message' (the summer anthem for 1982), Techno is throbbing in the funfair and, criminally, the roller coaster and water ride have been replaced by adventure golf (isn't that an oxymoron?). The beery, bleary youths who used to hunt in packs have also been substituted – by happy families attracted by the tamer rides.

Before arriving in Littlehampton I'd rung ahead and arranged to meet the funfair's owner, Gary Smart. I find him waiting for me at the entrance next to a larger-than-life bronze statue of Billy Butlin, who first opened the park in 1932 before moving on to his holiday camp down the road in Bognor.

'Did you know he was originally a showman in a travelling fair? Just like my grandfather. They were good friends.' Gary is already up and running, having dispensed with introductions years earlier. He's a good-looking, early middle-aged man dressed in jeans, T-shirt and Timberlands. 'Billy Butlin sold the park to Rank,' Gary continues the history lesson, 'and then my father, Ronnie Smart, bought it in 1977.'

'Wasn't Billy Butlin originally from Canada?' I ask.

'Correct.' Gary looks impressed. 'He was the first man to import dodgems and other amusements from North America. Most people these days only seem to know about his holiday camps . . . He eventually put funfairs into all his camps – that was his showman side. My own grandfather, Billy Smart, never lost that side either. Even when my dad, Ronnie, took over from Grandad, he continued to tour with our circus.'

Gary invites me into his office to take a look at the photographs that chart his personal odyssey. One is of a very young, disgruntled-looking Gary with Elvis Presley and Ursula Andress in Hollywood on the set of *Fun in Acapulco*. 'I was irritated because he ruffled my hair and said, "Hiya tiger."' On the other side of Elvis, Gary's elder sister appears to be in a beatific state of grace beside her idol. Another picture shows Gary swimming on the back of a killer whale with Prince Charles – 'That was later. When I served in the paratroopers.'

Gary's life had clearly been far from humdrum. His parents had met in the circus and he did his own growing up in it. 'Never knew anything else and absolutely loved it. By 1960 we had twenty elephants, seven lions, nine polar bears, six sea lions, twelve camels, seven chimpanzees, forty horses, twelve zebras, twelve Shetland ponies, twelve Welsh ponies, Highland cattle and even a few llamas. It was like my own private menagerie.'

By the time he was six, Gary had a team of four hands under him and responsibility for a 2-ton bull, as well as assembling and disassembling the vast big top. By the age of twelve, he hadn't yet lived in a house but had already attended twenty different schools.

'The circus was my home. Herman Buller the Tent Master made me a miniature big top, which I used to play with endlessly. Later, as an adult, I used to go to Africa to catch animals. Of course, I loved it . . . It was such a . . .' – Gary struggles for a word big enough to encompass his feelings and eventually settles on an overused cliché that in his particular case is apposite – '. . . such an *exotic* life.

'In every town we set up in, the girls would chase after us because we were different. And the local boys wanted to fight us for the same reason! Summer was the time we visited the coastal towns: Bournemouth, Poole, Southsea. In the mornings we'd take the elephants down to the beach and swim with them. We always started in a town the same way. We'd meet the elephants – which came by train – at the station and then proceed in a grand parade with all the animals, floats and bands through the streets. The whole town would march with us back to our site, where we'd tell them the times of the shows.'

Most of the audience had never seen such creatures. This was a time before overseas holidays, and overseas was brought to our shores by Smart's circus. 'In 1962 an audience of 21 million watched our annual Christmas show broadcast by the BBC – that's how big we were,' Gary brags unashamedly.

What's particularly interesting about Gary's life is that it was multi-cultural before this became either fashionable or despised; his extended family was Moroccan, Russian, French, Sudanese and German. 'We used to have football matches against the Arab kids who'd play barefoot but still beat us because they cheated and used their acrobatic skills!' Gary even learnt to like Hungarian goulash and to play the bagpipes.

Eventually the circus fell out of favour. There was an outcry about circus animals being cooped up in small spaces and being carted around the country. Overheads were crippling, and the circus was now competing with the African savannah and the British safari parks Gary's father had pioneered at Windsor. The animals were sold. In the end Gary stopped touring altogether and concentrated on the Little-hampton fairground.

The past decade's leisure revolution of VCRs and PCs; the competition from Legoland (located in Smart's old safari park), Chessington World of Adventures and Thorpe Park; the advent of cheaper flights abroad; the change in Sunday trading ('the funfair used to be the only thing open on Sunday apart from the church'); and even cutbacks in educational school trips, have all had a major impact on the park. 'Ten years ago we had 800,000 visitors a year. Now we have half that. I've streamlined the operation. You have to adapt or go to the wall. That's also why we renamed the funfair Harbour Park, to let people know it's not a white-knuckle place; that it's family orientated and beside the beach.'

Beyond Littlehampton I pull off the A259 and burrow down a leafy lane past flint walls and people sitting in the sun eating late Sunday lunches outside the Black Horse. The road expires with a sigh in a large car park beside the rural beach at Climping.

During the 1950s, when my family was living in Streatham, our holidays were spent hammering down to Climping – where we stayed in a friend's caravan – on my father's motorbike. My mother would ride pillion on the Triumph 600cc side valve and we three children would wrap ourselves round each other in the sidecar like bobsleigh riders. Once we had parked beside the caravan in a farmer's field, we'd race down to the beach, passing honking pigs that looked the size of elephants to a knee-high boy.

Today I saunter rather than race. Adulthood. In the car park a small café huddles against a wall out of the wind. Out on the shingle the sea has been whipped into a frenzy and trees complain loudly as their branches lash viciously like my old headmaster's cane. I look back across the wind-flattened farmer's fields but can read nothing from my past. The beach, however, is a different kettle of fish. The over-whelming smell of kelp provides olfactory memory prompts, while the cuttlefish, periwinkles and lugworms we collected have been rein-carnated and await the next generation's coloured plastic buckets. It is still a largely undiscovered and undeveloped stretch of shingle with sea kale sprouting between the pebbles' toes and yellow-horned poppy growing along the margins.

*

My next overnight stop is Gosport, which I choose as my Portsmouth base as it provides the best views across to the armada of historical craft moored in the harbour (in the same way, it's always best to stay on mainland Kowloon for the nighttime Hong Kong skyline).

I park and then stroll out on to the grass skirt of Ferry Park where I discover an evangelical love-in is in progress this Whit Sunday. A squadron of Salvation Army recruits listens rapt to a man in beard, striped shirt and sandals (Christ?) who's preaching into a microphone. 'Our Lord of Lord, King of Kings, is listening . . . Do you know God loves you just as you are? You don't have to go to university. You don't have to have qualifications to enter the kingdom of God.'

Someone with a chip against university students, I think to myself. A yacht zips by, keening against the wind, as a woman in a blue fleece takes over the microphone, singing, 'Jesu, Lover of my Soul'. Another woman sits beside a flower bed, swaying from side to side like Stevie Wonder. The harbour yawns; HMS *Victory* grimaces; HMS *Warrior* stands darkly mute and ready to blast them out of the water. Meanwhile, kids play on the rocks of the breakwater beside two fishermen knitting worms to hooks.

Another church member takes up the mic. Everyone wants to bear witness. 'I will love you alone. I will trust you alone.' Arms rise, hands stretch heavenwards, heads loll as the mantra is repeated. 'I will trust you alone. I will trust you alone. And I will give you all my worship.' Many in the congregation wave their arms as if bringing in fighter jets to land on the HMS *Invincible* as they proclaim in unison, 'Every day we are empowered by him.'

I turn the other cheek to the evangelists and travel a short distance to Explosion, a museum at Priddy's Hard dedicated to a different sort of power: naval firepower from gunpowder to the Exocet.

A new magazine with 8ft thick walls opened in 1777 at Priddy's Hard where 10 per cent of all munitions brought in would be tested below ground in the Proof House. The regular 'whump' was part of the soundscape that invariably left proofing workers stone-deaf by their retirement. The other stigma attached to the job in the 20th century was that workers in the loading area had to put up with being nicknamed 'convicts' because of the white woollen uniforms and surgical caps they had to wear, which had remained unchanged since the 19th century.

Bill Mansfield is easy to pick out in the Priddy's Hard museum because he's standing between a Gatling gun and a torpedo, dressed in that selfsame uniform his dad and he had worn all their working lives. Although long since retired, Bill occasionally comes in to help out or to give a talk. Today is one of those days.

'By the time my dad was working here in the 1920s, there was cordite and TNT as well as gunpowder,' he tells me. 'Things moved on even more quickly during my time but for some reason we kept the convicts' uniform!'

Bill was born in 1933 and started working in 'the Laboratory', where he primed cartridges, in 1948. I can't help wondering whether his white eyebrows and deep tan is down to the south-coast sun and sea or an accident at work. Bill had worked through the Suez crisis and the Falklands and claimed, 'You name it, if it went bang, I had something to do with it if Britain was involved.'

Quickly tiring of cannons, torpedoes, mines and muskets, I ask if Bill would mind if I took a picture of him. He readily accedes to my request but when I rummage my rucksack, I discover that my Canon SLR has gone AWOL. Panic. I take a deep breath and try to slow my thoughts. Think clearly. The video starts rewinding. I'd been taking pictures of the evangelists and had put the camera down next to me on a bench to make some notes. As usual, I got distracted and wandered off to the sea wall with my familiar rucksack on my back. But the camera was still on the bench.

I apologise to Bill and hurtle back in the car, only to find the Revivalist meeting is no longer reviving. The Garden of Gethsemane has been abandoned. I notice that a fisherman is still threading worms on the breakwater. I ask if he saw anyone pick up the camera.

'The Salvation Army took it . . .'

I'm dumbfounded. I may not be a believer but surely we share the same faith in the sanctity of personal property? I suddenly realise the fisherman is still speaking.

'. . . claimed it.'

'Sorry?'

The man excuses my rudeness or deafness and repeats, 'They made an announcement over the speakers about the camera but no one claimed it. Best check their centre up the road. Turn right at the Bingo Hall in

Crossways.' I feel ashamed. Casting doubt and aspersions, ridiculing the Good Samaritans who had taken my camera off and given it temporary refuge. I return to the car with my tail between my legs.

As I drive I feel a little edgy, a little spooked. Maybe I'm about to have my Road-to-Damascus moment. Like legendary blues guitarist Robert Johnson going down to the Crossroads . . . only he went there to sell his soul to the Devil in exchange for guitar mastery. A few years back I attended the Delta Blues Festival in Greenville and then followed the Mississippi north in search of Johnson's fabled crossroads. As I was driving out of Clarksdale I got a puncture, phoned round and found the only garage open on Sunday was Morton's, just a mile up the road. I limped in and on my arrival a guy in greasy overalls, carrying a monkey wrench, exploded, 'What took you so long, man?' I had driven directly there and only finished speaking to him on the phone five minutes earlier. He could see I was nonplussed so he pointed to the highway signs hanging over the intersection – 61 and 49. 'You can't make a tour of the Delta and leave without visitin' Robert Johnson's Crossroads, man.' I almost fell to the ground. How was he to know that I'd spent the morning looking for this exact spot?

Instead of the Crossroads, this time I'm anxiously looking out for Crossways. Eventually I find it, turn right at the Bingo Hall and park beside a redbrick Salvation Army church. Gingerly I open the door. Twenty to thirty heads in pews spin simultaneously my way, leaving their spiritual leader preaching to a congregation of backs. I have no choice but to explain myself. 'So sorry to interrupt but a fisherman [Peter?] down at the front at Gosport [Gosport and Galilee seem almost indivisible by now] said you might have picked up my camera.'

A balding man seated nearest the aisle, dressed in the white shirt and grey trouser uniform of his faith, smiles and then tells his comrades, 'I'll sort it out.' Together we walk back down the aisle like a couple who have just exchanged marriage vows.

Once outside, Mick McCorley gives me the news. 'It was actually one of the other churches that took it – are you a churchgoer yourself?'

'Not really.' I hide my atheism under a vague lapsed blush.

'Never mind.' Mick smiles warmly. 'I have some telephone numbers at home. I'll drive you there and we can check it out if you like.' I hope they are phone numbers connected with the camera and not my lack of commitment to the church.

In the study of his suburban home, Mick narrows his address book down to one name. 'Alan Smith. He should know.' He tries the number and leaves a message. I copy the number down and thank Mick for his help before he drives me back to my Nissan. I thank him once more and then return to Ferry Gardens.

I leave several more messages on Alan Smith's phone and also call the Gosport police station but nothing has been handed in. I fret. The camera has all the undeveloped transparency film from the trip so far with it in its bag. Finally I decide there's nothing more to be done at present and hop on a ferry over to the 15th-century – though you'd never know it – town of Portsmouth, the country's most important naval base (the Royal Navy was founded here by Henry VII in 1496 when Britain's first royal dockyard was established).

My ferry avoids two seemingly out-of-control yachts and then bucks in the wake of the Wightlink ferry. Moored on the far bank is the destroyer HMS *Edinburgh*, the aircraft carrier HMS *Illustrious* and the cat's cradle of 19th-century rigging that is HMS *Warrior*. The *Ark Royal*, just back from active duty in the latest Gulf War, is berthed further along, out of eyeshot. I decide to eat fish and chips in the late sun's rays overlooking the water, mulling over the next strategic move in reclaiming my property. As soon as I settle, pigeons attack in a pincer movement while others divebomb from overhead. You can never find an *Ark Royal* when you need one. Within minutes the shipload of grease that the cod and chips came wrapped in is slopping from side to side in my bilges, causing discomfort. I am under siege on all sides.

At 7.30 p.m. the mobile finally rings. It's Alan Smith returning my calls and, hallelujah, he has the camera. He apologises profusely for not having been in touch earlier. Alan had planned taking it to the police station after the evening service but on the way there he got my message.

'Can I come over and pick it up?' I ask.

'No, no, I'll bring it to you. I kept you waiting, after all.' I can't believe his kindness.

Weighed down with uncomfortable ballast from my supper, I make my way back to my hotel near Priddy's Hard where we've arranged to meet. Alan is already there with the camera. I offer him a beer at the bar in exchange but he declines. (Perhaps he's teetotal.) He hands over the camera and leaves. His reward will come in heaven.

The only problem, I discover after his rapid departure, is that he must have fiddled with the controls and somehow wound the film back to picture one. Back to the beginning. A clean slate, so to speak. I am a little anxious about what I'll discover when I have it developed.*

And so to Bournemouth. My friend Liora says Jews always holiday here because the sea smells of gefilte fish (fishballs). Down on the six miles of beach today a grandmother in a cardie with teacup in her hand peers out of her rented beach hut at a tattooed girl wrestling a boyfriend with a ring through his nose. Ten yards away a dad continues building a Taj Mahal oblivious to the fact that his children abandoned him half an hour ago. Beside the pier there are fleets of treasure hunters uncovering ring pulls with £600 metal detectors, and gaggles of foreign-language students singing Kamchatkan folk songs.

The whole world may be out on the beach but the resort remains resolutely as far from 'abroad' as it's possible to get. Amid the pretty flower beds and billiard-baize lawns in the Lower Gardens, picnicking families in candy-striped deckchairs watch Watership Brass performing from the bandstand. Unlike their continental cousins, who strip off at the drop of a hat, those basking in the sunshine here prefer to dress up rather than down. Women, shampooed and set and dressed in white Kay's sandals and floral frocks, sit next to husbands chomping salt and vinegar crisps, the outlines of their vests clearly visible beneath polyester shirts.

While many resorts rely on our nostalgia for British seaside tack to draw us back, Bournemouth rises, like its resident air balloon, above such things. It is the quintessentially English smart resort. Quintessentially Victorian. The Victorians believed in guesthouses, sensible beaches, sensible gardens and sensible shoes. Fortunately, sensibleness also breeds eccentricity. Ken Bailey, the England rugby cheerleader, whose career climaxed (you might say) when covering the topless Erika Roe at Twickenham, would often be found sunbathing in January, either in his trunks or a DJ, outside his beach hut.

* Three months later, when I get it developed after the trip, I receive a box of fogged transparencies – Alan had opened the back (looking for what? An address?) and erased my record of the gathering.

The town's best-known character now that Ken has sadly passed on is Madame Rosina. Weighing in at maybe 18 stone with a forbidding mass of black hair and rather intimidating masculine looks, Madame Rosina tells fortunes down by the pier. As I skirt past the signed photographs of Little and Large and Cannon and Ball (do they get a cheaper rate coming in pairs?), taking care not to landslide the gemstones and crystals on sale, I find Madame Rosina sipping Coke in her armchair. She takes my hand and starts stroking it. I concentrate on the crystal ball. 'Very sensitive, very intelligent . . .' (maybe there's something to this malarkey after all) '. . . You'll have more and more success the older you get.' She takes another swig from the Coke. 'You'll have no major health problems, retire at 55 and be very rich.' I leave as a committed believer. Who needs the Salvation Army or psychoanalysis when there's Bournemouth and Madame Rosina?

The town's eccentricity finds its clearest expression up at the Russell-Cotes Art Gallery and Museum on East Cliff. The imposing building – a mix of Italian villa and Scottish baronial – was built by John Fogarty in the late 19th century for Sir Merton Russell-Cotes and Lady Annie Russell-Cotes. Merton (1835–1921) was from Wolverhampton and had all the flamboyant excesses that new money could buy. At the time that Annie inherited her father's estate, Merton was a humble insurance salesman in Scotland. They relocated to Bournemouth, bought the Bath Hotel and made a few personal changes. It's amazing what a circumflex accent and a hyphen can do to a name. They set up home here on the cliffs amid an eclectic art collection trailing across the 78 rooms of the villa.

Inside the house today light floods through a stained-glass atrium over a plaster Parthenon frieze (made in Scotland). Near by is an alcove that is an imitation Alhambra, and the Mikado's Room where a small selection of the hundred cases Russell-Cotes had shipped back from Japan is on display. The most interesting rooms, however, tend to be the smaller ones where personal artifacts are displayed – a beaded necklace from Mauritius, a cast of the hand of Lady Hamilton, the axe that took off the head of Mary Queen of Scots, pieces of flooring from Mary's Holyrood Palace ('Given to me by the keeper Aug 18 1876'), a death mask of Napoleon – and, best of all, a piece of the galley that bore Nelson's body home to Portsmouth, which Russell-Cotes jimmied off with a penknife.

At the start of the same century in which the Russell-Cotes villa was erected, the town consisted of just one home (built in 1810) and a gorse and heather scrubland criss-crossed by smugglers' tracks. The resort started to develop in 1830 when the 'Marine Village of Bourne for bathing' was established by the Tapps family, who planted thousands of pines – Scots pine, Monterey pine, Mediterranean pine, black pine and swamp cypress – along the cliffs and down through the valleys. The smell of pine and the salty air made the place popular with those seeking a cure for respiratory ailments. It quickly became the resort for invalids and, because of the consequent fear of pollution, it resisted the arrival of the railways right up until the 1880s.

Today there must be around fifteen people swimming in the sea, despite the fact that it's an overcast, dank day. During an earlier visit to the resort a decade earlier, Steve Russell, the Senior Seafront Officer at the time, told me of a middle-aged couple who complained to him about the sea being too cold. 'They asked if I could do something about it. I told them I'd turn the thermostat up and they seemed happy with that.' Occasionally, however, eccentricity or gullibility finds its way to full-blown madness. Steve told me of several cases of males aged between fifteen and forty transported to such mental states after a few draughts of the sea air and/or several draughts of lager. One concerned a man in his thirties who was up on the pier readying himself to leap. 'I told him not to do it but there's no stopping them. He was six-foot-two and below him was an 18ft drop and three feet of water. Six foot two into three feet don't go. He dived headfirst anyway. He won't do it again. He's in a wheelchair for the rest of his life.'

I mumbled something about it at least serving as a warning to others but Steve just laughed. 'A week or two later another lad got badly injured. His brother watched him crumple and stagger about, clearly in distress, in the water. And then, roaring with laughter, he went and dived too. They both ended up in hospital.'

Apart from the loony leapers, Bournemouth appears on the whole a good deal happier than Brighton. It's greener, sandier, less pretentious, and you can park. The resort has three Blue Flags and six Seaside Awards, as well as five Green Flag Awards for its gardens. And then there are its wooded valleys, known as chines, that run to the sea on either side of the town. At lunchtime I walk down through leafy Alum Chine to Bournemouth's continental outpost, Vesuvio, where I order linguine al vongole and a Peroni. Then, after a long walk along the cliffs, I pop back to Vesuvio for its special ice cream. I'm almost tempted to stay on for sundowners and watch the stars come out.

Instead I slip back into town. Bournemouth by day may be almost terminally dignified, but with around fifteen thousand language students resident in the summer, it does have a nightlife to scupper the bathchair image. At 8 p.m., while beach-cleaning tractors are still discriminating between prone bodies and litter, the wine bars are already humming and clubs stocking up for the evening assault. I, however, head for supper at Westbeach, where the fish almost come in under the door on the lapping waves.

'The English migrate as regularly as rooks.'
Richard Southey. *Letters from England by Don Manuel
Alvarez Espriella* (1807)

'There are more saints in Cornwall than there are in heaven.'
Cornish proverb.

'The Druids' groves are gone – so much the better. Stonehenge is not,
but what the devil is it?' Lord Byron, *Don Juan* (1819-24)

Chapter Two: The Southwest

England Dreaming

As I clatter down a ramp onto a chain ferry in Poole harbour, it feels like a pivotal moment. I've just driven through Sandbanks, where footballers' wives live multi-million-pound Côte d'Azur lives on toy boats that cost the equivalent of a street in Stoke-on-Trent. The town has reputedly the fourth most expensive real estate in the world – John Lennon bought a home here for Auntie Mimi, Nigel Mansell recently sold one, Jamie Redknapp and Louise still own one, and if you fancy the Beach House it's on sale at £2.5 million.

Beyond the narrow mouth of the second-largest natural harbour in the world (Sydney's is largest), a low murmur of land rises from the sea and climbs into the Purbeck Hills. On the ferry, car windows are wound down so drivers can bronze their arms as they exchange news. They have to be sharpish, though, as the entire trip takes only a couple of minutes. My neighbour has just started telling me about a pub on Purbeck that has a dinosaur in its garden, when his voice is drowned by the ferry clattering up the arrival ramp. In a twinkling we have crossed from Metropolis Time to Mesozoic Time and a land sculpted 250 million years ago.

Purbeck is the 15-mile-by-6-mile knuckled tail of England's spine; where two degrees west (the Central Meridian) takes its dip into the Channel after its journey from Berwick-upon-Tweed. It also happens to provide a very neat chapter division between the busy urban corridor of the Southeast and the rural switchback of the Southwest.

Waiting to make the return trip at the jetty are a cyclist, four cars and two walkers emerging from wild heathland. Once clear of the ferry, I park beside a sign warning me to beware of wild deer roaming the road. A swamp that is an Indian headdress of reedmace and bulrushes leads me to Studland Bay and the finest beach in southern England. Offshore a shag hangs its wings to dry like the pterodactyls that once inhabited the area. Silver shoals shimmer beneath shafting sunlight and in the distance the slim vertical chalk stack of Old Harry stares longingly across the bay to the rest of its family clambering out of the water at the Isle of Wight's Needles.

Old Harry signals both the start of the 95-mile Jurassic Coast (designated mainland Britain's first UNESCO Natural World Heritage site in 2001) and the beginning of the South West Coast Path, a 630-mile seaside stroll through Dorset, Devon, Cornwall and Somerset. If, instead of managing just six miles today, I did the full 630, I'd climb a total of 27,000 metres – three times the height of Everest.

The trail could not make a better start as I track a barefoot couple traversing the Caribbean beach as serpent tails of sand are blown towards us from the opposite direction. Living in our cities, it's hard to believe such places still exist in England; that miles of wildness and open sky aren't mere childhood memories or adult fantasies. As waves gently break at my feet, it feels as if I've finally left London.

Like all Edens, however, Studland has its dark side. A kilometre-long stretch set aside for naturists (who have been using the beach since the 1920s) has seen a glut of incidents involving men, dressed in peak caps, shoes and nothing in between, masturbating in front of women. No one is risking exposing flesh today.

Tiptoeing between snakeskins of kelp and a scattered jewellery box of shells, I find myself singing for the first time on the trip. It has taken a wilderness to do it. In the distance a caravanserai of children edges slowly towards me out of a Fellini movie. A small dipping bird lands five yards away and then scoots further ahead as guide. Suddenly my mobile phone starts jingling in my pocket, shattering the calm and scaring the life out of me.

The call is from a sub-editor on a national newspaper. Apparently they have lost some travel copy of mine and want me to refile. 'Can you do it straight away, as we're running it this weekend?' I look at the waves rolling in beyond the blaze of sand and almost laugh. Then I realise I can actually do it. I return from the castaway beach to the car, connect my laptop to the mobile and send my words cascading into an office in London. Fifty years ago on Purbeck, indoor toilets were still a novelty and few families had seen a television.

I head up to the headland at Old Harry, where kittiwakes and guillemots are soaring above the cheese-grater stacks. Hundreds of feet below them, an underwater forest of kelp shimmies like a Hawaiian mermaid. Beside it a bevy of yachts on swinging moorings nose landward as if seeking their owners.

From Old Harry Rocks I drive across the chalk downs to Corfe Castle, where I've arranged to meet a friend of a friend who happens to have been entrusted with the National Trust's 60 square miles and 250 million years of stories on Purbeck, In 1982, the Trust was bequeathed an 8,000-acre Purbeck estate from Ralph Bankes. Allied to its Neptune Coastline Campaign (launched in 1965 to buy endangered areas of unspoilt coastline) purchases, it now manages 25 per cent of the coast between Purbeck and Lulworth Cove.

Doug Whyte suggests a hike along the southern cliffs, which we reach via an ancient track known as the Priest's Way that runs from Worth Matravers to Swanage. Few of the quarries on Purbeck, the stone from which once decorated Pisa and Bergen, still operate today. The major employer is tourism – poorly paid and seasonal – and with the influx of outsiders pushing up house prices, life isn't easy.

In cities we don't grow up with the idea that we have a God-given right to live anywhere, but according to Doug the people of Purbeck do. He claims to have met several who have never ventured beyond the 60 square miles of the island. Contrasted with the rest of the nation's current skittishness that sees Britons popping over to Benidorm, the Bahamas or Buenos Aires, such rooted provincialism comes as a shock.

A little further up the track at Spyway Farm, Doug greets one of his tenant farmers, Paul Earley. Near by, on the brow of a hill, a solitary tree is arthritically bent double from the severity of its life. Gales make the farm a bleak place and over the five years he's lived here, Paul's greatest challenge has been simply ensuring his Limousin beef herd survive winter. Fortunately the Trust is about to provide new farm buildings for the herd to overwinter under cover. While Paul and Doug discuss the changing seasons, skylarks chatter in the fields and swallows swoop like World War II Spitfires over whispering sorrel.

As Doug and I continue on our way, crossing fields grazed by hardy Exmoor ponies and meadows recolonised by wild flowers, Doug sums up the National Trust's current mission statement. 'The soil may be less productive now without the fertilisers and the rest but it's much more biodiverse so the flowers have time to seed and support insects which sustain the bird population and other wildlife.' It is a return to the countryside of our rose-coloured childhood.

The path takes us on to cattle pasture and an enormous bull passing slowly with his harem. At Dancing Ledge (located just a few metres from the end of England's two degrees west), Doug points to an artificially straight rectangular pool carved out of the wave-cut platform. 'That's where we were swimming with the kids last week. A headmaster from Durnford House blasted it out in the 1920s. He used to teach his pupils to swim here, pulling them along with sticks.'

Today, coincidentally, another school party is scaling the cliff wall, in harnesses and hard hats. Beneath our feet are blooms of yolk-yellow bird's-foot trefoil and a delicate pink icing of thrift. Doug bends to examine an early spider orchid, shows me caves in abandoned quarries that are important habitats for bat colonies, and points to the tracery of medieval strip lynchetts up on St Alban's Head where a skirt of shale is improbably crowned by a lonely 12th-century chapel.

On our way back to Corfe Castle, Doug swings into the Square and Compass pub in Worth Matravers. The whitewashed building is roofed in heavy Purbeck stone and the front garden is planted with an AC Cobra motorbike, flowers that sprout from milk churns, ammonites the size of truck wheels, and a huge wooden agricultural press. As Doug rattles the door, he tells me tantalisingly, 'They've got dinosaur prints in the back garden too.' The pub won't open for another hour and Doug unfortunately has to get going, as he is due at a parents' meeting in Poole.

At 9.30 p.m. Doug rejoins me after his meeting and we stroll the main street in Corfe Castle, passing grey Purbeck homes constructed largely of stone pilfered from the castle (Richard Fortey in *The Hidden Landscape* rightly calls the village 'the apotheosis of Jurassic stone'). The doors in the older houses, however, appear to have been constructed for pygmies, built in an era when 4ft 10in was enough headway for the average male. Doug steers us to the Fox as 'It's where the locals rather than the tourists drink.' During his earlier absence I'd already got a headstart on him at the bar of the Bankes Arms Hotel. There I'd been warned by an out-of-towner that inbreeding in Portland has led to some pretty interesting results 'and most of them are up at the Fox'.

As we enter the bar, a middle-aged man on all fours interrupts his barking to look us up and down. His female handler immediately yanks at his already tightly coiled lead. I look across to the bar counter expecting to see the pile of scattered keys that would confirm the place has been privately booked by the local wife-swap club.

'See?' the dog handler asks rhetorically. 'Works every time. Note the double-twist round the neck. It operates as a harness. We call that the *knee lead*.' She utters the words with reverence and awe. The woman is sharing her canine wisdom with a shaved-headed, tattooed *mutillato* and his Goth fiancée. The latter nods her head, admiring the efficacy of the stratagem. Whether she has a dog of her own, or is simply thinking about her soon-to-be husband, is not clear. Meanwhile the dog rises from the floor and resumes a seat next to his handler-wife.

Doug and I pull a couple of worn-down, worn-out stools up to the bar. The Fox has made no concessions to fashion, though it did start accepting Visa cards this year. Behind the counter real ales slumber under their doggy coats in a working space the size of a shoebox. At the far end of the room, next to the fireplace, a frosted-glass cover prevents wobbly-on-their-pins revellers from disappearing down a well. To avoid unnecessary redecorating expense, the wainscoting has been painted with nicotine. Magnolia waves crash across the wallpaper and in alcoves hunting horns, Toby jugs and small stuffed animals peer out. Three clocks scattered about the room each tell a different time, accurately reflecting the parallel universe of the Fox.

Landlady Annette Brown sits at a formica table with Dog Man and Dog Woman, plastic flowers blossoming eternally between them. Annette has a spray-can-fixed architectural hairstyle and a chin that has no need of a neck to join her head to her body. She runs the pub with her young nephew who's ensconced at the table with Mutilated Man and Goth Woman.

Doug and I politely listen to the lame dirty jokes being told by Annette's nephew. We also chat about Purbeck, schools and our mutual friend. Since their student days together, Doug had traded freewheeling bachelorhood for a Japanese wife, Misako, who, I'm told, is at home, 'Either spinning wool or giving someone reflexology.'

Doug's own time these days is taken up with building a new family home on the mainland, tending his sixteen beehives and carrying out National Trust liaison work. This majorly involves trying to keep all the interested parties – visitors, tenants, contractors and Trust staff – happy. The National Trust leases farmland on Purbeck to tenant farmers and provides them with sufficient inducements to accept lower-yield land and renounce devilish intensive farming practices and their concomitant pharmacy of pesticides and fertilisers. These inducements have included encouraging farmers to diversify or enter countryside stewardship schemes. One farm has developed a natural spring water bottling plant sideline, another a tearoom, and in the case of Wilkswood Farm establishing an on-site butchery so Paul Loudoun can sell lamb directly to the public.

When we finally exit the pub, Doug considerately closes the curtain at the front door, explaining, 'Looks like they're in for a late night.'

Back in my room at the top of the Bankes Arms Hotel, I stare out of the window over Corfe Castle, which stands like isolated sea stacks against the elements. Given a very unroyal seeing-to by Cromwell's sappers in 1646, tonight, silhouetted beneath rushing clouds, the castle continues to crumble slowly on its natural promontory between two rivers.

I sleep soundly and by 9 a.m. I'm burrowing alongside riotous hedgerows and slumbering Purbeck villages, eventually descending a beech and sycamore valley to the thatched village of Kimmeridge to greet the sea running in deep, regular waves, from the opposite direction. Kimmeridge's finger ledges, which once lay at the bottom of a deep tropical sea, are churning the water like a whisk. A couple of fishermen are chatting on the shore. The tide is in and there are few pools for exploring sea anemones and scuttling crabs. In the 16th century alum was extracted from the shale and used in dyeing processes; in the 19th century gas refined from shale oil was used to light Paris and the shale itself purified London sewage. Today we comb rockpools and jaw on the beach.

From Kimmeridge I skirt an MOD live-ammunition range where I notice red flags are flying. A sign declares the road to Lulworth Cove to be closed but a warden waves me through. 'Be sharpish and you'll be fine, the military has only just gone down.' The abandoned village of Tyneham is off limits, however, so I continue to Lulworth Cove, where I park and walk beside a stream tumbling through the deserted thatched village to a blueprint ice-cream-scoop cove. On the jetty a man is trying to walk a reluctant canine Methuselah with decidedly dodgy pins.

'Have you lived here long?' I ask.

'Twenty years – a newcomer. Most of us are and the town's none the worse for that. We come to live here because we love the place. Can you think of a better reason?'

I shake my head.

'There's a really good sense of community here among the incomers.' The man is in his late thirties and dressed in loafers, Chinos and a checked shirt.

'I think it's her last day.' He nods in the direction of the mangy black dog and then lowers his voice so his four-legged friend can't hear. 'Going to have to take her to the vet today. Been putting it off and putting it off. Last night she had a collapse and I thought that was the end. It was a shock, I can tell you, to find her still here this morning.' I commiserate and stare across the bay to the small proscenium entrance to the limestone amphitheatre.

'The rumpled cliffs are known as the Lulworth Crumple,' the man tells me, following my gaze across the natural rock contortions. 'To tell the truth, I feel a bit crumpled myself today.'

The next major headland along is a good deal livelier. The Georgian and early Victorian seafront terrace of Weymouth is basking in the morning sun, its toes stretched out in its sand pit. Prostrate sunworshippers are praying to the east and behind a windbreak I find Professor Guy Higgins and his wife Maggie sunning themselves in deckchairs, relaxing before Guy's first Punch and Judy show of the day.

Maggie is in white pedalpushers and a patterned pink top and has wavy shoulder-length hair. Guy, in blue shorts and sandals, looks as if he's already been in the sun too long, his face cracked into a hundred sun gullies. Like his puppets, his head, topped by an improbable bush of hair, appears far too large for his body. A little impertinently, I ask his age.

'Older than my teeth,' he replies elliptically.

'Seventy on 5 November,' Maggie interjects more helpfully. 'That's why he was christened Guy!'

Guy's fascination with Punch and Judy started at the age of seven when he attended a show in Weston-super-Mare ('I was particularly taken by Professor Rubin Staddon's high-pitched Punch'). Once back home Guy started making puppets, which his mother dressed (Maggie now handles that side of things). 'By the time I left school, I knew I wanted to go on the stage but my mother would hear none of it. Dad apprenticed me to an ecclesiastical wood carver in Powick, Worcestershire, but softened the blow by paying for me to have conjuring lessons.'

Guy subsequently joined the local Worcester Wizards Conjuring Society and before long was working as a magician, Punch and Judy man, impressionist and stand-up comic in small theatres and clubs. Bit by bit he escaped the day job as a cabinet-maker and since 1975 it's been mostly the Punch and Judy season here at Weymouth that has paid the bills.

The couple married in 1979 and have two grown-up daughters whose relationship with Punch and Judy pretty much mirrors everybody else's: spellbound until eight and then uninterested until they had children of their own. Now that the grandchildren are falling in love with Punch, their parents are taking their turn to wallow in nostalgia.

Despite the fascination of each generation with his art, Guy has had to move with the times. The current PC climate has meant less of Punch knocking seven bells out of Judy. His audience is also demanding that the show be generally 'Shorter, sharper and more vibrant, like everything else.' Guy's finest moment came in the 1980s when TV crews, the national press and coachloads of tourists flooded on to the beach to see his JR Ewing, the perfect modern incarnation of Mephistopheles. The crowds, he assured me, went wild for JR despite the fact that he had only one line.

Soon it's time for Guy's first show of the day. Watching the audience participation, it's easy to see why the timeless tragicomic archetypes have captivated audiences since the 12th century. When Judy leaves the baby with Mr Punch, she asks the assembled children sitting cross-legged in front of the miniature stage, 'Now if Mr Punch does anything silly, children, you will call Judy, won't you?' With one voice the kids yell, 'Yes!' Later I can hear the collective sharp intake of breath when the Devil appears behind Punch's shoulder.

Once, it was common to find piano, singing and dance teachers using the title 'Professor' but the convention has virtually vanished today. Guy claims he never used the tag himself until his peers bestowed it on him in recognition of his mastery. It took a long time coming but Guy's mentor had warned him early on that he wouldn't be able to understand the sleights of fortune – 'and let's face it, that's what Punch and Judy is really about' – and be a mature interpreter until he was fifty and had the wisdom.

I leave the crowd and continue my stroll through a town that Guy might like to believe owes its popularity to ER – Ewing, not Elizabeth – but in reality is more indebted to another royal, George III, who quite possibly earned his soubriquet – Mad George – on his frequent visits to the resort.

The sickly George arrived for the first time in 1789 and took to the bay in a bathing machine with two female dippers and a full band playing 'God Save the King'. Having immersed himself several times, he drank the sea water he was bathing in before returning to shore to eat cuttlefish shells and earwigs. Miraculously his physical condition improved even if the same could not be said of his mental state.

If George returned today he could swap the earwigs for the seaside staples – candyfloss, ice cream and chips. He could take a ride in a Victorian swingboat, join the kids digging to the earth's core, or admire the sand sculpture of Mark Anderson – a man who never outgrew sandcastles; the sandcastles just outgrew him. Pride of place today goes to a life-sized sand Mini Cooper out of whose window a bespectacled Harry Potter and owl are hanging. In previous years Mark, who was taught sand sculpting by his grandfather Fred Darrington (who pioneered the art in Weymouth from 1910 onwards), has chosen subjects as diverse as Tutankhamen, Buzz Lightyear and the Teletubbies. Today, unfortunately, Mark is competing in a sand-sculpting competition in Italy.

Beyond the prom lies the pretty harbour where the Black Death stole invisibly into the country from the Middle East for the first time in 1348. I notice a cannonball from the Civil War embedded in the wall above the women's public toilet in Maiden Street. Soon I am transported on the more savoury aroma of frying fish and chips into the queue at Fish 'n' Fritz, where a plaque declares 'National Runner-Up Fish and Chip Competition 2001 Paul and Julie Hay.' Alongside it are signed photographs of the stars – the Nolan Sisters, Hank Marvin, Rose Royce – who often nip across in breaks from summer shows at the Pavilion.

'Bobby Davro was the best,' Julie Hay behind the counter tells me as she empties a packet of coins into the till. 'He's really funny off stage. He came in with his wife and two daughters.' As I order my haddock and a pickled onion, I take the opportunity to ask what it is that Julie thinks elevates common-or-garden fish and chips to greatness.

'Well, that depends on who you're asking,' Julie says, launching into her culinary thesis. 'Different folk like different fish, for example. Southerners usually prefer cod and couldn't care less that we have to mostly use foreign ships fishing the colder northern waters to supply us. Then there's the Scots. Most of them, like you, prefer haddock. A lot of Londoners like rock salmon – only Europe has told us we can't call them that any more because they really belong to the shark family. But dogfish doesn't sound too enticing, does it? So we write it up on the board simply as "Rock".'

Regardless of particular fish preferences, according to Julie it is the quality of the catch and the batter that are the crucial components. Julie makes the batter on site from a recipe that was passed down to her by a veteran proprietor. She makes the humble mixture of flour, water and a pinch of salt sound like a magical elixir she's been entrusted with. 'Leave it to ferment and then scrape the top starchy layer off and it crisps up light, creamy and beautiful. Most shops these days use ready-made batter mixes, which is why ours is so sought after.'

I eat alfresco at the harbour (avoiding eye contact with the covetous gulls) and then decide to head across the causeway to explore Portland. The 'island' is reached via a short section of a 17½-mile shingle tendril (the longest in Europe) known as Chesil Beach, a tumulus of flint cobbles rising in places 35ft and on which everything from whales to a Spanish galleon have beached (in 1757 fishermen even claimed to have landed a mermaid here). Folklore has it that smugglers and fishermen are able to land in fog or darkness on Chesil Beach and know exactly where they are by the size of the pebbles. Today the largest of the pink, purple, cream and white stones still congregate at the Portland end where a gaggle of shops and a pub also huddle.

I park by the pub and walk up on to the sea defence that separates the beach from a freshwater reserve known as the Fleet. Three divers in dry suits are walking gingerly across the smooth multi-coloured pebbles, donning fins and reversing into the water under a deep blue sky. They turn and disappear beneath the foaming waves, off to investigate one of the innumerable wrecks that litter the bay. The last time the sea came right over the shingle bank, on 16 December 1989, pebbles smashed through the pub windows, tripping the electricity just as everybody was tucking into Christmas dinner. The Little Ship had already lost its bowling alley in a similar surge in the 1970s, when cars were also picked up and flung inland from an adjacent garage. When the sea rises permanently, Portland will become the real island it thinks it is.

I fail in my search to find a pebble pierced by a hole (considered good luck) but the stones are warm and comforting in my hand, like the marbles I used to keep in my pockets as a boy. I continue my walk up on to the limestone headland of Portland (which Hardy called the 'Gibraltar of Wessex'). Slowly the percussion of pebble on pebble that accompanies the expiration of each wave is replaced by a different kind of tapping. I follow the sound down a labyrinthine path through the blinding white sun trap of Tout Quarry, where vast cuts of fine-grained Portland stone stand like scattered sarcophagi.

In a clearing a dozen men and women are chiselling lumps of stone, inclining their heads, straining to hear the whispered stories of an underwater tropical paradise. Barry Discala, who leads the group, tells me they are members of a sculpture workshop run by the Portland Sculpture Trust, which was founded by a Burmese woman called Hannah. I discover that, like the rocks and Hannah, Barry's family had also migrated, though in his case from Italy. Who knows, Michelangelo himself may be a relative somewhere down the line.

As Barry talks, the tattoo of tapping continues in the dry heat. It could be Rome or ancient Greece.

'We're working with the most beautiful rock in the world,' Barry enthuses. 'That's why Wren chose it for St Paul's and why it was used for Oxford's Ashmolean, Buckingham Palace and half of imperial Delhi.' The stone is the classic signature stone for monumental architecture, as it's fine-grained and weathers practically white. 'If you stare into it, you'll see the food chain in the fossils. There's the story of the world in this stone. One day our era will be fossilised in stone too.' I stare at the piled rocks with Barry 'Plato', the ticked-off minutes of the end of some living creature's allotted time. At careers interviews in school when they ask students what they want to become, no one answers 'Fossils'.

Scattered about the sun-blasted site, and just five miles from Weymouth's Mr Whippy and swingboats, are works left behind by former students – *The Hearth* (complete with pouffe), *Climbing Figure*, *Still Falling* and, best of all, a lizard lazing on a rock beneath an all-seeing eye. An old quarry that became a boulder graveyard has been transformed into an open-air art gallery. Unfortunately there is also evidence that the Vandals – those that like to run amok with lump hammers – have found the site too.

Thomas Hardy called Portland 'The Isle of Slingers' because apparently the inhabitants were great stone throwers (with an unlimited supply of projectiles). 'Tophillers' used to throw stones down at 'Underhillers'. No one seems to know why.

The island, scarred with quarries and lashed by storms, hangs from England like a pirate's earring. Half an hour after leaving Barry, I'm relaxing on a bench with a crab sandwich on the southerly exposed oolitic limestone headland of Portland Bill. Banks of golden samphire and sunbursts of bird's-foot trefoil run to a derrick that's still used to lower fishing boats in and out of the water. I watch breaking waves leaping 12ft up as if stung by wasps, as kids deliberately get soaked and then squeal like victims. Today the sea is behaving itself but when it's in one of its tempers Portland Bill can be as inhospitable a place as can be found in England, with winds that can blow a man down and waves that crash 50ft in the air. Off the headland lies a treacherous current, the 'Portland race', which boils over steep shelves, 'a chaos of pyramidal waters . . . the master terror of our world,' according to Hilaire Belloc.

Three lighthouses stand on the headland within a couple of hundred yards of each other. The smallest, Old Higher Lighthouse, a snubbed affair built into a small complex of rental cottages, is the one I'm interested in. I knock at the owner's door and relay the greetings of a journalist friend who once interviewed her for a feature. Fortunately he made a good impression. Fran Lockyer makes tea and we take it out into the garden where we sit among the honeysuckle and geraniums she has cultivated over the two decades she's lived here.

When Fran bought the place in 1981, the lighthouse was in a parlous state. 'Following the death of my husband, my plan was to retire but somehow it didn't work out, as I've been doing B&B ever since!' Before its abandonment the lighthouse had been home to the family planning pioneer Marie Stopes who had outraged local residents with her eccentric and bohemian excesses. In the conservative world of Portland, scandal weighed more than celebrity and Marie Stopes' reputation as the author of the permissive bestseller *Married Love* was reprehensible enough but what were considered slatternly personal mores weighed even more heavily against her. According to Fran, who has become something of an expert on her predecessor, in the 1920s the local fishermen didn't take kindly to Stopes sunbathing naked between their beached fishing boats. 'They weren't too keen on her lying out starkers in her lighthouse either.'

The steps up into the lantern are almost vertical, and narrow with it, but up in the eyrie a comfortable circular sofa provides a 360-degree view and sunbathing opportunities wherever rays happen to fall. Two books on time lie opened on the sofa, *What is Time?* and *The End of Time*. There's also an identification chart, *UK Whales and Dolphin*, and a nautical chart from Berry Head to Portland showing offshore reefs. Beneath us in the garden, adrift between heron and rabbit statuary, washing turns slowly cooking in the sun.

In her second marriage, to the aviator Humphrey Verdon Roe (with whom she founded the first free birth control clinic in the British Empire), Stopes consigned her husband to separate quarters as soon as she'd conceived a son here under the stars at the age of forty. The phallic lighthouse clearly fitted the author of *Enduring Passion* better than the long-suffering Roe did.

'She had her last affair at the age of seventy with a man in his late teens and broke off with him eventually because, in Stopes' own words, she finally decided, "It wasn't quite nice."'

Fran reaches the end of the Stopes story with a fine final delusional obituary: 'She expected to live to 120 but cancer got her in 1958 at 78.'

Alongside bohemian and narcissist in the character appraisal should be added 'eccentric'. Once her son, Harry Stopes Roe, was old enough to walk, Marie togged him out in a dress because she feared for his genitals.

Later she forbade him from marrying a girl who wore spectacles because, according to Stopes, it would mean that any issue would be less than perfect (she never did accept his choice of wife).

When Fran first visited in 1959, she encountered the same suspicion and conservatism on the island. 'I tried to persuade the fishermen to take me out with them on their boats as I was a very keen fisherman but they said the boat would sink if a woman got on board. It took a long while to talk them round.' Fran's voice trails off and we stand in silence, staring out to the sea swirling round the belling skirt of the cliffs.

The next morning I continue eastwards along ever-shrinking roads and odd-named villages such as Buckland Ripers and Shilvinghampton. Abbotsbury, more literally named, dresses its prosaicness in delightful thatch and mellow stone. The overpowering feeling along the Jurassic Coast is one of déjà vu, of reliving seaside holidays as they once were. Inland, cyclists with backpacks (no doubt filled with lashings of ginger beer) disappear down narrow country lanes between hedgerows ablaze with wild flowers. Down on the beach dads ferry iceboxes and mums set up parasols while the kids search for the kite.

At the National Trust car park at Burton Bradstock (known to locals as Hive Beach), I decide to give my legs a stretch and follow the coastal path up to nesting herring gulls and fulmars on the eastern cliffs. If I'm lucky, I'm told, I might spot a peregrine falcon soaring or offshore dolphins playing. But I don't need the extra luck. Everybody out walking the carpet of pink thrift, wild chives and common mallow knows they're lucky simply being here. The sun's out. We're by the sea. What more could we want? The simple fact is that for large chunks of the population, the seaside is where we're happiest. We knew this truth in childhood with every bone in our body, but somewhere the kernel got buried under busyness. Up here on the cliffs, we remember. And so we all say hello and smile. The bastards, the things that go bump in the night, the thugs and polluters are all back home. The coast is the safe haven, our get-out-of-jail-free card.

Down on Charmouth Beach (where Danish pirates came ashore in AD 831 and butchered everyone in sight), excited children with a local ranger are trawling pools for plankton. Charmouth is one of the world's great fossil beaches, where you're pretty much guaranteed finding a belemnite if you're an attentive beachcomber. I tiptoe across rock pools crawling with crabs. I too prod and turn over seaweed, wondering if Charles II had time for the same before he fled the beach for France in 1651.

Inside the Heritage Centre I discover the cast of a 3m-long scelidosaurus (an early relative of the stegosaur unique to the Lyme Regis and Charmouth region) that was discovered in the winter of 2000 at nearby Black Ven by local fossiler David Sole (not the one from *Starsky and Hutch!*). In the Centre I also learn that the very first 'dragon' – the complete fossil of a meat-eating icthyosaurus – was discovered 189 years earlier at the same site by eleven-year-old Mary Anning.

I return to the car and set off to learn more about the pioneering palaeontologist in her nearby hometown Lyme Regis (which also happened to be a big favourite with Jane Austen, who set part of *Persuasion* here).

Arriving in town I become conscious of a conundrum: every new resort I visit, I seem to like better than the last. I preferred Ramsgate to Margate and Broadstairs to Ramsgate, and so it has gone on through Hastings, Bournemouth, Weymouth and now Lyme Regis. Brighton doesn't count because it's a city and has an altogether different feel; and Folkestone and Littlehampton are also omitted because they would ruin my thesis.

Lyme, layered in tiers on the cliff, has a dated and dignified charm – like Austen – that I just hope isn't ditched in the new millennium's seaside frenzy of reinvention. Outside the museum (it's 7 p.m. when I get here so it's unfortunately closed), ammonites, those enigmatic commas of stone beloved of Mary Anning, have been paved into the floor. The Catalan architect Gaudí believed such spirals of life were at the centre of all creation and were the inspiration for the Gothic church builders.

Behind the museum on Gun Cliff Walk, cannons promise a peppering to anyone but tourists sailing into the bay; but steps also disappear into the sea as a courtesy to mermaids. On this balmy summer's evening, the compact Georgian resort could not be in finer fettle. The boats in the harbour, lacquered by the late sun, have yawning views back along the green flanks and exposed ribs of the Jurassic Coast. On the small harbour beach, a scattering of locals are playing on the sands and an elderly man is taking a photograph of his dog. The mutt in Lulworth

Cove plods heavily back into my consciousness. I wonder whether it has surprised its owner by making it through another day.

Out at sea a final fishing smack makes its way back towards the Cobb, the 600ft stone breakwater protecting the harbour. According to the historian Holinshed, when the Cobb was first constructed Elizabethans complained bitterly at its absurdly high cost. If they knew the cost of the current sea defences (most recently overhauled in 1995), their Tudor wigs would turn grey. Over the centuries the Cobb has fired at smugglers and invading warships but has also provided the setting for the romantic scenes shot for the film version of John Fowles' *The French Lieutenant's Woman*.

The author, who moved to Lyme in 1966, started working on his novel on 25 January 1967, setting it exactly one hundred years earlier. The hero, Charles, is an echinoderm collector like Mary Anning (she died here twenty years before the book starts). Mary received little formal education and was commonly believed to have received her wisdom literally in a flash when a bolt of lightning hit her and three other children (she was the only one to survive). Her meticulous recording of extinct species and fledgling theory of geological evolution questioned the literal belief in the Bible and paved the way for Darwin.

Tonight it's not French lieutenants and their lovers strolling the Cobb but three teenage boys in wet suits topped by football shirts haring round the harbour wall and throwing themselves off at the mouth. It makes me think guiltily of my fourteen-year-old son Max and the life I should have given him. Instead of divebombing from a harbour wall at 8 p.m. on a silky night, he's probably sitting in front of the TV at home in London waiting for *Big Brother*. On the harbour wall, above a tangle of fishing nets and buoys, a sign admonishes, 'The Gods do not subtract from the allotted span of men's lives the hours spent in fishing.' Neither do they subtract the hours spent watching TV.

Beneath the sign an old red naval mine stands with a gaping mouth greedy for donations to the Shipwrecked Mariners' Society. A small fleet of rust-bucket scallop dredgers – *Spanish Eyes III*, *Sea Seeker*, *Stella Maris* – are tethered near by, their tired hoists raised heavenwards, pleading for retirement. A plaque on the wall offers up the skeleton of another life:

Admiral Sir George Somers K T 1554–1610
Elizabethan seafarer politician and military leader
As a merchant trader he flourished in Lyme Regis
Warring with the Spanish increased his wealth 1610
He died in Bermuda
His heart was buried there 1611
His body pickled in a barrel was landed on the Cobb
Shakespeare wrote the Tempest in tribute to Sir George Somers.

In between birth and death, Somers repelled the Spanish Armada and led a fleet to Virginia that was shipwrecked by a hurricane at Bermuda, where he founded Britain's first crown colony in 1606. I bet he didn't have time for *Big Brother*.

At 8 a.m. I park at the Holmbush car park at the top of Pound Street and set off to explore another English wilderness. On Christmas Eve 1839, 20 acres (and 6 miles) of chalk slipped off the shoulder of Lyme Regis into the sea. The landslide occurred during a particularly wet period when water had built up between the limestone overlay and non-porous Jurassic clays. Eventually the top slipped like a tablecloth off a highly polished table. The national nature reserve that the landslip bequeathed, known as the Undercliffs, is shared by badgers, roaming deer, 120 different species of birds and, today anyway, me. With its rampant ferns and midgies darting through sun motes, it conjures up memories of the Milford Track in antediluvian New Zealand. Although there has been little rain, there are still mini-quagmires to negotiate between glades of raking light.

The mixed-woodland rings with bird call, the most insistent of which distracts me from watching my footing and I slip between a hidden fissure and go over on my ankle. Fortunately I roll rather than fight and suffer no more than a dull soreness. On another rise an unstable ridge gives way and I surf down a gully. Again I escape in one piece. The narrow track bucks and plummets and twists and turns as if trying to shake me off, while exposed tree roots attempt to trip me. I feel as if I have stepped into Tolkien's Middle Earth.

The silence, each time I stop, is deafening to a city dweller. At one point I stand still and listen for several minutes. Slowly, behind the emptiness, a musical score emerges: the rustle of a rogue breeze sprinting through the leaves, a bee buzzing its fly-past, the squawk of a distant crow and background choir of songbirds. In time with my step, I find myself singing in my head the song I sang my kids whenever we entered a forest – 'Into the enchanted forest. Into the heart we go. Elves and dwarves and goblins, running to and fro.' During the three hours I spend in the enchanted forest, I encounter only one young couple out on a three-day hike along the South West Coast Path.

At Branscombe I take my first swim. I try not to flinch or prevaricate, for in that direction lies only a dry, shameful return to beach, tail between legs. It's forwards or backwards. My lower legs are already numb as I pluck up courage and plunge. The breath is punched out of me and I flail like a windmill in a gale. I cannot defrost the blood and manage no more than two minutes in the water. Ever since I can remember, my greatest pleasure has been that sudden daredevil plunge beneath the sea; particularly on baking days when I extend the cool drift underwater as long as possible, only returning to the surface when I'm gagging for breath. On my final plunge beneath the water and return to the sensate world today, three scuba divers surface with me.

Our desire to return to the sea that spawned us dates back as far as there have been written records. Alexander the Great descended into the Mediterranean in a glass barrel in 333 BC; in the early 17th century, James VII took a ride under the Thames in a prototype submarine powered by oars; and over the past two decades, my own desire to explore the two-thirds of the world free of sliproads and roundabouts has taken me on scuba-diving trips from the Sea of the Hebrides to the Mediterranean, Atlantic, Red Sea, Indian Ocean and the Pacific.

On the way out of the village, I pull into St Winifred's, one of Devon's earliest Norman churches. It was built, largely with the Saxon stones from an earlier church, between 1135 and 1150. With its virtually original wagon roof, crenellated tower with priest room (one of only fourteen remaining in England) and pretty hand-embroidered kneelers hanging on the backs of pews, it's a welcome distraction from the heat outside. What the church guide doesn't explain, however, is how it came to be named after St Winifred, a Welsh girl from Flint who, having rejected her local lord, had her head lobbed off in a fit of spite at the door of St Bruno's chapel. Apparently St Bruno, hearing the kerfuffle, appeared from inside and cursed the lord, who 'melted like wax'. Bruno then tidied up the mess and put Winifred's head back on so expertly that only a thin red line remained round her neck as a memento. Winifred then devoted herself to the Christian life. Well, you would, wouldn't you?

That night I'm back with haddock and chips on another promenade in England. The sea is dilatory grey beneath scudding cloud. Sidmouth's Regency homes bell and bow beneath their lead canopies – pinks, lilacs, pale blues and lemons. A few anglers are trying their luck on the beach, expansively casting floats, weights and hooks to the horizon. I sit looking seaward, along with a seagull who has taken on the role of being my minder by chasing off every other gull. Or rather, I sit looking seaward. Mr Seagull stares instead at me as pleadingly as my dog does at home when I eat. According to old sailor's tales, seagulls make the racket they do because they carry the souls of the tormented sea dead. These albatross-sized predators are without doubt the major drawback to holidaying in Great Britain. They splat-strafe everything in sight and then intimidate promenaders, blocking their way, hands in pockets, demanding chips or more strafing. It has to be said, however, that these promenade muggers are the only dangers when holidaying in a land where the risk of third-degree sunburn, shark maulings or jellyfish electrocutions is minimal.

It is 8.30 p.m. A man with painfully hitched slacks (slacks have retired to the seaside, by the way) is taking a picture of one of these ugly white sea camels. Each to his own, I suppose . . . The sea pancakes to the horizon and then rebounds across the sky in steel corrugations. It all looks and feels ominous. Turner knew that storms happen indoors as well as out. My mood is positively bleak.

What you can't escape when you travel, regardless of where you go, is yourself. It's an interesting phenomenon that psychotherapists and Relate counsellors are inundated with clients after the summer holidays. All year long people put off dealing with issues with the excuse of being too busy. But spend a bit of quality time together on holiday and the shit really hits the fan.

The black cloud that has descended on me this evening, however, is not down to drowning *within* the family but rather feeling alone because I'm *not* with them. Personally I prefer the word 'fug' – which I only learnt recently – to the more clinically nuts-sounding 'depression'. A yearning as deep and unfathomable as the sea is churning and turning in a cave. I try to pinpoint the genesis of the bad mood and realise it started when I opened the travel section of the *Daily Telegraph* and found my previous book *The Water Road* (surely the best travelogue of the past decade, if not century . . .) had *not* won the 2003 Thomas Cook Award. There is no justice in the world. I admit the cash prize would have been extremely handy, but more importantly the award would surely have put me in the Premier League for publisher advances. Plus, a little acclaim wouldn't have gone amiss either . . . As usual, the judges go for Ethiopia, Ecuador or Outer Mongolia, rather than a journey through one's own backyard where – I feel – more sense can be made of the tracks. Ho hum.

From being overlooked (ahh!), it is a short journey to feeling lonely. My own fug clouds are primarily wispy and solitary but some heavier brooding cumulus also lurks, demanding, 'What are you doing here and why?' If I feel lonely now, not yet even a month into my coastal journey, why didn't I feel the same on my *four-month* narrowboat jaunt for *The Water Road*? I search several mental drawers and finally decide it's down to the nature of the journey: the dislocation of the motor car and the alienation of the road.

Tarmacked roads are the varicose veins of England. The roundabouts, sliproads and lay-bys are alien landing strips, displaying a total disregard for regional difference and geology. As with the ubiquitous modern Barratt-land estates, there is no sense of having risen from any particular earth: the tarmac makes no distinction between Northumberland, South Hams, Kent or Cumbria. Lichen won't go near their synthetic hard geometry.

Pootling at 3mph at the tiller of a narrowboat, I felt very much a part of the linear village and had time for everything and everybody. In a car, however, the view is pinched by the window and you are cut off from everything whizzing by. Inside a car only impersonality, invisibility and expediency reside. God knows why Kerouac and Cassady made such a big deal of being on the road. Perhaps it was down to the drugs . . .

True, I have already met plenty of interesting people along the littoral, but I have never felt that same sense of belonging. The fundamental rootlessness of modern coastal communities will be underscored even more forcibly as I journey westwards through Devon and Cornwall. There are few outside Purbeck who believe they grew from the ground they're standing on.

A fug. And while I'm at it – I can get on a real roll once I get going – another depressing feature of my current fugdom is an increasing awareness that I'm growing into my elderly father, protecting my body as it makes its way through each day. The simple fall in the Undercliffs reserve I wouldn't have even noticed a couple of years ago.

A fug. I phone a friend back in London and whinge for an hour.

The lanes have shrunk to anorexic proportions. If they contract any more, there will be a metalfest as cars are crushed and left to litter and rust. In a week's time I'll pick up the tank – sorry, motorhome – from Paignton, by which time, I hope, Devon County Council will have widened the roads. Woe betide anyone coming the other way when I am out roaming in my house-on-wheels, for I shall take no prisoners. Perhaps, instead of driving, I should walk a fridge around the coast . . . Being someone who likes their adventures decidedly soft, however, I prefer a vehicle that carries the fridge for me. Adventures for the lily-livered, that's the ticket.

Another verdant valley soars up to a blue vat of sky and my mood lifts with it. Foxgloves, ferns and cow parsley provide an overly familiar guard of honour. The scattered villages along the East Devon coast use Beer and Salcombe stone, 'popples' (water-smoothed pebbles), and cob and thatch to create some of the prettiest hamlets you'll find anywhere.

During my pre-teenage years, our family had more holidays in Devon than anywhere else. Every year a day would dawn as exciting as Christmas when we would set out on our seaside holiday. By this time we had graduated from the motorbike to a funereal half-timber wagon in which we would cling on to leather straps for dear life as we careered round corners, plastic indicators whipping up and down as frequently as a pubescent boy's pecker.

At Ladram Bay, fulmars wheel over the red cliffs and a cormorant skims the mirrorlike sea. Again it's an absolute scorcher. Kids throw seaweed at each other and explore rock pools, dads loll in dinghies out of earshot in the millpond and prostrate mums sportingly feign interest in their darlings' discoveries. 'Do you want me to make you a cake, Mummy?' 'Oh yes please, Harriet.' Another castaway pebble cove.

Next up comes Budleigh Salterton, knee-deep in the retirement and nursing homes that have made it the richest town in Devon. Only two cafés are allowed on the pebble beach and the Ovaltine and cocoa served up in one is about as racy as the resort gets. In the shops along the Victorian high street, you're more likely to find winceyette pyjamas than beach paraphernalia. Among the stuffed seabirds and radioactive pebbles on display in the thatched Fairlynch Museum, I settle on a journal entitled *The Croquet Club – The First Hundred Years.* An entry in September 1939 establishes the inhabitants' priorities: 'Sunday afternoon play agreed. War declared.'

Its two most notable residents – the Pre-Raphaelite Sir John Everett Millais and Sir Walter Raleigh (who grew up on a farm out of town) – met momentously, though only metaphorically, in Millais' work *The Boyhood of Raleigh* (painted in 1870 and on permanent display at Tate Britain). It shows Walter and his half-brother, Humphrey Gilbert, sitting by the sea wall rapt in the stories of a local fisherman. That, of course, was before Walter went off shopping for tobacco, potatoes and El Dorado.

Both Raleigh's home in neighbouring Hayes Barton and Millais' seafront lodging (the Octagon) in town are closed to the public. It must be the only seaside resort in England that neither needs nor wants tourists. The only concession is a small plaque in the car park bluntly declaring 'This is Raleigh's wall.' If, like Winifred, Raleigh could have his severed head replaced and life breathed back into him, he could revisit today and sit rapt at the feet of car drivers telling of their adventures on the A376.

I leave the Jurassic Coast at Orcombe Point, skirting the canted boats on the mud flats of the Exe estuary before passing through the extravagant 17th-century Dutch gabled homes of Topsham (built from stone ballast carried from Holland in the holds of its wool-trading ships). Bird watchers are out, training their binoculars on things invisible to the rest of us. One tells me of a resident blind seal that has retired to the estuary because of the easy and safe feeding afforded by the protective sand bar. As the ferretlike man re-trains his bins, I ask what he's watching.

'Baby shelducks . . . They're unique.'

'Why?

'They're the only creature I know of, apart from humans, that are crèched. Their parents leave them altogether and they head off somewhere safe to moult.'

My swim today comes on the opposite bank of the estuary at Dawlish. With a shallower, calmer sea and another day's sunshine under its belt, it feels considerably warmer than at Branscombe. I thrash around for fifteen minutes and then retire to a banquette of shingle and sand to sit alongside a woman who promptly sends me to sleep with her knitting.

Unlike most resorts, Dawlish not only has a road running alongside the beach but a railway too and my snooze is disturbed as one of the Iron Horses gallops through. I walk under the railway bridge and pass in quick succession a whelks stall, a cheap and nasty pub, a tacky souvenir shop, and an amusement park predictably called Lost World Jurassic Park, where a fat man in his early thirties dressed in an England shirt is trying to pick up a cuddly toy with a grab-it crane. Outside the Bow Window Café, a chalkboard proudly announces 'Cappuccino and Espresso New**'. At Davidson's Toys families are stocking up on beach armoury – dragon kites, cricket bats, skipping ropes, juggling balls and power pistols. I am amazed to read in the local tourist literature that this unabashed bucket-and-spade resort was regularly visited by Dickens, who set part of *Nicholas Nickleby* here.

A crackling PA system draws me into the ornamental town gardens. At the top end, with the temperature in the eighties, the funfair has been abandoned for the beach and for a Beatles tribute band hammering through 'She Loves You' in the lower garden. Gulls squawk, three ducks go bums-up in the stream while black swans look on imperiously and call them chicken for not going right under. The annual Party in the Park is off at a canter.

Between the trees I watch a silver Bentley with a bride in situ skirting the perimeter. She stares across at the small crowd seated on the grass at the feet of 'The Beetles'. She asks the driver to stop. Perhaps she's getting cold feet, already yearning to be young and free again. Maybe her head has been turned by the topless guitarist, an Anthony Kiedis (of Red Hot Chili Peppers fame) lookalike with slicked-back long hair, shorts and boots. 'She Loves You' is followed up with 'Imagine' (with the high notes skipped). The bride steadies her nerves and orders the driver to continue on their way.

In nearby Teignmouth it's a regatta-on-the-water day rather than a party-in-the-park day. A flotilla of rowers is heading, hammer and tongs, into the broad estuary, sweeping beneath chocolate-truffle cliffs towards the finishing line. At the opposite end of the long esplanade, beefy males with beefy voices, in decidedly unbeefy swimming caps, scrap over a ball in the heated outdoor lido. Between these two whirlpools of activity, the rest of us ebb and flow. Another bride, careering round a corner on foot, clearly late for a date, almost knocks me flat. It's the wedding season. I wonder if there's a divorce season too – February, probably. An invalid in an electric chair, or motorised trolley, or whatever you call it, offers her a lift. Ungraciously, she declines.

Keats pulled into Teignmouth in 1818 to look after his ailing brother Tom, who had been drawn by the medicinal waters and the mild climate. While becalmed in port he finished *Endymion* and also wrote *Isabella*. There is certainly something uplifting about the fug-free resort. The pebbles of the Jurassic Coast that have progressively shrunk in size as I shuffled crablike sideways along the coastline have now been ground to coarse dark sand. Six women sit on the deck of their beach hut sharing bottles of white wine and laughter. Any more relaxed and they'd be comatose. In the next beach hut, three late teens are getting ready to go out. Next door a couple are finishing off a salad supper. Meanwhile the yachtees, done with their sailing and ready for some carousing, are storing boats and adjourning to the waterfront Anchor pub.

It's 8 p.m. and the sun is still strong enough for me to consider applying another lashing of suncream to my forehead. My stomach rumbles. It's Saturday. Biologically programmed, I ask someone to point me in the direction of the nearest Indian. The waiter, from Dhaka, discusses global warming with me. 'In the summer we already have the high seas and monsoon rains in the rivers in Bangladesh. We already have enough floods. We do not need this global warming.'

I overnight in a B&B in High Holcombe with views out over the bay. In just a few days, I'll pick up the motorhome. No more jammy dodgers in dodgy guesthouses.

*

The following sun-drenched morning stretches out seductively. I move
from coffee overlooking the harbour on the Georgian side of the estuary
at Shaldon to a short hike across the bucking downs above Labrador Bay
and a swim from the beach at Maidencombe. I feel in a beatific state. I
have, however, noticed of late that I've been getting some weird looks and
plenty of questions.

'On holiday?'

'Yes.'

'Alone?'

'Yes.'

A shuffle backwards follows, accompanied by the raising of an
eyebrow that suggests I've just been pigeon-holed as social pariah at best,
and paedophile at worst. The inquisitor avoids eye contact, staring at the
stigmata that have appeared between the deep furrows of my brow,
spelling out 'Sad Bastard'. Sometimes I tell the truth – that I'm travelling
over the summer round the whole English coast – but then they just stare
even more weirdly. People come to the seaside for fun. You don't have
fun on your own. Everyone knows that. Maybe that's why I got so low a
couple of days back – seeing everybody linked up having fun while I have
a relationship with a notebook. I look in a shop window to try to see my
reflection. Yup, 'Sad Bastard' is tattooed right across my brow.

Up on the hill above Torquay, I detour on to Babbacombe Down where
lobster-pink bodies are scattered amid municipal marigolds and hallucino-
genically vibrant pansies. The immaculately kept lawns are flanked by
restrained three-storey hotels, pubs and tea houses. Babbacombe emerged
as a popular early 19th-century winter bolt hole because of Torbay's fabled
mild climate (the marketeers claim you can spend a year here and never see
the temperature dip below 50 degrees). A compass on the headland informs
me that Teignmouth is at ten o'clock, Exmouth eleven, Budleigh Salterton
twelve (they're staying up late), Seaton one and Portland Bill two. A couple
of hundred feet below the lawns, laughter drifts up from the boomerang of
Babbacombe and Oddicombe beaches.

I have booked into the Imperial in Torquay and I decide to make the
most of it by checking in early. I've always scoffed at Torbay's
presumption in comparing itself with the French Riviera. But if you
happen to be sipping chilled white wine beside a hallucinatory blue

swimming pool running to Mediterranean pines that drop to a broad sun-splashed bay through which motorboats are zipping beside a mega-buck marina, it really could be Cannes. Only nicer.

Today the grand detached villas of the Victorian gentry still snooze in their 3-acre plots in the wooded hills whilst down below, the rest scrabble for elbow room flogging food, drinks and boat rides. The bookends of the mile-long Torquay seaside are the imposing Imperial and Grand hotels. Beyond the latter, Torbay gallops south – the usual resort detritus hanging to its swimming trunks – to the pink sands of Paignton and on to the rolled-up-sleeves fishing port of Brixham (for three hundred years England's leading fishing port and home of the Brixham trawler).

Kipling was not a fan: 'Torquay is such a place as I do desire to upset it by dancing through it with nothing on but my spectacles. Villas, clipped hedges and shaven lawns, fat old ladies with respirators and obese landlaus.' Tennyson, on the other hand, liked it a lot, claiming it was 'the loveliest sea village in England'. Nevil Shute felt pretty much the same way – 'a magic town built of high harbour walls and shining places beside the sea'. I am in the Shute and Tennyson camp when it comes to Torquay, though Paignton and Brixham can sail off to the south of France for all I care.

These days, however, Torquay could hardly be called a village as it's now the largest town in south Devon. Across the street from the Grand, between the rugby club and the sea, thirty women, resplendent in their bowling whites, are competing in the English Riviera Tournament. The grass has been cut with nail scissors to a smoothness that would not trouble a snooker ball. To avoid being slung out for being too scruffy, I decide to make an ally and sidle up to a Harry Secombe lookalike.

A little too much like a journalist, I open with, 'How long has the club existed?' Fortunately David Bateman, the club secretary, doesn't seem to notice.

'Since 1927, but the extension balcony we only got last year after we were paid for *Blackball*.'

'Black bull?'

David looks aghast. 'Don't you know *Blackball*? *Blackbaaaaall*.' He says it slowly for the divvy; unfortunately the delivery doesn't make a jot of difference. I wait.

'The film *Blackball*. It was at Cannes this year.' He nods his head and raises an eyebrow to impress. 'Mel Smith made it and it has

Johnny Vegas and Paul Kaye starring. Paul Kaye plays our boy Griff. Griff Sanders.'

'Who's Griff Sanders?

David's eyes positively bulge. 'He's who the film's about.'

The conversation is turning Pinteresque cartwheels.

'But who is he?'

'One of our members.'

I remain silent.

'He was the one that was blackballed.'

Silence.

'Griff's not exactly the sharpest knife in the drawer and the other players were winding him up at a tournament saying he'd never be picked for the county as long as John Smerdon was honourable secretary of the Devon County Bowling Association. Griff was younger than most bowlers and was different . . . a bit extrovert . . . inspirational, a prodigy at 25. But he'd been known to eat a bag of chips on the green between shots and had long hair.

'Anyway, he wrote on his scoresheet after the tournament, "John Smerdon is a tosser." He got a ten-year ban. Wearing the wrong socks could get a ban in this game but even so, ten years seemed a bit harsh. He said afterwards he should have murdered Smerdon instead and then he'd have been out in seven!'

Picking up on the incident, the *Mail on Sunday* wrote an article under the heading 'The Wild Man of Bowls' that kicked off a media frenzy. 'TV, radio, newspapers . . . the lot . . . They all came down. It attracted a lot of attention. Our club appealed against the ban and Griff got a short probation instead.

'In the film they give it the Hollywood treatment with Griff – or Cliff as he is known in it – going off with the secretary's daughter and then winning the South West Peninsula Cup, whatever that is.'

David is clearly keen to get away, to be on hand for the women bowlers if he's needed. I thank him for his time and say I'll let him get back to his crown green bowls. 'Not crown green,' he says huffily, 'that's fags and betting each end and cloth caps in between! North of Staffs is crown green; we're flat green – the genteel game of the South. It's different.'

Shamefaced, I toddle back along Agatha Christie Mile (named after its most famous former resident). Just below the Imperial I join a crowd peering into a vast fishing net that seems to have been carelessly dropped by Poseidon. Inside, penguins are settling in, or rather not settling in. These migrants have come from just up the road at Paignton Zoo but seem as disoriented as if they'd arrived straight from the Antarctic. They moved in a fortnight ago and have another month to calm down before the £7.5 million attraction, The Living Coast, opens to the public. In the meantime, as soon as any of the staff come within 50 yards, the penguins shuffle as one further up their small beach. They are also steadfastly keeping well clear of the cool lagoon waters, despite the heat.

Down in the inner harbour, old timers are behaving pretty much the same way, peeved at the multi-million-pound harbour improvements that have reduced the hours available for putting to sea. Newer boat owners are happier with the arrangement. The new sill and lifting bridge has made the harbour area more pedestrian friendly and as they rarely go to sea, they couldn't care less about reduced sailing hours. Now that their floating palaces are tethered to pontoons, they don't even have to get their feet wet when popping aboard for their nightly G&Ts. Some of those who do actually make it to open water probably shouldn't. One 'sailor' has apparently had the coastguard out twenty times so far this year. Another virgin boater, when asked by the harbourmaster if he had a radio, showed him his stereo system. He was found to have no ropes on board ('Didn't think I'd need them') and when asked if he had flares, thought he was being asked about his wardrobe.

The last time I was in Torquay, I took a cruise with Bob Ould, then aged 67, and his nineteen-year-old grandson Mathew (the sixth generation of the Ould family working the harbour). As on every other morning in the summer they had got up at 7 a.m. to start work and wouldn't knock off until 10 p.m. In the winter, when the tourists left, they fished. I remember Bob raising his meat-cleaver hand as we were leaving the harbour, pointing to the concrete car park. 'That's where the fairground used to set up in the summer and behind it was the old Cherry Walk. Lovely.' Bob, with an accent as thick as Devon cream, did his best to champion the resort but even Mathew, too young to regret anything, was wistful about the changes.

A decade on, Bob, his son Mick and his two grandsons Mathew and Nathan, still work the harbour, but they have sold the pleasure boat and returned to what they know best: fishing. Theirs is the last full-time fishing boat operating out of the marina.

From my balcony at 9.45 p.m. I watch Bob's boat furrowing homewards to a garland of welcoming lights strung round the bay and reflected on the sea like candles on the Ganges. I can hear the sea gently lapping 100 feet below me and a low murmur of voices from the rock edge. A gull is beating its way vigorously, as if late for an appointment. Maybe he too is holidaying alone and pretending he's got someone to meet.

As I watch the furrow of Bob's returning boat, I think of other lives I might have led. If I'd traded in our London home, I could have owned a smart waterfront mansion, joined the yachting masters of the universe and grown into a grouchy old salt while my children leaped from harbour walls or rode surfboards. I find myself increasingly drawn to Hinduism with its millions of gods and millions of lives. Reincarnation would be great but only in human form, thank you very much. I have no truck with life as a lizard but I definitely would like a few more turns round the block as a human. One more proviso, though – I take my family with me.

The lights continue their dance of Shiva in the mirror sea. Still dressed just in T-shirt and shorts, I have another glass of chilled wine out on the balcony. The sky is washed in a pink glow. Tonight it feels a very precious world that we inhabit. A world we gamble too recklessly with. Maybe if Bush converted to Hinduism, and renounced his Christian escape-hatch-to-heaven faith, he'd take a little more care of the world he's destined to return to.

By 10 p.m. the sun is starting to wimp out and the moon to rule the roost. The waves get up a little. Two boats pass in opposite directions, kiss and move on. A couple of days back, the world was hell; today it's heaven. That's life. What's the difference? My sap was low. I had a fug. Sun and moon, heaven and hell. Maybe I need help. Maybe I should book an appointment with my wife, who happens to be a psychotherapist – or 'psycho' for short. Maybe I should open another bottle.

The regular set of waves spread expansively. Perhaps they've come from Cape Horn and have experienced a little weather on the way. The seventh wave isn't the biggest, by the way (contrary to what I was always led to believe). That's a myth. It all depends on the pattern. The ocean breathes in and out once every twelve hours (give or take six minutes).

The story of the seventh wave may be a fiction, but Torquay – the Queen of the English Riviera – really does get more sun than most. Around 150 hours more each year than even nearby Exeter. Other inequalities of weather include the fact that the coasts of Devon and Cornwall get half the rain of the inland moors and its buxom hills. The east coast does even better, receiving a third of the rainfall of Cornwall. There's always someone better off. And someone worse off.

When my allotted two days of being spoiled in the Imperial are up, I descend a perfumed tree-locked valley to the Kingswear ferry, where I hitch a ride across to Dartmouth's jagged tiers of pastel-coloured terraces layered on the far bank. It's a clammy day despite the breeze and the Parish of Dartmouth Summer Fete is in swing amidst its pot plants and fairy cakes. A vicar carrying two bottles of Scotch to the tombola wishes me a good morning. Also in attendance is a rather suave fifty-year-old in naval uniform. Only it isn't naval. The three-maces insignia decorating Rob Trowbridge's sleeve does, however, have the weight of history.

'The post has existed since the 14th century,' the small neat man tells me. 'Originally we were Sergeants of the Mace to the king. Richard I stole the idea from the French, whose king was always protected by mace-carrying bodyguards. We were the bodyguards to the English king (he makes it sound personal) until Henry VII replaced us with beefeaters.'

Rob Trowbridge is the Town Sergeant, the custodian of Dartmouth's regalia and in particular the mayor's chain and processional maces. 'If the mayor falls into the sea, it's my duty to save the chain. The mayor is replaceable,' he chortles.

I buy a 19th-century copy of *Things Seen in Madagascar* by the missionary James Sibree from a second-hand book stall and then drive on a couple of bays to the crescent of Blackpool Sands, where I pull into the beachside Venus café for coffee. Manning the counter is owner Mike Smith, one of the major players in moving Devon in an increasingly green direction. Mike now has three cafés. The one here on the beach at Blackpool Sands and another at Bigbury-on-Sea stay open at weekends all year round. The one at East Portlemouth, however, closes from the end of October. 'No point opening when no one's there,' Mike explains. 'Fifty per cent of the town is holiday homes and they're usually empty.' The statistic comes as a shock. But the decimation of Devon and Cornwall's seaside villages is something that will become a litany as I travel west.

Everything Mike sells at the cafés is phosphate- and chlorine-free. He uses paper straws, cooking oil is recycled, energy-saving devices are used on lights and fridges, 'and the cardboard is converted into donkey bedding.'

Mike's green passion has also been brought to bear on South Hams Green Lanes Project, which has raised cash to open old abandoned smugglers' paths and farmers' tracks that fall outside any other funding. 'Ten thousand pounds has been raised and the project has restored twelve lanes so far,' he enthuses while simultaneously catching sight of his brother-in-law, a spry middle-aged man in shorts and 'Blackpool Sands' polo shirt who's marching past the boogie boards and wet suits of the seafront shop. Mike waves him over.

'Geoffrey owns the land and his family have lived in Dartmouth right back to the 15th century,' he explains by way of introduction, before adding, 'And the road – the first to be tarmacked in Devon – was laid by Geoffrey's grandfather Robert Newman.'

Sir Geoffrey Newman thrusts out a firm hand for me to shake.

'My grandfather was irritated by the sand from the dirt road – that's why he did it.'

Sir Geoffrey then quickly moves on to inform me that Blackpool Sands was where England's last stagecoach stick-up took place, in 1873. His family is perhaps the best known of all the Dartmouth seafaring families and his hauteur and height give him an imposing presence. 'The sea was the major thoroughfare up until the 19th century,' he begins, launching into his history lesson. 'You couldn't trust the roads. Mind you, you couldn't trust the seas either – there was an underground smugglers' passage from the beach but so far we've only been able to locate the exit up in a field up in Stoke Fleming.'

The Newman family operated a triangular trade taking goods to settlers in Newfoundland, returning with dried salted cod as ballast to Portugal ('It's called *bacal* there and is still very popular') before turning homewards laden with port wine. The family's influence at sea extended to carrying Letters of Marque, which permitted them to carry guns and attack enemy vessels. There was no shame attached to piracy in the days when Thomas Newman introduced himself as 'Merchant and Privateer'. The Crown, of course, got a share of the booty.

The family established a summer home at Blackpool Sands in 1790. After World War II Geoffrey's parents established an ice-cream

concession and then a car park when they noticed more people had cars
and were exploring. Now the family imports around 30 tons of dressed
sand virtually every year 'because people like to build sandcastles'.

In the Slapton Monument car park at Torcross, I pull up beside a black
Honda Civic and an amphibious Sherman tank. Overhead argumentative
gulls are cursing each other's parents; behind me a ribbon of shops faces
down the sea; and out front an archipelago of water lilies provide frogs
with hopping stones across the ley.

Ken Small, a large man clearly uncomfortable with his bulk, sits in the
front seat of his small car rubbing his swollen belly. His equally large
former wife (they're now divorced) sits alongside him finishing her
Tupperware-boxed lunch. The book that has been his life lies neatly
stacked in paperback and hardback piles on the rear seat and in the open
boot where there's also a framed letter signed by Ronald Reagan dated 12
April 1988, which reads: 'The tragic loss of lives in April 1944 vividly
reminds us that freedom is not free.' The driver's door is flung wide,
letting in the sun, the passenger door closed to the chill sea breeze.

A showcard for Ken's book, *The Forgotten Dead,* leans up against the
black tank Ken was responsible for rescuing from the sea. Beside it stands
a granite monument commemorating around a thousand US marines
who died when German E-boats got in among the fleet during rehearsals
for the Normandy landings in 1942. For decades the truth was kept from
the public and it is largely down to Ken that it ever came to light and
parents were finally able to mourn at the site of their sons' watery graves.

Ken, who lives alone with his cat in a bungalow in nearby Strete,
recently completed a course of chemotherapy only to find the cancer had
not moved out but instead found sanctuary in his lungs and liver. He's
been told he has 'five hours, five days, five weeks or five years' to live and
that he should enjoy whatever time he has left. He lights another
unfiltered cigarette and takes a sip from the plastic cup of beer beside
him. No point giving up anything now. Each day he returns, as on
virtually every other day of his adult life, to park beside his big story,
flogging *The Forgotten Dead* to visitors.

Ken claims to have sold more signed copies of a single book – 280,000
– than any other author in history. Today, however, he hardly has the
strength to lift a copy or turn his head to talk to me. A malignant smell

has moved into the car. 'I just don't have the energy, physical or mental, at the moment. A TV crew came down the other day and wanted to film a two-minute slot. You can't do this story in two minutes – you need an hour minimum. It's a massive story.' Whether Ken is referring to the American tragedy or his own is unclear.

Ken's ex-wife tries to offer solace where there is none: 'You never know in life.' Ken almost smiles. A miracle is all that's left. 'Sometimes these things just stop of their own accord.' The couple are clearly still good friends despite their divorce. Ken's soulmate scrapes the last bits of salad from the dish out of the door and the pair return to staring through the windscreen, lost in their separate thoughts beside the piles of *The Forgotten Dead*.*

The American debacle wasn't the first military incursion into the area. In AD 851 the Danes rampaged through Slapton, and a succession of foreign armies and pirates have subsequently followed in their wake. But things are different now. The next breaching of Slapton Sands may well be the last.

On the rear window of a second car parked beside the ley, a sticker demands 'Save Slapton Road'. Leading off from the car park is the threatened arrow-straight sliver of tarmac that local residents have been up in arms about ever since a recent sea inundation made it impassable for several weeks. The road runs beside the precarious shingle ridge of Slapton Sands that separates the sea ('the Barre of sand betwixt sea and lande' as 16th-century topographer John Leyland described it) from the 180-acre freshwater lagoon, the largest natural lake in the West Country.

When I last visited the area three months earlier on a walking trip, gabions had been erected as a pathetic defensive wall and a truck was tipping shingle in a vain attempt to turn back the sea. They might just as well have screamed at it. The sea, meanwhile, continued – and continues – to nibble.

Three months on I notice the gabions have vanished. A local shopkeeper tells me that the council just moved them one day after having spent thousands installing them. One spring tide, one watery massif from the right direction, one great sigh and it will be all over.

Beside a stile into Slapton Ley, local Field Study Council assistant reserve manager Nick Binnie is checking on a newly planted hedgerow

*Ken Small lost his battle with cancer on 15 March 2004.

flanking the National Nature Reserve. As we look out over the reed beds
to ornithologists with binocular eyes staring back at us, Nick succinctly
and unsentimentally sums up the past and future. 'During the last ice
age, the sea level rose and deposited shingle along the shore, sealing off
the freshwater lagoon. Soon it will all go back. Historically the time span
is the blink of an eye. A new saline ecosystem will quickly establish itself.
It will reinvent itself. We may think it's a big deal but there's nothing to
be done. The relationship between the land and sea is in constant flux and
coastal communities have no choice but to adapt or perish.'

The council is now at the consultation and feasibility stage for taking
the road inland despite clamouring local protests. Whatever happens, it's
unlikely to make any difference to Ken or to the two seagulls that are also
doing some reinventing of their own, using the barbecue spit as a giant
nutcracker to smash open snail shells.

I make my way back across the car park and into the Start Bay Inn,
where I'm served fresh scallops cooked in garlic butter. They may well be
the finest I've ever tasted.

The publican owner, Paul Stubbs, aged 61, proudly tells me he
brought them up from the ocean floor himself. Paul dives once or twice a
week with the previous owner, Laurie Anderson. 'Three of us usually go
down together and we bring back seventy to eighty dozen scallops a dive.'

Propping up the bar on another stool is Robin Steer, a taxi driver who
gave up fishing for cabbying three years earlier. When I ask if he misses
the mariner's life, there is no hesitation. 'No,' he replies bluntly.
Sentimentality has found no home in Robin's memory regarding his
former exposed, hard and dangerous life. 'We started at three most
mornings and got back to port at six in the evening. Sometimes in the
early days we caught as much as two ton of crab but later there was no
competing with the big fleets out of Dartmouth. Personally I prefer
sitting in my car on dry land listening to the radio to listening to a Force
Eight howling at sea.'

Improving the quality of life is also the motivation for the army of
migrants who have settled in south Devon from the Southeast over the
past two decades. South Hams covers 342 square miles, and 38 per cent
of the total district has been designated an Area of Outstanding Natural

Beauty (AONB), with more award-winning beaches than any other district in England. 'Ham' is old English for 'sheltered place'; the coast here enjoys one of Britain's mildest climates and is industry free apart from Plymouth. Why shouldn't those of us inhabiting less gorgeous corners of the realm want a share of the spoils? It's the same dream of a better life, albeit from a less privileged starting point, that brings asylum seekers to our shores. On leaving school everyone may head for London's fabled streets paved with gold but as soon as they can, they cash in and move to South Hams. This coast is where we keep our dreams.

In a *Sunday Times* article, South Hams was designated Britain's holiday-home capital with more than 11 per cent of all homes in the local authority area being occupied for just a few weeks of the year (the second-highest concentration is Berwick-upon-Tweed with 8.5 per cent). Along the actual coast the figure is considerably higher – in Salcombe 44 per cent of the town is holiday-home occupied.

Wherever I go over the next few days, walking the coast or driving through villages, I hear the familiar though displaced accents of London and Essex. The voices, however, do not belong to the super-rich who can afford two or three homes as investments, but to those who have cashed in everything and headed west like the 49ers, seeking a better life.

At Lannacombe Bay I chat with a middle-aged man with long silver hair waxing his surfboard out of the back of his camper van. He has relocated from Bethnal Green. I ask if he works in the area. He stares at me long and hard, assessing the likelihood of me being a tax inspector, finally deciding the unlikelihood merits a half-guarded reply. 'Not officially. I walk the dog, I surf, I canoe . . . Semi-retired you might say.'

At the Providence Inn in East Prawle, the urchin-thin new tenant confides that he sold his home in East London less than a year ago for £300,000. With the proceeds he bought the pub and upstairs accommodation.

Outside another pub, the Cricket at Beesands, I chat with a man named Dan, dressed in smart Goretex Kelly Anderson jacket and green wellies, who's accompanied by two Labradors. He tells me that, unlike most incomers, he lives here all year round. 'I walk the dogs for a living now.'

There is a cost to the incomers' new lives, however, and the tab is being picked up by the locals as house prices rocket and young families are forced further inland from the increasingly child-free coastal villages.

Inside the Cricket I meet with Frank Crocker. Frank has lived in the same pebbledash seafront terraced cottage all 84 years of his life, although he gave up earning a living as a fisherman – launching his boat straight from the shingle beach – more than three decades back. The fleet of twenty boats that were still operating when he retired have all followed Frank into retirement. It had withstood storms and plagues of octopus but had no way of competing with Dartmouth's larger mechanised trawlers.

Frank has watched the fishermen retire and die and the youngsters move to the cities as their parents sell the family home to incomers and retreat to flats in Totnes. Frank's flattened vowels are stretched as if caught in a storm at sea. He bought his own small terraced home for £50 and it's now worth £250,000 ('Baaaaarmy money'). He still lives just three doors from the pub he pops into every day. 'Only two pints mind, that's why I've lived so long.'

When Frank started fishing there was no sea wall and the waves regularly crashed through his house. Frank had seen the foreshore washed away by storms and roofs lifted off but nothing has decimated the village like the holiday homes.

'Never know your neighbour from one week to the next. It's all "grockos" (outsiders) now. One house they let for £750 per week. You could have bought the whole village for that when I was a boy!'

As I stroll the shingle beach, clearing my drowsy head from the beer, I ponder the pace of change. The sky is heavy. Does it mean bad weather or weatherless days? As a city slicker, I wouldn't know. If men don't fish and if farmers don't farm nor villagers grow out of the soil, who will be the guardians of weather folklore? 'If clouds look as if scratched by a hen, be ready to reef your topsails then'; 'Red sky in the morning, shepherd's warning'; 'Rain before seven, clear by eleven'; 'A bee was never caught in a storm'; 'Swallows high, staying dry; swallows low, wet will blow'; 'Seagull, seagull get out on the sand, we'll never have good weather with you on the land.'

Up above the holiday-let fishermen's cottages and abandoned lime kilns, I pass primitive orthostat boundary slates and wade through waist-high undergrowth that has covered an abandoned mine that Frank and other village boys played in as boys. Exhausted after their labyrinthine adventures, they would rest on the cliff edge, imitating the adders sunning themselves on the rocks below. I doubt very much the wilderness hears the patter of children's feet these days.

In the next bay south from Beesands, a derelict pub totters precipitously above the burrowing sea. Soon it will go the way of the rest of the village of Hallsands, which was stolen by the sea – 37 homes, a pub, chapel, post office, grocer, baker's and coastguard station – on one night of 26 January 1917. It is an eerie place with just a few still remaining walls stretching upwards from the water like desperate arms seeking salvation.

It was not the combination of the ferocity of the easterly gale and the unusually high tides that was the major cause of Hallsand's eclipse. The principal factor was the cavalier sea-dredging of 650,000 tons of protective shingle bed from Start Bay, which was used to extend the Royal Navy dockyard at Devonport.

While sewage and industrial discharge are far less of a problem today than they were twenty years ago, thanks to greater investment in treatment and tougher mandatory EC water-purity standards (disposal at sea was banned altogether in 1998), aggregate extraction for construction work can still have devastating consequences, as it did at Hallsands.

After the Hallsands catastrophe Eliza Ann Trout, a fisherman's widow, along with daughter Ella and her three sisters Patience, Clara and Edith, were temporarily housed in the nearby village of Bickerton. One day Ella was checking her crab pots when she saw a German submarine torpedo a cargo ship. Ella rowed a mile out single-handedly to rescue a crewman clinging to a piece of driftwood and was rewarded with an OBE for bravery. More importantly, she received a gift of money from the grateful family of the crewman and the Trouts used the windfall to build a new family home and guesthouse.

Money, however, was still tight, so the four sisters dug the foundations themselves and laid the water supply and concrete building blocks before hiring a builder. Most of the food subsequently served to guests was also caught or farmed by them. After Patience and Ella died, Gertrude, a German girl who was employed as a cook, but in fact seemed to do virtually everything, quit and business declined. Edith closed the hotel in 1959 but continued to live alone as a recluse with the guest tables all set

for dinner until her own death nineteen years later. The property has new
owners today and has been converted into holiday flats.

Living in our inland cities and towns, protected from storms such as
the one that hit Hallsands, we only rarely get glimpses of nature's
power. October 1987 was one such occasion, when oaks that had been
burrowing their toes ever deeper into our parks and gardens for three
centuries were yanked up like daffodils and strewn across the landscape. I remember as a child in Hong Kong fearing for my life as our
apartment block shook when Typhoon Mary swung through. The
following morning the newspapers all ran front-page photographs of a
tanker that had been plucked out of the harbour by the winds and
deposited in Nathan Road.

Most offshore beds, as in Start Bay, are owned by the Queen. The
Marine Holdings (the Crown Estate's second largest business) include
about half of the foreshore (the land lying between mean low and mean
high water) around the UK, 55 per cent of the beds of tidal rivers and
estuaries, and almost all the seabed out to the 12-mile territorial limit.

According to an unpublished 163-page report commissioned by the
Association of British Insurers (on work carried out by consulting
engineers and the Met Office based on the 1990 Sea Defence Strategy),
if a storm tide as lethal as the one that struck southern and eastern
England in early 1953 hit again, up to two-thirds of our storm barriers
would be likely to fail. This would result in far greater loss of life today
than half a century ago for two reasons: firstly because of the larger
populations working in danger zones, and secondly because of the
absence of a large standing army stationed close by that could provide
emergency rescue work.

In the report Professor David Crichton of the Benfield Greig Hazard
Research Centre, part of University College London (and fellow of the
Chartered Insurance Institute), claims that Scotland, where no flood
defence grant has been refused since devolution, is far better prepared for
such an eventuality.

As a result of such a tidal surge, more than nine hundred sea defences
would be likely to fail on the west coast, inundating 824 square miles of
land. A total of 438 sea defences on the south coast and 318 square miles of
land are likely to be breached, and 431 storm barriers and a colossal 1,000
square miles on the east coast. The risk of flooding on the eastern seaboard

is exacerbated by climate change and the tilting of tectonic plates that are expected to boost storm surges by 4ft 7in by 2080. The estimated insured losses of such a catastrophe would be around £20 billion. Such storms generally occur once or twice a century.

The worst in recent history happened exactly fifty years ago as I write.

It's only another couple of miles from Hallsands to Start Point, where I exchange the Nissan for one of two ex-lighthouse keepers' cottages at the end of a remote peninsula. I'm grateful the lighthouse is 90ft tall and painted white, because if it were any smaller I wouldn't have been able to locate it down the maze of country lanes hidden between high hedgerows. I guess ships at sea feel pretty much the same way.

Start Point Lighthouse was one of the most remote in mainland Britain when it was erected in 1836 and needed a live-in workforce of eight to operate it. But in 1993 it was automated and the lighthouse keeper pensioned off (he now works as a guide at Torre Abbey in Torquay). Today a computerised box does the work and never gets tired or curses its lot. The two adjacent cottages have been converted, like much of the rest of south Devon, into holiday lets by Trinity House. Around twenty of its remaining 71 lighthouses (chartered by Henry VIII in 1514 to protect the welfare of 'our true and faithful subjects, Shipmen and Mariners') now have their adjacent cottages available for holiday hire.

I arrive at dusk and by the time I've eaten and sorted my stuff, night has fallen and the lighthouse is at its most impressive. I stand outside the cottage, spokes of light spinning above me like a celestial chariot travelling the star-studded sky. From the edge of the knowable world, where the light dies 20 miles out, wild white horses gallop across the infamous wrecking reef of the Skerries. Scattered somewhere within the arc of light are the invisible carcasses of hundreds of wrecks – warships, submarines, fully rigged clippers, fishing smacks, Phoenician galleys, steamers, U-boats and even a salvage ship. In one night alone in March 1891, eleven ships went down in a rare snow blizzard.

I retreat back inside the windproof, battened-down cottage where I can still hear the wind howling and whimpering at the door to be let in. Beneath my bedroom window a vestigial stone boundary wall veers drunkenly off the cliff. Spindrift crashes from the rocks below like

drifting snowflakes. I decide to turn in and burrow beneath the comforting duvet. I lie there, listening to the wildness outside. On mainland
Britain only the Lizard juts further south into the sea than the Prawle
Point headland. There is something comforting in the knowledge that the
one-eyed lookout will stay up all night, keeping its beady watch like a
vigilant parent, as I drift off to sleep.

Some time later, hugely disorientated, I am woken by what I at first
imagine is the bleating of a lost lamb. Slowly I realise it is the doleful
sound of the fog horn honking mournfully for the thousands of
deckhands on the armada of shipwrecks. I peel back the curtain and look
out to sea but fog has swallowed the infamous sandbanks of the Skerries.

By daybreak the fog has lifted. The sun is out and sheep have quit the
warmth of the drystone walls to graze the bucking fields. I set out, with a
spring in my step, to join them on another stretch of the South
West Coast Path.

As I quit the outcrop on which the lighthouse sits, I look down at a
couple of cormorants perching on lichen-stained rocks, hanging their
wings to dry. In 1581 Henri Muge was hanged in similar fashion, chained
with arms outstretched on the fissured gneiss and abandoned as a warning
of the penalty for piracy (seven years later, when they lit the Armada
beacon, bits of him were reputedly still hanging there). The roller-coaster
path leads me past old smugglers' caves and abandoned mines concealed
in the gorse and bracken behind porcine-sounding promontories –
Gammon Head, Pig's Nose and Ham Stone. Less than a mile from the
lighthouse, I discover one of those golden-sand, Famous Five coves that
Devon is renowned for. Children, long gone, have built a den out of
driftwood, beside which a line of sea-sculpted rocks stand sentry.

Several miles later, I skirt a hut at Gara Rock that served as a coastguard station from 1847 and which for a short period in the early 1970s
became the smallest pub in Britain, catering for three customers at a
time. Above it, on the precipitously sloping baize, are the raised lines
of medieval strip farming still visible above the breaking surf of
Rickham Sands.

The weather and the empty sandy bay are too much to resist. I descend
the slope, throw off my clothes and am in the water in a matter of
seconds. Five hundred yards offshore a buoy marks the spot where, in
1996, jewellery, ingots and six hundred gold coins were recovered from a

sunken Barbary Coast pirate ship that had come seeking white slaves but instead only found an early unmarked grave. I spend a castaway half-hour in the bay and then walk the final three miles to East Portlemouth, where I await the ferry and its skipper, Steve Smith, who will transport me across to Salcombe.

Having met Steve on an earlier walking break, I'd rung ahead to arrange to spend some time together. When Steve finally appears with shaved head and beatific smile, he looks like a Buddhist monk instead of a ferryman. I've timed things perfectly: he has just one more return trip to make before calling it a day.

Slowly we make our way across the mouth of the estuary. Waiting at the jetty on the Salcombe side is a female teenage shop assistant in an overall awaiting her regular commute home. She chats easily with Steve, while I sort out my camera and snap away. Back on the East Portlemouth side, the girl is replaced by a group of dog walkers.

Having dropped his last passengers, Steve moors up and hands in his takings before leading me up through Salcombe's stacked terraces to the home he shares with his mother and stepfather. It's about 5.30 p.m. I sit in the small rear patio garden with a beer while Steve showers. Eventually he rejoins me and we make our way back down to the harbour where we board a small battered white fibreglass speedboat. Steve pulls the umbilical of the outboard. It explodes into life and we head out on to the ever-narrowing mouth of the ria (long narrow inlet), avoiding a minefield of moored yachts, most of which are used even less than the holiday homes.

The flotilla of shellacked wooden hulls and sun-speckled fibreglass boats finally peters out and gives way to a sublime stretch of waterway flanked by wooded hills. 'Mrs Waterhouse's home up there.' Steve points to a thatched home coyly peeking through its leafy fringe, one of only a handful occupied year round along the entire East Portlemouth shorefront.

Goodshelter Creek veers off to starboard with billowing fields rising above it. We, however, sail dead ahead, following the main wooded channel known as South Pool Creek.

'The last wild bear killed in England was shot in East Portlemouth,' Steve announces as we pass an old lime kiln half consumed by undergrowth. Fifteen minutes later the outboard's power falls away dramatically as if starved of petrol and we start limping rather than cruising. With the engine muffled I decide it's time to eke out the story of my skipper's great adventure.

In 1994, at the age of 27, Steve set out with an old college buddy, Jason Lewis, to attempt the first human-powered circumnavigation of the world. This much I already know. As we pootle safely and serenely up river, I ask how he felt about crossing the Atlantic in what amounted to a pedalo.

'Well, it was 26ft long, weighed 1,000lb unloaded and had a covered hammock in the bow for taking turns sleeping when either of us wasn't pedalling. Hardly a pedalo!' As he speaks Steve tinkers with the engine, trying to coax it into the robustness of his ocean-going vessel. 'The hardest bit was pedalling rather than resting, not because of the physical exertion to my legs – it's a far more efficient method of water propulsion than rowing – but because my body was always listing one way or the other. You could never attain an equilibrium and relax and so there was always a tension in the body.'

After 4,500 miles and 111 days, the pair arrived in Miami. Steve then set off on a bicycle bound for San Francisco, where he was to rejoin Jason, who was making his way there on a pair of rollerblades. Unfortunately Jason's journey took more than a year as he was hit by a car in Pueblo, Colorado, and was confined to hospital while they mended his shattered legs.

Eventually, in 1998, the pair commenced the first Pacific pedalo leg to Hawaii. This took a more reasonable two months. It was then Steve's turn to interrupt proceedings. He'd lost the will and enthusiasm for the journey and decided instead to set up a self-sufficient commune in New Zealand. Jason continued alone.

By this time our own limping journey has brought us to a jetty at South Pool. We tie up and start walking up a deserted lane to the waterside Millbrook pub.

Steve spent six months in New Zealand ('The commune never worked out') and then moved on to Australia, where he studied under a Zen master, Hogen Yamahata. In 2000 Steve returned to Salcombe, where he has worked as a ferryman ever since, transporting people from land to land while he rootlessly inhabits the middle watery element and continues his Zen studies. Jason, meanwhile, continues pedalling and paddling round the world.

'There's not a lot of difference, really, between sailing the ocean and sailing the creek. On a four-month journey across the Atlantic, you move so slowly it would drive you mad if you thought about your destination and where you are in the journey. In Salcombe if I focused on the endless repetitive futility of the short cross-harbour journey, I'd go the same way. You live in the moment and depend on nothing further.'

At the Millbrook pub Steve orders us fisherman's pie and we sit on a small terrace overlooking a stream. When the pie arrives we move inside to the trinkets, barometers and trophies that mark the publican's life. Steve's only memento of his epic journey is the manuscript he's been working on that he hopes to find a publisher for soon. Later, as we make our way back to the boat, lost in private thoughts, I ponder the dissimilarity of our two journeys: Steve's Herculean, my own safe as houses (Hallsands notwithstanding); one global, the other local; one arduous and personally challenging, the other rather indulgent but hopefully of interest.

On board Steve turns from his own epic to tell me about Joe Login, who, as the skipper of a Salcombe crabbing boat, was reputedly the last man in England to be convicted of piracy. When tensions were high because French fishermen were encroaching local waters, a French trawler ploughed through the *Dolly Ann*'s string of crab pots yet again. Joe had had enough and ran amok, boarding the French boat and trashing the crew and equipment. He was later arrested and convicted.

It is now 10.15 p.m. but the day has still not quite turned over to night yet. In the penumbra we journey back down the ria, its waters a mosaic of pale busy patches whipped up by the wind at bends, and luminous deep pools in protected lees. The incandescence is watched over by brooding woodland and a single star. Steve shivers as the temperature plummets. Soon, however, the coldness seems to leave him. It reminds me of a time in Saharan Algeria when I camped out in a gorge in the Tassili (a national park the size of Switzerland) with one of the Blue Men. It was night and I was dressed in all my clothes and had my sleeping bag pulled up round my neck too. Mohammed, meanwhile, sat alongside me in his cotton djellabah. 'Aren't you cold?' I asked. Mohammed laughed. 'The cold comes in here . . .' he pointed to one hand then ran the finger across his body, switching hands to point to the other hand, 'and it leaves here.'

Steve seeks out a seal that lives on top of crab pots. 'Not around. Must be out fishing.' Buoys bob like corpses in the crepuscular light. Finally Salcombe comes into view, its harbour lights writing cabalistic messages on the water. We pass a moored yacht and can hear the clinking of cutlery being cleared in the galley accompanied by a contented murmur of French voices. I decide to stay the night in town and to return to Start Point to pick up the car tomorrow.

Tomorrow, ever reliable, dawns. The morning is dull and drizzly but Salcombe is all neatness and prettiness. Four-wheel drives pull up on kerbs in the pinched streets so their owners can run into deli-cafés for lattes and bagels. Salcombe Coffee Company, Sea Chest (nautical leisure wear) Cranch's Pantry, Fat Face (surfer beach gear), Chattels (designer home accessories) and Salcombe Chocolate Factory are a few of the wedding gifts celebrating Salcombe's marriage to tourists and incomers willing to pay £80,000 for a double garage and seven figures for their dream home.

Inside the Maritime Museum, a salty dog's sea chest below the Tourist Information Centre, I overhear two friends conjuring up a litany of hotels that have vanished over the past two decades: St Elmo's, Great Gates, South Sands, Bolt Head, Grafton Towers, Castle Point. Who needs hotels when everyone has a holiday home?

I continue walking the wildly bucking coastal path, rounding the shattered prismatic rocks of Bolt Head, heading west. Offshore between Bolt Head and the equally desolate Bolt Tail, the most dramatic stretch of the walk, seventeen wrecks have been discovered, their shattered bellies spewing everything from Roman pottery to Portuguese coins. In Thomas Pynchon's novel *Mason & Dixon*, an 18th-century sailor bound for the New World exclaims, 'Aye, and that's the Tail of the Bolt where the Ramillies went down but the year February, losing seven hundred Souls . . . This is League for League the most dangerous Body of Water in the world . . . Sands and Streams, Banks and Races . . .' Looking at my OS map, I notice the Ramillies site is still marked clearly a kilometre from Bolt Tail.

Bantham Bay and Thurlestone Sands have been the setting for some of the most infamous acts of piracy. One renowned case concerned the

Chantiloupe as it returned from the West Indies in 1772. On learning that the ship was about to run aground, Mrs Burke (a relation of the parliamentarian Edmund Burke), bent on saving her precious jewellery, bedecked herself in everything she could. Her relief at being pulled from the sea by helping hands soon turned to cold terror as her frenzied rescuers hacked off her sea-swollen fingers to get at her rings. Her body was buried in the sand like so many before her. Even today locals claim that bones from unmarked graves are exposed during storms.

At Hams End the smell of kelp and brine lead me to Bantham. In high summer the single-lane road is clogged with cars heading for its golden sands. Today, however, with the cloud curdling above a chill wind, the road's deserted. What human life that exists is holed up in The Sloop. A previous owner of the pub had been a notorious wrecker and rigged up the interior to resemble a sloop with walls leaning outwards like a hull and the bar requisitioned from boat timbers. With its low beams, stone-flagged floors, table skittles, freshly caught fish, spotted dick and 12 per cent Churchwards Scrumpy, it's the kind of place walkers start dreaming about miles from base. At The Sloop I phone a cab to take me back to Start Point where I pick up the car and drive to Bigbury-on-Sea.

Standing at the boot of the Nissan in a car park above the beach at Bigbury-on-Sea, throwing my only smart clothes into a holdall, I'm almost blown over by the gusting wind. Beyond a watery causeway lights are already lifting the gloom inside the Burgh Island Hotel. I phone across and ask for the tractor transfer to carry me across the inrushing tide. It is to be my last night in a static home. From tomorrow I shall be taking my bedroom, kitchen, toilet and living room with me. It seems appropriate that my final night will be spent on an island still lost in a 1930s fog where people dress up like Noël Coward and Agatha Christie.

An hour later I'm showered and changed and making my entrance into the hotel cocktail bar through a forest of tuxedos and garden of fine gowns. I slink to a table as inconspicuously as possible in my crumpled beige linen suit (personally I'm impressed I have anything better than shorts).

'Gary McBar's my name,' the waiter introduces himself. 'Well, the surname's just a nickname . . . I work in a bar and I'm from Fife. Geddit? Mc-Bar.' Gary has been serving cocktails at Burgh Island for a decade now and with consummate professionalism immediately puts me at my ease. 'Saw you walking about earlier with your rucksack. What a transformation!' I try to read the implication: I'm a tramp and shouldn't be here, or I have transformed myself from ugly duckling into a beautiful swan? As I look around the room, it would appear that all the penguins from Torquay have escaped and are holidaying at the hotel. I am the only tuxedo-less male on Burgh Island.

I stare out at waves cresting the side of the seawater pool. The mist has temporarily lifted and what's left of daylight is streaming through the arching windows, dancing with the artificial lighting and palm fronds on the wooden floor to the popping of champagne corks. Tonight the past seventy years have been erased. We're bound for New York on our transatlantic liner, unmoored from the prose of our lives.

From the restaurant a sugar-sweet male voice boards the melancholy shipwrecked raft of a clarinet playing the introductory bars of 'Night and Day'. The maître d' appears at my shoulder and escorts me into the dining room. There is to be no sunset tonight. Instead a marbled mist once more rolls over the cliffs. We are adrift at sea. But I am also adrift in a sea of couples and once again I feel the stigmata blistering my forehead.

Romance suffuses the air. Even the current owners first came as guests to be married here. It's that kind of place. The band launches into 'The Very Thought of You'. Couples entwine themselves on the dancefloor; others cup hands across tables as the sea rushes in. Eyes swim dreamily. Candles flicker in wine glasses. I'm tempted to glide solo across the floor as I used to at Manchester's Twisted Wheel in my teens. But I don't. I'm still on the first bottle. Others are ahead of me, bodies canting on the alcoholic swells.

Burgh Island is not what I expected. I thought it would be tacky, contrived and stuffy. For once tuxedos don't belong to tired and drunk conferencers, and the majority of those happily marooned here this evening even look to be under forty. The best pair of dancers, however, is a svelte couple in their sixties, their only handicap the man's unfortunate facial tic that makes him look as if he is about to sink his teeth into his partner at every turn. Nosferatu in a tuxedo.

'Anything Goes', Cole Porter's witty anthem for an era, brings the first set to a close. During the band's break Billie Holiday's 'God Bless the Child' plays and almost brings a tear to my eye.

When guests finish their meal, they have no TV in their rooms and so they have to think of something else to do. I invite myself upstairs for a last cocktail. I'm in the Agatha Christie room (she wrote *And Then There Were None* and *Evil Under the Sun* on the island) with Art Deco fanned mirrors, rough silks, walnut veneer, geometric wallpaper, a poster of Hedda Hopper as Cleopatra, and a Bush radio that I'd love to slip into my holdall. Through the mist I can see the light of the Pilchard Inn, the only other building on the island. I almost expect the band to materialise on the lawn playing 'A Fine Romance'.

With a yawn and reluctance, I hitch a lift with the sea tractor back to the mainland the next morning. The driver tells me that sometimes guests have to lift their feet or risk a soaking. Not today – the tyres, as big as continents, are turning through no more than 18in. As I take one final look back at the hotel, I make a mental note to return to this time capsule with my wife to celebrate a special occasion (a Booker, a Pulitzer or maybe her birthday).

My next port of call transports me from the 1930s to today: the modern city of Plymouth, which rose from the rubble of the Blitz in the fifties after eighty thousand homes were pancaked. Most of the city is thus predictably bland and nondescript. What remains of historic interest is shoe-horned around the harbour and up on the Hoe (the grassy headland overlooking Plymouth Sound). I start my tour at the latter, where in former times I might have expected bear baiting, cock fighting or an execution by way of entertainment. It was here, too, on the immaculate lawns of the Plymouth Bowling Club, that a breathless messenger in 1588 blurted out to Sir Francis Drake, 'The Spaniards are coming, the Spaniards are coming!' At the time a southwest wind was blowing into the harbour, marooning Drake's fleet. So, with nothing to be done, he famously replied, 'We have time enough to finish the game and beat the Spaniards too.' A saying almost as legendary – I said almost – as Dirty Harry's 'Make my day, punk.'

A bronze statue of Elizabeth I's favourite takes pride of place on the Hoe, striking a casual, rather mincing pose. The outline of Drake's muscular calves is visible beneath a slight ruffle in his tights, while one hand rests daintily on a hip and the other on a miniature world he spent three years circumnavigating and pillaging (the first sea captain in history to complete such a journey, as Magellan died on his homeward leg). Four hundred years after Drake's voyage, a second Francis, with the surname Chichester, became the first man to sail the world single-handedly when he returned to Plymouth in the diminutive *Gypsy Moth* in 1967. This Francis too was knighted by a Queen Elizabeth.

Beside Drake is a second statue depicting an anonymous young pilot, one of many who spent endless nights in the sky attempting to prevent the Luftwaffe reaching the city. At the end of the war, however (assuming he survived), there were to be no financial spoils for him to enjoy in old age from his acts of heroism.

Dominating the grassy headland is Smeaton's Lighthouse, which was moved here brick by brick from Eddystone Rocks, 14 miles offshore, when it was replaced by a more modern structure. The one relocated on the Hoe was the third to stand on the treacherous rocks. The very first, a wooden Heath-Robinson affair, used sixty candles to guide shipping and somehow managed to avoid burning itself down. From somewhere dusty and musty, I hear my sister singing a child-hood sea shanty.

> My father was the keeper of the Eddystone Light
> And he married a mermaid one fine night
> Out of this union there came three
> Two little fishes and the third was me
> Singing yo-ho-ho
> The wind blows free
> Oh for the life on the rolling sea.

At least, I think that's how it went.

From the Hoe I descend the hill towards the River Plym. Halfway down, at an elbow in the road, the Royal Citadel, home to the 29 (they pronounce it 'two-nine') Commando Regiment Royal Artillery, hunkers. I'm in luck. It's Tuesday afternoon, the only time of the week the garrison is open to the public. The baroque gateway is festooned with Roman legionaries in rather effete uniforms not too far removed from Drake's outfit (the original Citadel was run by Sir Francis so maybe this is where he got his dress sense).

A young commando dressed in far more seemly macho fatigues and machine gun guards the entrance. He looks no older than my fourteen-year-old son Max. I walk the ramparts squinting out to sea with the cannons. A Brittany Ferries booze cruise is heading homewards heaving with its swag from Roscoff. Inside the walls the army camp appears deserted apart from a soldier in fatigues walking the ramparts. I interrupt his stroll to ask why the place is so deserted.

'Everyone's on leave after the Gulf,' the young officer replies. Of course. A few innocent months back, soldiers not long out of short trousers would have been buffing their vehicles beneath us on the parade ground. Today the returning combat vehicles appear as battered as their recent occupants must have felt in Iraq. One jeep has two ominous webs of shattered glass radiating outwards from central impact points on the windscreen. The unit returned several vehicles and four men lighter, the latter killed when their helicopter was brought down by 'friendly' American fire on the very first day of operations.

'Our job was to provide fire support for the infantry. The helicopter was on a recce when it was hit,' my companion informs me.

'Were you there?'

'No, I've only just joined, which is why I'm here and everyone else is on leave. My brother is still out there with another unit on counter-insurgency detail. Fortunately that's what we're best at in Britain, unlike the Americans, because we have all the experience from Northern Ireland.' I get the impression Lieutenant McCaffery is trying to reassure himself more than he is me.

Having just completed his commando training at Sandhurst, he's happy to tell me his name but will give no information regarding his brother's unit or where they're based. We look down into the parade ground to hide embarrassment at his understandable reticence. A line of BV206 all-terrain vehicles stand in identical camouflage to that Lieutenant McCaffery is wearing.

He neatly changes subject: 'The BV206s don't take kindly to 50-degree heat that melts boots. The new Viking is much better; it can operate comfortably from minus-50 to plus-50 degrees.'

Lieutenant McCaffery disappears for tea in the mess and I walk across the parade ground, passing the helipad, the officers' mess (redolent of a

Scottish baronial home) and a soldier in civvies watering plants outside
the guard house.

Charles II – who is said to have single-handedly fathered the British
aristocracy – built the Citadel to overlook and protect Sutton Harbour.
But he reputedly made sure the cannons pointed landward as well as to
sea because he didn't trust the town after it had sided with the
parliamentarians during the Civil War. Nearly four hundred years later,
young men are still being sent from this same garrison to war. Only the
technology of killing seems to have advanced.

From the Citadel I continue winding my way down the hill to
the Barbican (the oldest part of Plymouth) and 'The Mayflower Steps',
where the Pilgrim Fathers set sail for the New World on 6 September
1620. Half a million colonists subsequently followed in their wake bound
for North America, the Antipodes (mostly convicts), the West Indies and
South Africa. Raleigh also sailed from the harbour in search of El Dorado
and, returning from South America without the promised gold bullion
(some believe he actually buried it at nearby Hooe Lake), was taken to the
Tower of London and beheaded.

Joining the Forces is still a tradition for Plymouth's young males – apart
from the Citadel, the city also has a naval base (mostly submarine) at HMS
Drake. But these days the service industry is a much bigger employer and
the Barbican's waterfront terraces are heaving. I am tempted by the
Nepalese cuisine on offer at The Three Crowns but decide I need to shun
heavy lunches or I won't fit in my truck driver's cabin. Today is the day I
pick up my motorhome. Unfortunately I think I've put on about 14 stone
in weight since I left home. I consider going the whole hog and maybe
even getting a few tattoos and a string vest, but steady my nerve.

Outside Kerr's showroom back in Paignton, I am shown the Swift
Sundance 6306 motorhome ropes. There are many of them to unravel
and, what with loading, it takes the best part of two hours before I'm
ready to roll. Fortunately my baptismal route is a reasonable-sized road
back to Plymouth. As my grip on the wheel and stress-locked jaw slacken,
I start seeing some advantages to my new house-on-wheels. With the
price of property today, perhaps in a decade the motorhome will become
the new starter home for adults. Considering our current rootlessness

and passion for road building, it would seem a logical progression. My meditation on the advantages of movable homes doesn't last long. Shortly after crossing the River Tamar beside Brunel's mid-19th-century railway bridge (the single track still being used by the London-Penzance line), I suck Cornish air for the first time and the road shrinks. Once more my knuckles turn white gripping the wheel and my teeth clamp as I fret about how to fit my new 2.22m-girth (with mirrors folded), 3.1m-height and 6.99m-length down a rabbit warren.

Somehow I manage to reach Polperro, a town that defines the Cornish aesthetic high ground of pretty and quaint. The small town is an old hand at selling beauty and has it down to a T. Alleys dive off in every direction, seeking out ledges on which to perch another half-dozen cheek-by-jowl cottages. A miniature train runs through the town, making it accessible for weighty or lazy tourists. A sign in the absurdly pretty harbour proclaims 'Polperro Harbour is a fine example of a Cornish fishing port and is entirely self supporting. The trustees are anxious to maintain this without further commercialisation, will you please help us with your generous support. Thank you. P.H.T.' There is a slot below wide enough to take a folded note or cheque. I imagine that whoever wrote it had the middle finger of his free hand pointing heavenwards at the same time as he drafted his charitable plea.

There is something about Polperro that makes me bilious and Sid and I flee the place an hour after arriving. Sid, by the way, is the name I've given to my moving home – Sid Sundance – as he (and it is a he) did not offer any name of his own when we were formally introduced in Paignton.

Sid seems to like the narrow lanes better than I do and runs his wing mirrors through the hedgerows on either side singing as we rattle along. Unfortunately, everywhere that looks to be a fine overnight camping spot has unfriendly signs warning 'No overnight camping'. Fear of gypsies, no doubt. The signs, together with the extortionate daytime double-fee charge in car parks for motorhomes, are clear indications that I have joined a mobile leper colony. There is a similar bugger-off sign in the National Trust car park at Frogmore but I decide to ignore it, putting my own middle finger up at the attempted breach of my human rights. The car park immediately exacts revenge by assaulting Sid's rear with a raised bank. I hope I get the hang of the motorhome soon or there won't be much to return.

The only other humans sharing my new car park home are a couple with a baby in a white Combi van who appear a little sneery about the *Queen Mary* on wheels that's gate-crashed their isolation. As they're unresponsive to my sizzling social gambit ('Are you from round these parts?'), Sid and I make do with each other. I enjoy being able to cook once more and am back to my staple stir fry – throwing in a lemon grass sauce – and rice. By 9 p.m. the couple next door have turned in. By 11 p.m I've finished washing up and unpacking my kit bags; the only thing I appear to have forgotten is the car mobile phone charger. My fixed rear berth is as big as our double bed at home. There are light screens and midgie screens as well as curtains. Everything tilts and folds. It's all very ingenious, if a little complicated at the moment. Having done with domestic chores, I slip outside and relish being camped in deadly quiet countryside beside a field of silhouetted hay reels and a pin-cushion sky.

The following morning I am woken by bird song and walk beneath the vestiges of a feathery moon into a leafy tunnel that emerges into a field overlooking a succession of bejewelled coves. On a green ledge 20ft above a cradle of shattered rocks, a couple of campers are stowing their tent before continuing along the South West Coast Path. A wise choice of holiday, but I don't know if I'd like to be camped where they are when a sou'wester blows in. I manage to scramble down to the crystal-clear water of Lantivet Bay and wake myself with a swim. The campers wave as they traverse the coast path above me.

Once back on the road, as gently as possible, I tell Sid a few home truths about things I'm already finding irritating about him. My major grumble is that his brake is too close to the accelerator. As it's our first full day together, Sid decides to fight for mastery. He claims there is nothing wrong with the location of his pedals; that the fault lies with the size of my foot that hits both pedals simultaneously, frightening the living daylights out of everybody. Chastened, I try to ingratiate myself by telling him how grateful I am that his bulk has made me reduce my speed. He's uncertain if I'm taking the mickey. I assure him I'm not: I'm simply seeing a lot more now that I've slowed down and been lifted several feet in the air.

The bike tracks that pass for roads the further west I head are, however, proving increasingly tricky. One verdant lane perfumed with honeysuckle leads us down to the car ferry at Bodinnick. As I edge forward in the short queue, at any moment I expect someone to stop me, laugh and send us back the way we came. Surprisingly the ferry doesn't flinch, let alone sink, as we transfer our bulk on to it. It takes us from Daphne du Maurier's imposing white home (still inhabited by her brother) across the deep harbour to the stacked hillside of Fowey with its half-beams and colour wash. Beyond it the Cornish Alps rise in the distance, no more than a small burp.

Our family often headed this way on summer holiday to Mevagissey's Pentewan Sands. The first time we came, we were living in Wiltshire and I was probably aged seven or eight. Dad requisitioned a 160-pounder tent, army-issue camp beds and pack rations and bundled them all into the Austin 12 Shooting Break, before carefully spooning a half-pint of graphite in with the oil as a protective measure after fitting a new engine. En route one of the copper pipes fractured and oil spewed everywhere but the garage mechanic said it would have been a lot worse without my father's precautionary measure – a woe-betide-you tale that Dad subsequently liked to drop into conversation at every opportunity, whether salient or not.

Our Pentewan Sands campsite was located right next to the beach and at night there would be a mad charge to be first in the queue to the fish and chip van as soon as it was spotted breasting the hillside into camp. The chips remain the finest – Boteroesque and slightly limp – I've tasted to date. I like to think they were cooked in dripping, however carcinogenically evil that is currently viewed. Occasionally, in those long-gone days when you were permitted to do most things, we even caught our own mackerel and barbecued them on the beach. When it came to packing up, all the wooden tent pegs had to be clean enough to eat with, and then laid out to attention in orderly lines for inspection. There was a drill for everything. Now it seems I have grown into my father and my kids joke about their own father's operating systems. My sister still claims that everywhere else she has holidayed since Pentewan Sands has been a letdown.

Today the Pentewan Sands Holiday Park is an altogether grander site with its own restaurants, swimming pool and clubhouse alongside the deep sandy beach. Unfortunately the chip van no longer calls. And despite my early arrival at 2 p.m., there is no room at the inn as a rally of motorhomes from Wiltshire has booked all the available plots. The

receptionist suggests I pitch up at their sister site at Heligan. I swap the
private beach and drying wet suits for an altogether pleasanter, intimate
location with dipping hills and the sea just a distant rumour.

The couple camped in front of me own a tiny tent and a K-reg Ford
Granada. They're in their early thirties, look surprisingly suave and have
picked an admirable spot with views to the sea and nothing in front of
them to break the spell of their romance. They sit on a lawn that slopes
to a barley field that dips to a valley, which in turn gallops to a thin blue
sea rushing to a pale blue sky. The couple are on their second bottle of
champagne and their pitch probably cost them £7 or £8.

In Cornwall, so far, I have passed through a trinket box of knicky-
knacky perfect fishing villages that have probably seen a 50-plus turnover
in populations over the past twenty years. Fishing villages first started
appearing with the advent of commercial fishing in the 15th century in
places such as Mevagissey, Bude and Newquay when quays and
breakwaters could protect fleets. The function of these chocolate-box
coves may have majorly shifted to the leisure industry but the physical
appearance has changed little. Mevagissey, with its half-drained inner
harbour, is a perfect example, its necklace of kelp hanging from mooring
ropes like flayed skin and its walls decorated neatly with stacked nets,
buoys and anchors. I sit watching kids charging down steps straight into
the paddling pool left by the retreating tide. In the central deeper
channel, a line of boats buck restlessly, all impatient to be let off their
leads. I notice that fishermen returning from their trawlers in row boats
stand at the stern sculling in a figure-of-eight with a single oar, the same
way I was taught as a teenager in Tenby. I presume the style originated
at a time when harbours were heaving and there just wasn't the room for
oars extending on both sides.

All the town's hand-painted wooden pub signs seem to depict
fishermen with beards and pipes, though I have yet to see anyone
remotely similar. At Celtic Knot I am offered two Cornish pasties free if
I buy ten. I decline. In a grocer's window I mull over items for sale – two
small armchairs, a fishing rod, candle-making equipment, a door baby-
bouncer. Someone is also in need of 'A man to lay my lino for bathroom
and washroom'.

Back on site I cook another stir fry, this time with a green Thai curry sauce (a considerable improvement on the last). I eat slowly, enjoying the same view as my neighbour in the tent but with a bottle of Sauvignon Blanc instead of champers and a girl.

Steve and Jan, the site managers, appear in the doorway. I offer them a glass of wine and we sit outside, enjoying the balmy evening. I learn that the pair took flight from homes and jobs as soon as their children left. 'We had a dream of the open road,' Steve explains. The couple travelled to Portugal, Spain and Morocco over winter and worked the summers for several years until they somehow found themselves on a campsite – a halfway house between a fixed home and the open road. Steve's aim is for them to own their own site eventually. Jan, however, seems less enamoured of the vicarious transience offered by a campsite. They quickly down their glasses and continue on their nightly inspection.

When they've gone my thoughts turn to the honeymooners (for that is what I have decided they are) camped in front of me. Smoke from a barbie drifts across their tent. The squaw and her brave head back under canvas with the remains of the bottle and their glasses. It's only 9 p.m. Grazing cows slowly work their way across the far field. The credits run.

With my romantic leads turned in, I return to the romance – or the illusion of it – of the open road. Neil Cassady's drug of choice. For me, driving is not an open road. Walking is an open road. Narrowboating is an open road. But on tarmac only a bicycle or a motorbike can approximate an open road. Any four-wheel means of transport is merely a means to an end. As Miller (played by Tracey Walter) says in *Repo Man*, 'The more you drive, the less intelligent you are.'

In Cornwall, as in Devon, the major risk at this time of year (late June) is not car pile-ups but seagull muggings. Down in the village of Pentewan, outside the Ship Inn, a sign warns 'Due to the seagulls and crows being so vicious we strongly advise you not to eat outside in the garden.' All the way along the southern coast, I've seen them flapping and swooping like Hitchcock extras on unsuspecting punters seated on harbour walls. Suddenly the punters are under siege, one arm arching protectively across food as they used to do as kids in the school canteen. The problem, of course, is that gulls like chips too. And fish even more. Where there is a rash of chippies, so there is a rash of gulls.

*

At Lizard, Britain's most southerly outpost, I drive the tank straight up on to the village green and am relieved to find that the car park operates on a donation scheme rather than £100 in coins for the first half-hour like everywhere else. Flanking one side of the green is a ribbon of craft shops selling shell-encrusted mirrors and local Cornish stone fashioned into trinkets and jewellery. Outside one of the scattered bungalows, four jars of homemade marmalade await buyers. Next to it, on a nearby telephone pole, is a flyer announcing the welcome return of The Sex Slaves, who are due to play Treveddon Farm 'very soon'.

At Lizard there is none of the gentrified flower arranging of England-in-bloom villages. It is an untamed place that bedazzles with extravagant flowers and exotic plants that would only survive indoors anywhere else in the country. After the chocolate box of exquisite coves I've been passing through, Lizard's wildness is like a cool shower after a hot, dust-filled day.

From the hamlet I follow a snaking lane to a coast path lashed on three sides by the sea. A foot from oblivion stands a simple wooden cross on which three letters spell out DAD. Did he walk or did he fall?

Beyond the headland the land breaks up in its plunge beneath the waves. Between these isolated islands drift eddying archipelagos of seaweed, uncertain which way to turn. There is an unmistakable feeling of having arrived at the end of things. To my left the remains of an old lifeboat ramp jut suicidally into the air. Above it stands a lighthouse (there was an outcry at the intrusion into the lucrative wreck-looting industry when the first one was built in 1619) and the southernmost café on mainland Britain, The Southerly.

A succession of bays provide flat sedimentary slates and shales that make perfect skimmers for bouncing off the belly of the sea; volcanic and igneous heavier rocks such as basalt that sink beneath the water as soon as they hit; and serpentine rocks (so named because of their 'snakeskin' markings) that separate the two as skimmers but are out on their own when it comes to tourist trinkets.

The Lizard promontory and the much-valued serpentine rock originally hatched through the earth's crust from the bottom of an ancient sea called the Rheic Ocean, 30 degrees south of the equator. The land eventually semi-settled 50 degrees north, just in time for the last ice age and the flooding of the English Channel. I say semi-settled because in reality it continues to drift, like the rest of Europe, 20mm a year away from America (however much Tony Blair would prefer it to be travelling in the opposite direction).

Some 370 million years after that first major upheaval, I pop into Shipton's Cornish Stone Shop where I chat with the owner Zena Browning (née Shipton) a fourth-generation Lizarder who's been selling the stone for thirty years. Dressed from head to toe in red, Zena tells me, as she wraps a customer's book on crop circles, that the problem is not with finding customers these days – the whole of Cornwall has seen an upturn over the past decade – but finding craftsmen who can work the stone. School leavers are reluctant to devote the time required to become proficient turners. It doesn't help either that parents encourage their kids to go away to college and seek better jobs in the cities.

Zena wraps two more items – a polished serpentine ashtray and an ornamental piskie (pixie) for a Portuguese customer – before turning her attention to another local issue she feels even more strongly about. Apparently a small group of locals are trying to ban cars from the village green despite the fact that they've been parking there since the first four-wheelers appeared more than a century ago. 'They want to make it into a picnic area with a *bund* - that's a raised bank – to prevent cars getting on to it. They want a traffic-free village. Which will mean the traffic continues on through the village to the headland, causing massive jams there in the summer.' Zena is incandescent at the stupidity of the idea. 'It's not just that our businesses will suffer. We don't want the natural setting spoiled either. Where did you park?'

'On the green.'

'Exactly. See, it keeps the cars back from the coast. Every morning before I start work, I walk our dog on the cliffs and my husband swims. We don't want cars clogging the headland more than they already do.'

Back on the green Sid is snuggling up with a motorhome girlfriend who has ignored the vast empty spaces and sidled up to him. All that's missing is a giant drive-in movie screen.

The A3083 north has plenty of bikers on it today, licking the grass verge as they bank at bends, leathers crackling with excitement at the winding

open road. I follow them, and a web of country lanes, to my friend Gill
Charlton's home, Ennis, near the village of St Hilary.

Gill hears the tank approaching and comes out to greet me from her
converted Georgian farmhouse at the end of the lane. Unsurprisingly,
she appears a little frazzled this morning because the sky fell on her head
– or rather the ceiling in the four-poster bedroom fell *almost* on the
heads of a couple of friends ('Thank God it wasn't paying guests'). Gill
distractedly runs fingers through her hair and a cloud of plaster rains
down. 'We've been trying to clear the debris. Now I've got to find a
plumber.' She invites me indoors for coffee.

In the kitchen a neighbour's son, Jack, aged seventeen, is fixing
breakfast as Gill's cook is on holiday. Jack dropped out of A levels
recently and took his surfboard off to Bali for a couple of months. Now
he's working to repay his dad the money he borrowed for the trip. Gill
has given Jack instructions to ignore the pandemonium reigning all
around and focus on serving immaculate breakfasts. He manages like an
old pro and the guests get their breakfasts just ten minutes later than
usual despite the chaos Jack's working in. Gill, a stickler in all things, is
mortified by the tardiness but full of praise for Jack. Fortunately I know
her of old and reassure the young kitchen hand that Gill is simply a
perfectionist. For several years when I was chief travel writer at the *Daily
Telegraph*, Gill was my boss.

While Gill organises a plumber, I wander the grounds and meet an
American father and young son peeling back the pool cover despite the
stormy skies overhead. They are clearly enchanted with the place. Next
I meet Laura, an expatriate Parisian living in London whose hair is
covered in dust and loose plaster. Laura has known Gill more than a
decade and they have even had the same boyfriend (though not
simultaneously). I ask her if she had been in the room when the ceiling
came down.

'No, it was another room occupied by some other friends of Gill's. I'm
sharing with my younger sister, Julie. She's still helping, clearing out the
last of the mess while I take a break. Gill is dropping us for a coastal walk
in ten minutes if you'd like to join us.'

Half an hour later I'm dropped with Julie and Laura at the end of a lane
that leads us down to Prussia Cove (named after an 18th-century smuggler
who modelled himself on Frederick the Great, for some reason). A sea mist

has stolen the coastline. We follow the track through the steam bath. Julie, I discover, is in the first year of a degree in business studies in Paris ('I'd like to do something related to fair trade when I graduate'). Ten minutes later the mist curtain rises on an ominous band of rain rushing across the bay. Thunder rumbles and soon light rain starts falling. We are clearly going to get soaked. Julie spots a pony near by and attempts to persuade it to transport her by lying across its back like a saddle. The animal doesn't budge, even when encouraged by a slap on its rear accompanied by the French equivalent of 'giddy-up'. We continue on foot.

Rounding Cudden Point we behold an offshore granite crag rising from the water, crowned by a 14th-century castle enclosing a medieval church dedicated to the Archangel Gabriel who appeared to fishermen here in AD 495. In 1135 a Benedictine community settled on the island and reminded themselves of their home on Brittany's Mont St Michel by naming the lonely outpost St Michael's Mount.

A mile or two later, we arrive at Perranuthnoe, where we've arranged to meet Gill in the snug Victoria Inn for lunch. Over warm fish soup and a bottle of Sauvignon, Gill recounts the denouement of the Fawlty Towers incident. 'The plumber found that a faulty junction only installed a year ago was haemorrhaging water.'

Like many before her, Gill has discovered that when you leave the rat race for somewhere prettier, the rats often travel with you. She is now responsible for wages, upkeep and everything that goes wrong. I can't resist reminding her that she'd quit London and her manic travel desk for a saner life five years earlier.

On the pub walls there are a number of dramatic photographs. One shows a 30ft basking shark weighing 6 tons that was landed with a single harpoon by Harold Dennis from a tiny wooden boat off Porthleven on 6 June 1934. Another is of the oil-spewing *Torrey Canyon* stranded on Seven Stones Reef in 1967. A third is of violent waves lashing the lantern of the Wolf Rock Lighthouse (located 8 miles southwest of Gewnnap Head).

Back at Ennis, Gill starts planning our evening sortie. Ominously she has decided to leave the car at home. Drinking sessions back in London invariably ended with me nursing a monumental hangover and Gill still up for more at 3 a.m. Gill rings the local taxi driver whose wife asks if we can wait 25 minutes so her husband can finish his dinner. When Jolly

Roger the taxi man turns up in shorts and sleeveless shirt, he looks as contented as if he's eaten five dinners.

Roger was born in Shepherd's Bush in 1948, moved to Rhodesia when he was eighteen months old, then relocated to Penzance when his father bought a hotel in 1960. As an adult, he continued the itinerant lifestyle, moving to Berkshire and Ealing before returning to Cornwall six years ago 'having found nowhere better'. For the first two years back on his home patch, Roger and his wife ran their own B&B. It wasn't easy. 'You live well for ten weeks and then you starve for the rest of the year.' Driving your own taxi is a more reliable business.

Porthleven is a bare-knuckle kind of a place. Three churches hunker around the harbour. God's final abode – the old fishermen's chapel – stands defiantly facing down the elements on the outer harbour wall. The houses flanking the waterfront are not cutesy but pragmatic, square-jawed, unadorned Victorian semis with just an occasional painted plaster scroll to brighten up the place. As we walk towards the pub, Gill bemoans the recently erected railings protecting clumsy pedestrians from a fall into the drink. 'Health and Safety. Only one car's gone in as far as I know and for that they spoil the whole look of the place.' Fencing-in is something Gill feels strongly about. Getting away from fences is what drew her down here.

'At Land's End they've erected railings too, just because stupid tourists step back too far when having pictures taken, or get taken by a swell when they clamber down to lower platforms. It's a nanny state.'

Inside the Ship we find Chris and Sue, the proprietors of our lunch-time stop, the Victoria Inn, propping up the bar. It's their night off and they stand us a drink. Over a rather fine crab mornay, Gill tells us how she used to visit Ennis two or three times a year on holiday and when the former owners decided to sell up, she made a snap decision to buy. She borrowed £340,000 from the bank and sold her flat in Pimlico to meet the £480,000 asking price. 'I got an 18th-century dream home, a half-converted barn, 20 acres and a successful business. What would you get in London for that?' Not a lot.

The next morning I follow up Gill's disaster with the ceiling, with a mishap of my own when a lorry whips round a corner and smashes Sid's passenger mirror. I find it lying in the street, a spider's web of discordant images. Somehow I manage to fix it back on to the van: it may now offer several lanes behind me where once there was one but it's slightly better than nothing at all, as a motorhome has no inside mirror to aid reversing.

Frazzled, I eventually reach Newlyn, a small town on the shoulder of Penzance that I'm reliably, though improbably, informed is England's most important fishing port in terms of value of fish landed by British-registered vessels (Hull and Grimsby land more, but predominantly on Icelandic-registered ships). The harbour is quiet. A few trawlers are buddied up, bitching about their crews who have deserted them for the pubs.

In the public toilet I notice a slot in the wall for used syringes. Smuggling has been a way of life from the early Middle Ages and is still a way of death too (Newlyn is reputedly topped only by Liverpool per capita in drug-related fatalities).

Seeking more edifying fishermen's tales, I pop into the Pilchard Works, a working factory and museum, where my attention is immediately drawn to a black-and-white photograph of trawl nets straining to contain a catch. It was taken in 1905 in St Ives when five boats landed 13 million fish and it took eight days to clear all 1,100 tons. Adjacent to the photograph is a recent colour shot of one of the superefficient, super-expensive Breton sardine boats.

When the Common Fisheries Policy was being established in 1978, the French fleet got 62 per cent of the Channel cod quotas and the Cornish got just eight. Brittany historically landed more cod than us – which is what the EU quotas are based on – but they also lubricated their figures a good 25 per cent according to just about every fisherman I've talked to. The result is that while the French trawler legally hauls mountains of cod, alongside it a Cornish boat will be having to throw its catch back into the sea. Because of the restriction the Cornish boats understandably want only the biggest and best cod, and to find the best 100 kilos they're permitted to land, they'll probably sling 300 kilos overboard – once the fish's eyeballs and bladders have exploded from being out of water. A logical conservation policy, then.

The owner of the Pilchard Works, Nick Howell, has not had a good day. Earlier I had seen him driving a 1928 green Model A Ford through the town. Soon afterwards, 'Some young bastard ran into me and scarpered before I could get his number.'

Nick's own salt pilchard business has been faring better than the cod fishing fleet and his Ford. When he bought the works in 1980, it was the only one left operating in Cornwall. What made the difference was a crucial makeover for the humble pilchard that led to a significant breakthrough on the domestic front. As the fish had such a bad image in Britain (due to its being marketed solely in tins swimming in tomato sauce), he switched from the second to the first part of its Latin piscatory name – *sardine pilchardus* (mature sardine) – rebranding it as the Cornish sardine and making it more acceptable to a younger generation of customers. Marks & Spencer and Waitrose were soon hooked.

In the adjoining black-tarred processing warehouse, Terry Tonkin is expertly packing a traditional box of the salted sardines as carefully as if it were a wedding gift. Terry is dressed in yellow overalls and wellies and has a fine pair of snow-white sideburns travelling due south from his peaked blue cap. He is seventy and has been packing pilchards for 35 years. 'It's a disgrace really. I keep asking Nick to let me retire but he won't let me go!'

In the museum shop I buy a postcard of a 1926 painting entitled *Girl on a Cliff*, of a seventeen-year-old beauty sitting on a rock . The cashier tells me the model was none other than Terry's mother and it was painted by Harold Harvey, a member of the Newlyn School. The group were much influenced by the French Impressionists, choosing to work *en plein air* rather than in studios. 'A canvas by Stanhope Forbes recently sold for £1.2 million,' he tells me with a wink of the eye.

Quitting Newlyn I slip through Mousehole (pronounced 'mowsel'), where figs, peaches and apricots flourish outdoors and the 'downalongs' (the name given to those living on the seafront) have cashed in on their coveted harbourside cottages and moved to their reservation up on the hill. Mousehole is followed by Penberth Cove, where Phoenician merchants used to pop in to buy tin, and Porthcurno, where the first telephone link to Bombay was completed in 1870.

I rejoin Gill at the virtual theme park that's grown up at Land's End, where a banner, a little parochially, declares 'The edge of the world'. The site – known to the Romans as Belerion ('Seat of Storms'), and as Pen an

Wlas ('End of the Earth') by the ancient Cornish – is the last word in 21st-century tawdriness. The most westerly point on the British mainland, located 874 miles from John O' Groats, is to junk and tat what the southernmost point at Lizard is to beguiling wildness.

Fortunately we don't have to walk far to escape. From the next headland, above Sennen Cove, Gill points out the Isles of Scilly, thirty miles offshore. In another cove huge smooth white boulders lie scattered as if abandoned by giants who grew bored during a game of marbles (in a couple of days I'll discover similar stones sculpted by Barbara Hepworth in her St Ives garden). One minute we're walking a carpet of pink and lilac wild chives, bloody cranesbill, campion and foxgloves; the next we are in a yellow drift of tormentil, St John's wort and dyer's greenweed. A century ago many of the plants that grow here would have been hanging to dry inside cottages, for just about everything had a use then – the fragile pink flowers of the common centaury, for instance, were once thought to remove freckles.

Down in Priest's Cove we watch a fisherman launching his boat into a shimmering sea and then assist an elderly man who's had a dizzy spell from being out in the sun too long. Meanwhile a young boy, locked in his own pleasure and oblivious to all, sings as he splashes in his natural seawater pool. Gill and I make our way up on to the headland above the cove to the ornate brick boiler stack of the Cape Cornwall Mine. Beneath it a plaque marks the location offshore of England's only genuine cape (defined as the meeting of two oceans or channels). We skirt the promontory and the wreck of a chapel beside which stands a lonely grave on whose headstone is written, 'You made your dreams come true.' We then turn inland and loop back to the car, passing a number of irregular moorstone Celtic field boundaries.

On our drive home Gill decides we should pop into the Penzance Arts Club, located in a Georgian building that was formerly shared by the Portuguese and Russian consulates. We sit on a small deck, overlooking the harbour and St Michael's Mount, and are joined by one of Gill's friends, Martin Val Baker, who owns the RAINYDAY Art Gallery. Sitting at the adjacent table is Carol Innocent, who owns the Innocent Fine Art Gallery in Bristol and is down 'trawling for new treasure'.

'You mean nicking my artists,' Martin corrects her. Clearly there is history between them. Martin has been exhibiting contemporary local artists for eleven years and is still struggling. Carol's pillaging visits probably don't help. Penwith (the Land's End Peninsula) has long been an artist's colony but it has seen a huge influx of artists in recent years – Martin estimates there are now as many as a thousand working in the area.

Carol provides the historical overview: 'Artists have sought the special light here from the turn-of-the-20th-century Newlyn School to the mid-century St Ives School.' Gazing out at the multi-coloured trisails criss-crossing the indigo bay, I am indeed struck by the luminosity of light – it's as if you suddenly discover how to open a window after a lifetime looking through glass.

Martin provides an irreverent rider: 'You get a lot of crap artists too. Like New Agers and illustrators who think they can paint.' He takes a swig of his beer, which seems to quell the attack. 'There are some gems, though.'

'Like who?' I ask.

Martin lowers his voice so Carol can't hear. 'Chris Hankey. He moved down from Bristol three or four months back and paints Turneresque seascapes beautifully. He has two kids, his wife's an artist too and they have to earn £800 a month just to pay the rent on their cottage. Most artists have to turn their hand to something else. Terry Frost used to work as a waiter in town. They may come to paint the warmth of the sun but invariably they find themselves eking out an existence and living on the edge.'

Martin adeptly licks a Rizla and pops his Golden Virginia roll-up into the corner of his mouth while fishing a lighter from a pocket. He first moved to Cornwall at the age of three with his father, Denys Val Baker (after the latter's divorce from Martin's mother, Pat Kitto), who was a writer and mixed in the arty set. One of his father's earliest books was entitled *British Art Colony by the Sea*. In all, Denys Val Baker had 110 books published, including 26 autobiographies. 'He found the auto-biographical formula worked particularly well so he wrote two a year until his death in 1984.'

Somewhat predictably, Martin, who is now 57, attended art college after finishing secondary school. 'I studied at Falmouth but wasn't much good,' he admits with refreshing honesty. As the bones of his life continue to be revealed, we discover we have a connection. In the 1950s Martin often used to spend his summers with his mother, who was living in an artists' community in Heligan Woods. One year my father-in-law, the poet Dannie Abse, visited the community. Martin believes Dannie had a fling then with his mother, Pat. Extraordinarily, he also claims that when Dannie was a first-year medical student, he dated Martin's step-mother, Jess Val Baker, in their home town of Cardiff.

As we chat our way through the balmy early evening, the Scillonian ferry slowly bisects the bay heading into port from the Scillies. 'That was where I last holidayed,' Martin switches tack, following the ship's progress beneath a sun that's still high in the sky.

'Where?'

'The Scillies. Fifteen years ago.'

'What, you haven't had a holiday for fifteen years?'

'Nope. Why bother? Everyone comes here for their holidays. There must be a good reason.'

Martin is the antithesis of the itinerant: rooted so deeply in Penzance, he rarely strays far. Dressed in black T-shirt and battered, shapeless blue trousers, he reminds me of the dishevelled actor and director Colin Welland.

Many of Martin's contemporaries left with dreams of a better life in the big cities and drifted back in their forties and fifties. Others, born elsewhere, migrated to Penzance with dreams of richer lives and traded in their degrees to become plumbers and builders – the skills that are most needed in the Southwest.

Like the majority living in the area, Martin does several jobs. Apart from running his own business, he produces an annual guide to Cornwall's galleries, promotes bands and also organises Penzance's summer 'Little Festival'. 'Basically I book all the bands I like so it's not that onerous. This year it was Ben Waters' Boogie Band, The Andy Shepherd Trio, Waterson Carthy and – for the second year running by popular demand – a five-piece Senegalese band known as Jalikunda Cissokho.' Martin is particularly proud of the fact that he was only £200 out of pocket at the end of the festival. 'That was a record . . . the best yet . . . maybe in another decade or two I'll be in the black.'

*

In the morning I bid Gill farewell and then drive across to St Just, the most
westerly town in England and home to the finest pasty-maker in Cornwall
(McFadden's). I eat my pasty sitting on a granite block in the stone
rectangle of Plen an Gwary ('Playing Place'), where medieval mystery plays
were performed until the early 17th century. As I munch, I notice a series
of holes in the granite blocks and wonder if they have something to do with
the performances. A local puts me right. 'No lad, they've got nothing to do
with mystery plays. They were put there by miners who had races during
the annual fete to see who could drill six inches down fastest.'

Heading in a northeasterly direction for the first time, I discover my
first genuine classic coast road. Most coastal routes get a sniff of the sea
and then immediately burrow inland but the B3306 snakes a ridge
halfway between coastal cliffs and sweeping moorland. Between them
crumbling 7ft-thick walls make a snail trail across fields cleared of forest
three thousand years earlier. Venerable farms built of cut granite dot the
landscape alongside a postindustrial sculpture trail of abandoned mines.
Their chimneys stand like tombstones at the edge of hunkered mining
villages hewn out of slate and brown millstone grit. With the demise of
mining, farming and fishing, the towns are now festooned with signs
offering B&B and 'Cornish palms for sale'.

At Zennor I visit the 12th-century Church of Serena, where carved
mermaids adorn an ancient chair, recalling a tragic local tale of the
doomed love of a local man for a creature that was half-girl and half-
fish. It comes as no surprise to learn that DH Lawrence worked on
Women in Love here during World War II until he and his German
wife Frieda were ordered to leave because of their suspected pro-
German sympathies.

In St Ives (founded by St Ia, who reportedly journeyed here from
Ireland on a leaf), I park to the west of town and descend a steep hill past
a cemetery packed with occupants jockeying for the best views over the
long sandy beach. Surrounded on three sides by the sea and drenched in
a light that is reputedly the finest in England, St Ives has long been the
art world's rural capital. Those who retire here for the air and sea seek
west-facing homes; artists, however, will sell their souls to get a north-
facing aspect, for that is where the light is fabled to be purest of all.

Down on the shore I arrive at the Tate, which though not in the
Guggenheim Bilbao league in terms of extravagant, gravity-defying

architectural ambition, does happen to perch beside a beach on which two flags are fluttering with the imperative 'SURF' emblazoned upon them.

With consummate timing I have arrived in town in time for a Barbara Hepworth retrospective, marking both the centenary of her birth and the Tate's tenth birthday. What is most striking about the exhibits, apart from their continuing sense of modernity (many were created fifty years ago), is the lurking presence of the sea and the coast's special luminosity in every deep-lustred wood carving and enigmatic stone. Sensual curves and piercings allow light to radiate through or gather in bowls transforming objects into bedazzling bays and dark, unfathomable caves.

Hepworth spent most of her adult years in St Ives, working in a studio on the other side of town, where she died in a fire in 1975 at the age of 72. After the busyness of the Tate and the resort's crowded alleys, the Hepworth Museum and Sculpture Garden on the other side of town is a real oasis. In an upstairs room a schoolboy stares quizzically at an eyeless Buddhalike child (*Infant*, 1929) carved in Burmese wood. Other class-mates, dressed in matching yellow sweatshirts, sit on the floor listening intently to one of the staff who is showing them how to make a curl of paper that can lock on to its tail but doesn't roll when laid on a flat surface.

Out in the garden large objects balance on top of each other, as if by the same miracle that leaves one rock impossibly perching on another on a beach when the tide peels back. Most are pierced, allowing light to flood through them. Each seems to have its own sense of equilibrium, set in a frame of lilies, white roses, Japanese anemones or whispering ferns.

St Ives, a six-hour train slog from London, can feel wonderfully out on a limb at times but at others – especially on summer days like today when there's a surge from the land – it feels like the hub of Europe with its Babel of tongues echoing down the narrow, cobbled streets and across the granite quay. The lanes constantly twist, offering unexpected sea vistas. The houses too all seem to face in different directions, as if a giant had dropped glue on the hillside and then emptied a sack of houses from the sky.

Despite its charms and obvious attractions, with nowhere to stable Sid for the night I decide to quit town and drive several miles east along the pristine sandy bay to St Ives Bay Holiday Camp whose statics, tents and tourers (that's us) are scattered across an extensive Site of Special Scientific Interest (SSSI). As I stand on the final crest of dune, watching surfers paddling out towards the setting sun, a wave of contentment passes over me. It feels good to be staying on a rural campsite instead of cooped up inside a guesthouse.

I spend 26 June beachcombing, swimming and cleaning the van as I have an important guest arriving. Then, after lunch, I travel a few miles inland to meet my fourteen-year-old son Max and our family dog Lucky off the train from London. I arrive an hour and a half early. It's a month since I left home and I can't wait to see him. It's just a shame that my seventeen-year-old daughter Larne won't be coming too – she plays lead guitar in a punk band called The Cherry Bombers and they're playing a gig over the weekend. My wife Susanna, however, will be joining us in a couple of days on a budget flight from Stansted to Newquay.

As soon as Lucky hits the platform, she starts bouncing up and down like a rubber ball, preventing me from giving Max a proper hug. My son seems to have had yet another growth spurt and now stands less than an inch from overtaking me. The journey has taken for ever and the friends have been cooped up too long. We head north, stopping first for a walk and a Cornish ice cream and then for fish and chips, which we eat in the van by the side of the road with cars streaming past.

Max is impressed with the proper sit-down dining quarters and table. His sleeping arrangements above the driver's cab also meet with his approval – 'It's great I don't have to slide it away . . . that it's permanently out . . . because it means I won't ever have to make the bed.' But he is particularly taken by the folding tap in the kitchen sink and also the longer-handled tap in the bathroom that pulls out from the sink to function as a shower. Lucky, meanwhile, has taken up residence on the front passenger seat, giving a low growl to anyone who passes. God knows what Sid makes of it all.

Having stashed the rubbish and cleared away, we briefly join the A30 and soon pull into Beacon Cottage Farm on the outskirts of St Agnes. The working farm is the best campsite I've checked into so far. The site has a couple of washing machines in addition to the usual showers and bathrooms (with soap and toilet roll provided – not the case in some of the ropier places), and just a handful of tents and caravans sharing our sloping hill and long sea views.

At 9 p.m. Max, Lucky and I walk a carpet of purple bell heather and western gorse to the ghostly remains of the Wheal Coates mine, its gaunt engine house and chimney silhouetted against the bay. One hundred yards further on, precariously perched halfway down the cliff, the Towanroath engine house stands in spectacular desolation. With the proximity of the sea no more than a hundred yards away, it's hard to imagine that the 600ft-deep shaft and tunnels were ever dry.

Once a thousand people in St Agnes were employed in the local tin mines, spending most of their daylight hours scurrying along the seams like rabbits in darkness while all this beauty awaited outside. Each time they ended a shift they must have felt like Lazarus. Although the mines have long since stopped operating, it's believed there are still massive seams of untapped tin here. If they ever became commercially viable once more, I guess it would be a hard call for many to choose between unemployment and the prospect of one-third of your life spent underground.

In classical times the Greek writer Diodorus described the local tin-producing community as, 'especially friendly to strangers and, as a result of trading with foreign merchants, civilised in their dealings'. From the Bronze Age until its 19th-century heyday, Cornwall was Britain's – and for a time the world's – most important tinmining area. The last mine closed as recently as 1998 but the pits remain so historically important that UNESCO is considering awarding them World Heritage status.

As we continue walking the cliffs, 100ft beneath us surfers are still catching waves. It's 10 p.m. The flat sandy beach stretches in both directions to more empty serried bays. It's said that thirty parish churches by day, and twelve lighthouses by night, can be seen across both Cornish coasts from nearby St Agnes Beacon, 629ft above sea level.

Surf beaches now stretch right up the north Cornwall littoral. The undisputed capital of surfing culture is Newquay, with eleven different beaches and more surf shops per square mile than anywhere else in the country.

Max and I pull into town the next morning, parking on the western headland before descending the hill to the BSA National Surfing Centre on Fistral Beach. For some reason Max is strangely reluctant to have a surf lesson. He's already an advanced open-water scuba diver, a good skier and loves the great outdoors in general, so this really isn't like him. Maybe it's the gangly adolescent age, the reluctance to be a learner at anything any more. He decides to sit out the lesson and walk Lucky instead. I pick up a wet suit and surfboard and head off across the beach with ten others who have booked the same beginner's lesson. Two more BSA groups are already being put through their paddling paces further up the beach (and that's from just one of at least ten surf outfits operating in Newquay).

All the instructors are bleached blond, young, good looking, as trim as their boards and therefore bastards. One of them, an Aussie who should be able to judge such things, is eulogising 'Fistral Beach is a beaut' to his group. Our instructor is Kieron, who has been teaching in Newquay for four years and hails from North Wales. Needless to say, like all the other bastards, once he has slipped into his body-hugging wet suit Kieron becomes a god.

I peel on my less-than-flattering rubber and buddy up with Brian, an engineer from Sheffield. We carry our two boards between us across the long beach. Adonis is out ahead, leading the way; beyond him waves curl and crash. When we reach our designated patch of beach, our nervous, self-deprecating banter under Cornish-cream skies is called to a halt as Kieron sends us off on a short jog. When we wheeze back in, we are instructed to stand in a semi-circle behind our boards. First we are taught the names of the different board parts and their functions. I instantly forget this essential bit of information, which makes it tricky for me to follow subsequent instructions once Kieron allows us into the water. Fortunately our first task is a simple one – to propel the board forward before sliding on to it and riding the wave in on our bellies. Simple enough, as long as your body remains in the right place. Next we add a little paddling before catching the wave.

And then it's time for the full surf. Kieron runs through the sequence: look behind, push the board ahead, glide on to it, paddle, look behind again and when the wave closes take three strong strokes (without rocking) before popping up on to the board slightly crouched with arms stretched ahead and behind for balance. And bingo.

Bingo, however, is a long time coming. Kieron reminds me of the Silver Surfer, my favourite Marvel Comics hero. I, on the other hand, am more like Bambi on water. The first curling lip of sea is past me before I have even got properly on to the board. The next time I'm weighted too much to one side and the board leaps from under me and into the air like a hooked marlin. Slowly I improve and by the end of the session I manage to get up three times, which I'm rather proud of. I return to dry land elated after the £25 two-and-a-half-hour session and resolve to do a full course next year.

Back at the Portakabin that the BSA outfit is housed in (until it moves up to its swish new home in the town's £2.1 million international surfing centre later in the month), I chat with Barry Hall, the manager. Barry tried his first surfboard at the age of six. He has been teaching in Newquay for a decade and has noticed a huge surge in the sport in recent years, particularly among young women.

'It's down to the cult surfer's chic flick *Blue Crush*. It brought so many female surfers in there's now pretty much parity between the sexes.' The female of the species has apparently been deliberately targeted by both Hollywood and clothing manufacturers. 'Women spend more on clothes than men. Fact. Surfing's about the most fashionable sport on the planet at the moment – fact – and a lot of it's down to the clothes – Quiksilver, Mambo, Billabong, Oakley, O'Neill – they're all mainstream high-street fashions these days.'

Barry is in his early thirties, has blue shades nestling in his hair and he's dressed in a blue T-shirt and blue shorts. Clearly a man who takes his work togs seriously. He is tanned and attractively weathered, like everyone else here. The other big change Barry has noticed over the past decade has been in the surfer profile. 'This week I've a heart surgeon booked in for one-on-one lessons and I've also got another professional coming in from Spain on a private course. They're both in their forties, which incidentally shatters another myth – that it's just teenagers that surf.'

Just to prove Barry's point, at that very moment a couple of forty-somethings park their sixties-style, split-screen VW camper 30ft from us and start releasing the bungees holding their boards to the roof. The doors are left wide and Nickelback is blasting out of the speakers. Pretty soon the couple are on the beach joining all the other upright seals walking in every direction, each one of them carrying a surfboard beneath a flipper. Out to sea experts zip along the curling lips of waves while beginners wipe out theatrically. Hepworth would have made something memorable of such a landscape. So would Turner. What they produced, though, would probably have as little in common as the lives of those who formed our beginner surfers' semi-circle two hours earlier.

I catch sight of Max camped with Lucky, chatting with one of the guys from Beach Rescue. I head down to join them. Kelvin Kilday and Max are talking dogs but I manage to hijack the conversation and nudge it towards drownings and Baywatch rescues. I'm surprised to learn that Kelvin rarely has to hit the water despite the fact that upwards of twenty thousand people – a fair number of them in poor states of alcoholic disrepair – attend the big surfing events.

'Is this a typical swell today?' I practise my new surfer's speak and Max rolls his eyes.

'Yeah, pretty typical. Maybe one-and-a-half feet.'

I'm hugely disappointed. 'One of the surfers told me it was three feet.'

I blanch, 'Must be a beginner. Surfers measure from the back of the wave rather than the front so when you hear of a six-footer in Hawaii, it's probably about twenty feet to nonsurfers.' Max grins.

For many years Kelvin travelled the winters, following the surf and cheap budgets, to Mexico, Sri Lanka, Brazil, Oz, Indonesia, Belize. 'The kids teaching surfing these days do the same thing. It's a great life if you're young and single.' I can see Max mentally adding surf instructor or beach rescue to his list of future careers alongside ski instructor, dive master and football coach.

We wish Kelvin a quiet day ('No question of it, mate') and head down for a swim. As we splash about and throw a ball to each other, Lucky darts about frantically at the water's edge, desperate to join us but unwilling to get a soaking. We move on up into town in search of lunch.

Kelvin may be happy with the new availability of latte in Newquay but the town seems to be suffering schizophrenia: street signs declare 'Alcohol-free zone' in an attempt to keep the drunks from rolling in the gutters, while the Beach Nite Club, Fun Pub and others offer cheap double shots to oblivion. Newquay is the capital of stag and hen nights as well as the entire country's post-GCSE school's-out revels. The town's endless summer party has led Viscount and Lady Long, who inhabit a private outcrop, to demand that the council introduce a by-law to stop the nightly naked debaucheries that commence around 2.30 a.m., 100ft below them on Towan beach.

Max is less than impressed with the town. 'It's just like London but smaller and with a seaside. I'd rather be somewhere remote like we were last night.' That's my boy.

We quit town for another beach campsite and the next morning pick up Susanna from the airport at 7.50 a.m. The flight has cost just £30 (about the same as the train) and taken 25 minutes, but she had to be up at 4 a.m. to make it. Despite the ungodly hour, she looks surprisingly fresh. As we hug, Lucky goes through her bouncing-ball trick again. It's strange to have company sharing the motorhome. Susanna takes up the passenger seat, while Max is relegated to Lucky's quarters at the table seats.

Virtually everything along this coastal stretch is National Trust owned or managed, an AONB, Heritage Coastline or all three. Unlike Cornwall's south coast, which softly seduces with gentle valleys and lush gardens, north Cornwall exhilarates with its rugged cliffs, silver surf and golden beaches. In summer I find it hard to imagine anywhere I'd rather be, especially with three-quarters of the family with me, skylarks chattering in the fields and the air suffused with honeysuckle and wild thyme.

At Padstow I leave Cornwall's 'Ps' behind – Pentire, Perranporth, Porthtowan, Portreath, Pendeen, Porthcurno, Paul, Penzance, Perranuthnoe, Porthleven, Porthoustock, Porthallow. Beyond Padstow moving up through the alphabet will come the 'Ts' – Tregurrian, Trenance, Treyarnon, Trevose Head, Trevone, Tredizzick, Trebetherick, Trelights, Trewalder, Treligga, Trebarwith, Trewarmett, Treknow, Tintagel and Trevalga.

It's hardly surprising Padstow has been renamed 'Padstein'. Rick Stein's presence is everywhere – the Seafood Restaurant (with thirteen bedrooms upstairs), Padstow Seafood School, St Petroc's Hotel & Bistro, Rick Stein's Café, Stein's Seafood Delicatessen (where you can get a crab pasty for £2.95) and Stein's gift shop. Soon the Rick Stein show plans to roll into Newquay with a new hotel and two restaurants to drag the town up by its surfer straps.

While Susanna takes Max to buy some cargo pants, I slip into the Crib Box Café Portakabin where Geoff Meacham has been sizzling bacon on the griddle virtually every other day for the past sixteen years. Between a white cap and apron, Geoff stares professorially out over specs that rest on the bridge of his nose. He displays no visible envy concerning Stein's success when I ask about the maverick chef. Not everyone feels like Geoff, however. Some of the dwindling pool of indigenous inhabitants berate the new fancy ways, the fancy restaurants and fancy incomers. The cardinal sin in Cornwall, as in the rest of England, is success.

Nowadays people book weekend breaks in the Southwest just to eat at Rick Stein's. At 1.30 p.m. I rejoin Susanna and Max (Lucky is keeping Sid company back in the car park). It's the second time I've eaten at Rick Stein's and it doesn't disappoint. With original works by major artists serving as wallpaper, and light pouring through the windows over rustling linen and glistening glasses, we take two hours eking out every last drop of pleasure from the occasion.

After lunch we take the ferry across the Camel estuary to Rock, where teenage Hoorays from London party in their big villas between surfing and sailing. It is a world away from Newquay but still there are tell-tale signs of the outdoor booze predilection of visitors in the signs declaring the beach, skinny street and air to be alcohol-free zones. John Betjeman lived here and is buried at St Enodoc, which also used to be buried up to its armpits in sand. Apart from churches there's a sailing club, a chandlery and Di's Pantry where you can order the finest delicacies – on account, naturally – to be delivered to your door on arrival. The only restaurant I come across is Mariner's Rock. It has a broad terrace and wind-away glass frontage, redolent of the languorous newspaper-and-spritzer lifestyle of the South African Cape. Everyone seems to know everyone here and they all dress from the same Boden catalogue. Men in beige shorts and polo shirts carry oars to their dinghies while reminding their five-year-olds – who have halos of white hair and are dressed in sailors' matelots – 'Be careful, Thomas.' The adults almost certainly came as five-year-olds themselves, as did their own fathers before them. The place is as snug and satisfied as a private club.

There are people like me everywhere along the coast, with accents as thin as the Thames. When you encounter a clotted-cream accent, it comes as a shock. And it comes as an even bigger surprise to find a living eccentric still surviving anywhere near the sea these days. While Susanna and Max spend an hour or two trawling surfy shops such as Boo and White Sail, I revisit one such fossil I'd met on an earlier Cornish trip.

Ed Prynn lives in a bungalow a mile outside St Merryn. The only difference between Ed and his neighbours is that he happens to have Stonehenge sitting in his garden and is dressed in the white robe of a druid priest.

Over the past four decades, Ed has squeezed on to his front lawn a number of monoliths he proudly calls his rock sculptures. Taking pride of place is an 18-ton dolmen he calls *The Angels' Runway*. One night, according to Ed, he was woken by an angel who sat on his bed complaining of nighttime navigational difficulties and bemoaning the lack of safe landing places in the area. Ed, always eager to help, constructed his dolmen as a landing strip. 'The angels run up the capstone like them Harrier jets on aircraft carriers and jump off,' he explains. 'Soon I'm going to rig up some fairy lights so they can see it better after dark.'

Ed's 'rock sculptures' have transformed a nondescript suburban garden into an occult fantasy sufficiently intriguing to passers-by that the 67-year-old now supplements his disability pension (Ed is partially sighted) with donations from visitors. The contributions may not amount to much, but then Ed's needs are modest apart from the occasional boulder he might require shipping from the Preseli mountains or somewhere further afield.

The most exotic stones are a pair of émigrés from the Falklands. During the war with Argentina, Ed wrote to Governor Sir Rex Hunt asking if he might spare a rock or two for a memorial he wanted to erect to the war dead. St Merryn's cynics laughed on hearing about the letter but were silenced when two quartz rocks weighing a ton each arrived, having been transported 8,000 miles on the HMS *Lesterbrook*.

Ed believes his Falkland Memorial has special powers. But then, he believes all his stones have. Each of the seven that make up the Stone Circle (Ed's personal Stonehenge) are named after powerful women in his life and it is from these women, Ed claims, the rocks get their energy. 'Great Auntie Hilda, named after the seventh of my mother's father's sisters, is strongest of all – the seventh sister is always lucky,' Ed explains.

According to Ed, the most popular 'sculpture' with visitors is the Rocking Stone. 'People stand rocking on it for hours for good luck.' To underline the point, Ed jumps on board, his white druid's robe swaying rhythmically round his ankles, his shock of white hair iridescent in the sun. 'It weighs more than ten tons and rocks like a feather in the wind. Now tell me that's not magic.'

Another monolith, an Italian marble slab called *Judgement Stone*, apparently got its power from the sea, having been washed by it daily for more than a hundred years before being dragged by tractor from a nearby cove. Ed believes it has enormous power. 'In some future time all the world leaders are going to be drawn by it to my home to heal the world's sickness.'

One political figure has already called in. Unfortunately Ed didn't know who Dennis Healey was when he paid an impromptu visit ('"Who be you?" I asked him – embarrassing it were'). Others have been invited: Prince Charles' brief, polite apology is pinned to the garage wall and alongside it is an even briefer note from Margaret Thatcher – 'I called but no one was there.' Ed had invited the former prime minister when she was holidaying in nearby Constantine Bay. 'Unfortunately my mother made me go and do the shopping and I missed her,' Ed shakes his head.

Sharing the garage wall with these apologies are plaques dedicated to benefactors and to an assortment of celebrities whom Ed and girlfriend Glynnis believe have made 'a positive contribution to life on earth'. The Hall of Fame quickly outgrew the garage and now slate plaques cover every inch of the bungalow's facade. It is an eclectic collection – Harry Houdini, Benny Hill (Ed's voice sounds uncannily like Benny Hill's 'Ernie (The Fastest Milkman in the West), Frank Ifield, Sir William Hesketh Lever ('I like Sunlight soap'), and a Billy Butlin redcoat named Jonathan Cowling.

Ed encourages me to climb through the marriage stone. 'Shame your wife's not here. It's a fertility stone and many ladies climb through it with tremendous results.' I tell him our two teenage children are more than enough for us. 'Well, if you ever decide to remarry, I do marriage contracts too. My tip to newlyweds is to not go too heavy to start: just get married for a week; if it's going good, have another week, and then a month.'

The marriages take place in a grotto Ed has dug 10ft underground. As we descend the stone steps, he sagely informs me that the grotto is the womb of Mother Earth – 'We do rebirthing here too.' In the central circular chamber is a lingam fertility stone. 'We call it *The Dreckly Stone* 'cos it guarantees you better luck *dreckly* . . . I came up on Ernie premium bonds not so long back after a visit. It were only £50 but we tore our clothes off and thanked the stone.'

As we enter Ed's bedroom, a black Collie called Roly runs out. In the centre is a pine four-poster bed that appears too large for the room. Above it is hung a purple lurex canopy decorated with sequins in the shape of a well-endowed fertility god in a clear state of excitement. 'I did that,' Ed's partner Glynnis proudly informs me. 'It's a celestial bed – makes you sexier.' She smiles and lifts a candlewick bedspread that conceals a mammoth crystal sleeping beneath the mattress. 'That's where the power comes from.' Draped across the mummified crystal is the lead of an electric blanket that, I suppose, serves as back-up if the crystal fails to warm the love-makers up.

After our tour of the bungalow ('the most photographed in Cornwall' according to Ed 'and possibly in the whole of the UK'), Glynnis leads me across the garden with a twitching hazel stick. She's trying to locate their underground spring. 'Every time I stray into the Stone Circle the stick has a fit.' She demonstrates and the stick does indeed become possessed. 'See, see – that's the power of them stones,' Ed excitedly exclaims before insisting on dancing with me inside the circle. 'Keep your eyes on the tops of the stones, Paul. D'you feel it, d'you feel it?' I feel dizzy.

Ed now has plans for a new sculpture – 'It's going to be a big log and I'm going to call it *Big Dick*.' He's also planning a tea room, which he'll call 'The Happy Fanny', after his great-great-granny Fanny.

As I leave Ed and Glynnis' bungalow an hour later, Ed waves me off with the words, 'There, you're a druid now so make sure you come back for the next sun dance on the summer solstice – it'll be great fun but watch you don't get no mystic mania. Some people can go over the top a bit.'

When I meet up with Susanna and Max and tell them what I've been doing, they think I've made it up. Max in particular can't believe that people like Ed and Glynnis exist. I thank the Angels of the Runway that they do. In Victorian times tourists came to see the pixies in Cornwall and spoke reverentially of Padstow's patron saint, St Petroc, a man who removed a splinter from a dragon. Local miners, meanwhile, feted a saint who died falling into a well in an advanced state of inebriation at the age of 206. There is a tradition to uphold and Ed's doing his level best to uphold it.

We head out to our overnight camp at Mother Ivy's, a model clifftop campsite whose undulating lawns are broken into twenty pitch corrals separated by dry-stone walls topped by banks of mauve erigeron. It shows what can be done with a little planning and care. The private sandy beach the site abuts is among the best I've seen since starting the trip. Max and I play with Lucky beside waves crashing round reptilian outcrops.

Later, while I'm cooking back in the motorhome, Tom Fairhurst, one of the security men, pops his head round the door on his rounds. He tells me that a couple of days earlier he'd stopped someone marching through the site dressed in just walking boots and a rucksack. 'He said he was walking from Land's End to John o' Groats bollock-naked as a protest.'

'A protest about what?'

'Not sure really. About clothes I think. He mentioned something about personal freedom. Anyway, I cleared him off and a day later he got arrested for the fourth or fifth time since leaving Land's End. I reckon it's going to be winter before he reaches Scotland and his nuts will be frozen solid.'*

After an early swim on Saturday morning, we arrive in Tintagel for a coffee-and-cake breakfast at Primrose Cottage Café. The owners, Avito and Julie Nunes from St Albans, spend their summers working long hours in the Primrose and then, as the last tourist leaves, they pack for their apartment in Avito's home state of Goa. Avito and Julie are not the only recent arrivals in Tintagel. The owners of Wyldes Café, opposite, are from Nottingham. Londis is run by people from Cambridge; the fish and chip shop is owned by a couple from Peterborough and they own the bakery too.

The locals with history mostly live in the main village, a mile inland – farmers with huge tracts of land or property owners with holiday lets. But the really big money these days is in car parks. Instead of farming sheep, they open their fields to paying cars and fleece the visitors.

As we enter the English Heritage site of Tintagel Castle, legendary birthplace of King Arthur, my daughter rings on the mobile phone. When

*He actually completed his journey in late January, just as temperatures plummeted below zero.

I tell her where we are, Larne reminds me of my old bedtime story, a bastardised Arthurian legend I called 'Arthur and the Egg Cup'. The epic stars Guinevere and Sirs Lancelot, Gawain, Galahad and Perceval, all of whom take it in turns to scour inhospitable mountains and enchanted forests inhabited by ogres and trolls in an attempt to find Arthur's favourite eggcup, which he'd lost en route to a friend's castle in Liverpool.

It's often been said that the Round Table is the root of our democracy. Similar ideals of chivalry, mystical wisdom and heroism rooted in the Arthurian legends continue to be played out today in *Harry Potter, Dark Materials* and *The Lord of the Rings*.

Archeological finds show goods were being traded at Tintagel as early as the 4th century. The discovery of the 'Arthnou' stone, a 6th-century inscribed slate, further fuelled speculation that a Dark Ages royal palace may once have stood here. There is, however, no solid evidence that Tintagel was ever the seat of the historical Arthur, a local Cornish chieftain of Roman descent who repelled Saxon invaders at the siege of Mons Badonicus around AD 500.

Whatever the truth, the setting is truly dramatic. Doomed buttresses of a 12th-century blackstone castle cling for dear life to cliffs long since orphaned from the mainland. Hundreds of feet below, shattered boulders are scattered like bones. Despite the lack of historical evidence, the eyes can still play suggestive tricks when spindrift provides a muslin veil across Merlin's Cave and the sun glistens on the scattered stones, transforming them into knights in armour slain on the battlefield.

Today the threat to Tintagel comes not from invading Saxons but from an army of Japanese knotweed creeping insidiously through the valley, silently suffocating local inhabitants. The other dark invasion is from the industry that has grown up on the back of Arthur – the ugly redbrick Victorian hotel on the headland called Camelot Castle, the King Arthur's Arms, King Arthur's Bookshop and Celtic Legend souvenirs.

The stretch of the A39 from Fraddon (southeast of Newquay) through to Bideford was renamed the Atlantic Highway in spring 2002 but it is a complete misnomer as it travels far too far inland to get even a flash of the sea. More deserving of the designation is the humble but more sinuous coast-hugging B3276 from Newquay, the B3314 from Padstow and the

B3263 out of Tintagel. The latter eventually feeds into the A39 for the final gallop into Bude and across into north Devon.

Our next port of call is Clovelly, a vertiginous honeypot cove so perfect that they charge nonresidents for the privilege of entering it. Beneath us silver-grey roof tiles sledge their way down to a 14th-century harbour where fixed cannonballs, requisitioned from the Armada, serve as mooring rings on the wall. A couple of tourists are heaving their suitcases up the cobbles looking close to cardiac arrest (donkeys and sledges are the only transport that can fit down its skinny, precipitous main street).

Charles Kingsley wrote *Westward Ho!* here and the village was also the inspiration for *The Water Babies.* The remarkable state of preservation of the 16th-century fishing village is largely thanks to Christine Hamlyn, who owned the village from 1884 to 1936 and devoted her life to protecting its integrity.

The designer fishermen's cove has sensibly located its gardens at the front of its stone cottages so tourists don't have to crick their necks peering over walls to admire the show-off red fuschia, yellow lilies and pink geraniums. Roses climb cottage walls, lobelia hang from baskets, and purple and pink petunias overflow boxes and tubs. It is unquestionably the most exquisite of villages but I cannot imagine living in such a museum. Don't the inhabitants tire of everyone and their dog peering into their parlours (as I do with Lucky, admiring the delicate tea service inside Donkey Shoe Cottage whose colouring and design perfectly matches the pale mauve hostas in the garden)?

In the post office you can arrange for Cornish clotted cream to be delivered by post. And at the Cottage Tea Room you can order 'Lady's Tea'. A cloying bucolic tweeness creeps across this village in which everyone sings from the same tourist hymn book. At different points I recognise Spanish, German and Scandinavian languages before an entire coach party of Italian students muscles into the fresh shellfish shop as I'm queuing for smoked mackerel and cockles.

We eat our picnic on the harbour wall, staring up at the Japanese knotweed, which is winning its battle over the fuschia, valerian and bindweed on the cliffs. It is our last meal together. We head back up the hill to the motorhome at a snail's pace, our tardiness not purely down to the 45-degree incline.

I drop Susanna, who has to get back to work, at Barnstaple station and try to distract myself by picking up a newspaper. In it I read that a railway guard, Declan Rankin, aged 31, has been arrested for using and dealing cocaine and ecstasy while responsible for passenger safety on the Paddington First Great Western train that reached Penzance on Friday at 4.30 p.m. The same train that Max travelled down on.

On Monday morning Max and I make our way to the Alverdiscott Estate on the shoulder of Bideford, where a mechanic fixes a new wing mirror to Sid and pushes in the mangled metal trim at the rear that was mashed by a hit-and-run. Business over, we head for the long sands of blue-flagged Woolacombe Bay, which greener-than-green Jonathan Porritt numbers among the world's ten finest beaches. It is flanked by a scrum of instantly forgettable cafés and shops. One of the latter serves all-day breakfasts – I restrain myself – and seventeen flavours of ice creams including Christmas Pudding flavour (not bad, actually).

Beside a rocky promontory at the far end of the bay, two unshaven men are hauling in a net that pulses with bass and mullet. Max cringes as I try to engage them in conversation. We talk about the fish and the coastline, both of which I'm assured are the finest in the land. At 71 Roy Lancaster, with his ponytail and Hawaiian shirt, resembles the American folk singer Willie Nelson. Roy owns the Woolacombe Bay Hotel, which stands imperiously beyond a line of lemon, pink and royal blue Edwardian guesthouses. His son Rudi owns and runs the large caravan site up the hill. I comment on the fact that Roy's choice of flamboyant and informal clothing is somewhat unusual for a hotelier.

'Well, I'm a seaside hotelier,' Roy replies unabashed, never having forgotten why he gave up being a fishmonger in the East End to move west in the fifties. 'Anyway, oddness rubs along well in Woolacombe. Behind the memorial to the Americans who rehearsed their D-Day landings, we've got a former U-boat captain living quietly. And did you know Barricane Beach is almost entirely made up of shells carried over by currents from the Caribbean? All sorts get washed up here.'

Max and I hire wet suits and boards and hit the waves. Further out to sea other wet-suited experts sit on boards, hovering like dragonflies, waiting for the right wave. For two hours we are pummelled, drink half an ocean and giggle like the schoolboys that only one of us is. Neither of us manages to get up on the raggedy waves, but it doesn't matter. The sun's shining, we're in the sea we both love, and we're playing.

As we finally head back to the beach, I become aware of a searing pain in my left foot. I sit on the sand and peer into the hard pad of skin where there appears to be a long splinter wedged. The throbbing gets worse and I hop my way to the lifeguard post. 'That'll be a present from a weaver fish,' a young lifeguard tells me with a broad grin. 'They've got a razor-like spine and appear as the tide's going out. It's left its poison as a calling card. It'll hurt like hell for a bit, but don't worry, it'll get easier after 24 hours. You could try leaving it in very hot water for twenty minutes.'

Back in the van I do as I'm told but quickly get bored. The pain has already started to subside anyway. An hour later I've forgotten all about it. I still haven't forgotten the fun Max and I had, though.

As the coast edges round the headland and bears right to meet the Bristol Channel, we arrive at Ilfracombe. Beside the twin peaks of the new Pavilion Theatre (known locally as 'Madonna's bra'), Ilfracombe Museum has somehow managed to ignore fashions, eschewing hyper-interactive exhibits. Maybe the heady formaldehyde is what first brought Damien Hirst to town. Following Stein's success in Padstow (and new venture in Newquay), Hirst is planning to join the culinary high table with a restaurant seating 150 here in Ilfracombe. Max and I join a posse of schoolboys marvelling at a shrunken pygmy head and a pickled two-headed kitten before rifling drawers of impaled moths and butterflies.

Only one schoolboy is known to have cultivated an aversion to the town. Unfortunately the German child, briefly educated in the resort in 1870, later took on the title Kaiser Wilhelm II. Who knows, World War I might well have been down to the local Ilfracombe lad who punched Wilhelm on the nose when he caught him throwing stones at a bathing machine.

The drive across the edge of the Exmoor National Park is a glorious switchback of empty hills and misanthropic farmhouses. A heather-and-gorse hedgerow accompanies us for a while and then disappears, leaving us with more unbroken views of rolling moorland. Inland a sign points to Oare and the moorland church where Lorna Doone was shot on her wedding day. A second sign declares we have crossed into Somerset. I pay £3 to descend a preposterously steep road through an oak forest that leads to the 15th-century harbour of Porlock Weir, where surf shops are traded for hiking shops.

At Minehead (the terminus of the 630-mile South West Coast Path) the tide is right out and the banks of the Severn estuary heaped with mud that was formerly sold for cosmetic face masks. Max and I stare north across the sludge-coloured Bristol Channel to South Wales' Glamorgan Heritage Coast, where my parents-in-law have a second home. Max's grandfather, Dannie, claims to have been conceived in Ogmore-by-Sea and knew even then that he never wanted to leave the place. Max and I try to decide whether the steaming fumaroles belong to Port Talbot. We then scan for the dunes flanking Merthyr Mawr, and Randolph Hearst's St Donat's Castle. The coastline appears close enough to step across.

'You don't get seagulls in Wales,' Max says mysteriously.

'Yes, you do,' I correct him.

'Well, I haven't seen them. They're English.'

Lucky looks up imploringly, seeking a ball to chase. Max obliges. We're running out of time. Soon the pair of best friends will be on the train heading back to the metropolis. In front of Merlin's amusement arcade a man is prospecting in short sleeves despite the chill, waving his metal detector from side to side as a blindman does his stick. People gather up cricket stumps, ravel kites, fold windbreaks and snap shut garden chairs. We have run out of Southwest.

We slip through Bristol's thick urban coat to Temple Meads station and Max departs with dishevelled revellers returning from Glastonbury's annual music festival. I turn back to my moving house that is not a home because it lacks the family that would make it so. It is itinerant, like the waves. Sid and I quit the dark shameful secret of Bristol, a port that grew to prominence and wealth on the wealed back of the slave trade. We make our way across to the M5 and set a course due north.

'The highest purpose of a civilisation was to create meaningful forms of leisure, for its citizens – and for the individuals the ideal to be sought was leisure as an exploration of the good life.'
Blackpool postcard quoting Aristotle

Chapter 3: The Northwest

Mudflats and Arabian Sands

I am making my sprint for the Northwest under the cover of night partly because I find driving in the dark comforting, but also because the curtain conceals the oceanless state of England's western flank.

In Tenby, on the coastline nicked by Wales, I got my first real job, aged sixteen, as a deckhand on a pleasure boat taking visitors to Caldey Island (the Italianate home of a small cell of Cistercian monks). While Nobby Stiles was skipping round Wembley with the World Cup, I was enjoying my own delirium, romping with one of the passengers in the sand dunes. Formative experiences.

Tonight an orchestral sunset sits upon the puffed purple pillows of Wales. A new mood settles on me as Sid and I cruise to the tenor sax of Coltrane. To my right wheat-coloured Gloucestershire stretches weatherless and rooted, far from the nibbling sea. At night even arterial roads can be invested with beauty. Two Jersey cows wander across a bridge and stare down, collecting car numbers.

I feel a strong sense of a journey, of leaving one place and not yet arriving at another. For the past month I've been stopping at every distraction, and have never driven more than 50 miles in a day. But tonight is different. There is time for a rhythm to build as I drive, without stopping, the length of the M5.

North of Wolverhampton, as I pull off the M6 into a Moto service station and park up for the night, I wonder if unofficial raves still erupt in the car park like the one I happened on at two in the morning during a diving jaunt to Oban a decade back. The tarmac that night was an alien landing strip, car spotlights anointing two hundred metronomically jerking heads as techno blasted from a wall of speakers in a white pick-up truck.

Tonight the car park is all functional regularity: Fords and Nissans, segregated trucks, and one very flash American motorhome snoozing in a corner out of the way. A sign declares 'Two hours parking free'. Beneath it is another informing anyone wanting to overnight that they should pay £6 or risk a £60 fine. I pony up the £6. I reckon I've spent well in excess of £100 on parking alone since starting this trip. With Sid gobbling a pound's worth of diesel every five miles, plus the cost of campsites (between £9 and £18), motorhoming may not be the most economic option when it comes to touring.

I scramble up into my double berth at the rear of the vehicle. No one next to me and no one up front either in the van tonight. Families are always only on loan. On the plus side, it does mean I won't have to tiptoe around in the morning. Lying on my bed, looking out of the window, I watch car lights strafing walls and hedgerows. I feel another energy surge, knowing I'm heading somewhere altogether different. As the son of a soldier, I spent my entire childhood on the move (we never stayed anywhere more than three years) and have continued an itinerant life as an adult, working in a bar in Spain, teaching in Algeria and Cyprus and backpacking for a year in Asia. That all happened before I had kids of my own, though. Mind you, I did quit teaching promptly when our first was born and hit upon the job of travel writing to provide me with my occasional nomadic fix.

During the night I occasionally wake to traffic humming its dirgelike *laus perennis* to the gods of the motorways – Pirelli, Michelin, Mr Ford, Mr Peugeot, Mr Nissan Micra. When I finally get up the next morning, cars are busily breakfasting at the gas station. When we make our slaves imitate us, it's hardly surprising we imagine a god who shaped us in his image.

With the rain hammering from a grubby sky, I feel cosy scooting up the M6 in a vehicle that's also a home. It reminds me of the time, aged thirteen, that I first camped in the Lake District with friends and could hear the rain beating on the canvas 2ft from my head and yet was still

Outside his Gravesend barber's shop, Tony McGuire waits for customers.

Patriotic outfits for the organisers of the Ramsgate 50th Anniversary Coronation Party.

Three thousand years of defence: The Iron Age hill fort has gone but the remains of a 95-foot tall Roman lighthouse, the tallest Roman structure outside Italy, still stands beside the church at Dover Castle.

Artists and architects have moved into Dungeness, making it a highly sought after southeastern bolt hole.

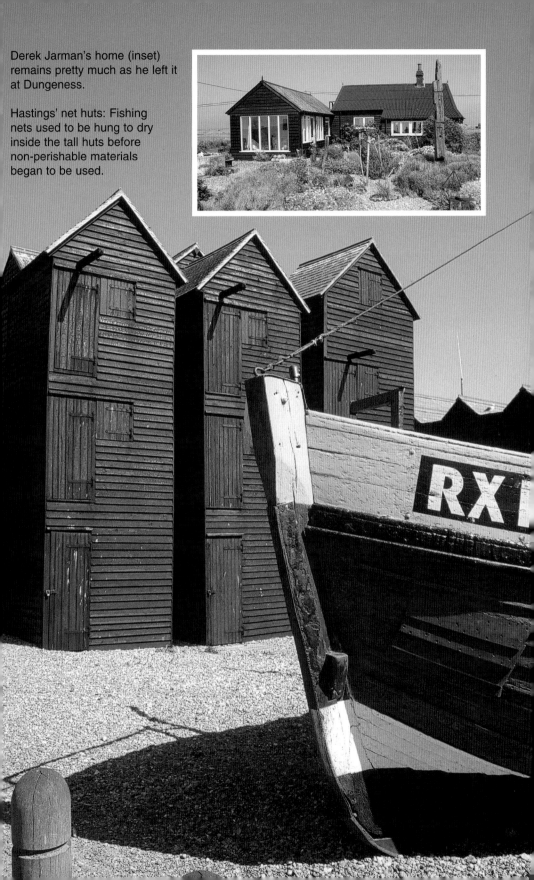

Derek Jarman's home (inset) remains pretty much as he left it at Dungeness.

Hastings' net huts: Fishing nets used to be hung to dry inside the tall huts before non-perishable materials began to be used.

Peter White on Hastings Beach with the fishing boat he was recently forced to sell.

Left: Souvenirs of a Bournemouth holiday.

Professor Guy Higgins (inset) prepares for his first Punch and Judy show of the day on Weymouth beach.

Old Harry's Rocks on Purbeck (main picture) signals both the start of the 95-mile Jurassic Coast (designated mainland Britain's first UNESCO Natural World Heritage Site in 2001) and the beginning of the 630-mile long Southwest Coast Path walking trail.

Dancing Edge, Purbeck.

Trout Quarry, Portland (below).

Teign estuary at sunset (bottom).

The Costa Brava? No, Torquay from the Imperial Hotel.

Blackpool Sands – one of the finest beaches in the Southwest.

Steve Smith, Salcombe ferryman, who once pedaloed across the Atlantic.

An unusual hotel transfer is required to get guests across to Burgh Island (below).

Polperro provides the tourist blueprint for the perfect Cornish cove.

Above: Terry Tonkin packing pilchards in Newlyn.

Left: Children playing in Mevagissey harbour.

The author gets weighed on brass beam scales by Jake Edmondson at the Haysham Institute, Morecambe.

Right: Remains of Wheal Coates tin mine near St Agnes.

Max Gogarty and Lucky at Mother Ivy's Bay.

Clovelly – a town so impossibly pretty, they charge tourists an entry fee.

Right: Dorothy Middleton and Norman Casey in the ballroom of the Blackpool Tower.

Storm clouds gather over Blackpool Prom (below).

Right: Dyker John Brassington repairs a wall on the England-Scotland border in Northumberland.

Berwick-upon-Tweed, a handsome coastal town that has changed hands thirteen times between Scotland and England (below).

The remains of Lindisfarne Priory on Holy Island (left).

Below: Lindisfarne Castle upon its cockle-shaped basalt crag.

Above: 10 pm: Approaching Bamburgh
Castle.

Phil Wood and a Saxon teenager get
acquainted in the grounds of Bamburgh
Castle (right).

Puffins on Farne Islands (above).

L. Robson's 100-year-old smokehouse – home to the Craster kipper.

Tommy Rudlands and friends relax in the Salsbury café after the early morning auction at the new Grimsby Fish Market (right).

Below: Robin Hood's Bay – Grade II listed from top to bottom.

Left: Ernie and Karen Child at the Great Yarmouth Potteries.

Hunstanton Cliffs (below) – a layered cake of cream, strawberry and chocolate (white and red chalk plus brown carrstone). The town is the only one on the East Anglian coast that faces West.

The beach huts of Southwold, which can sell for £40,000-plus (bottom).

deliciously warm and dry in my sleeping bag (it didn't last – by dawn we were soaked).

I arrive finally at the port of Liverpool, which was granted its first charter in 1207 by King John, who saw its sheltered creek as a favourable embarkation point from which to send his troops over to Ireland – a particularly ironic historical fact in view of the mass exodus in the opposite direction as a direct result of subsequent Irish colonial policy. I slip past the anodyne waterfront of Albert Docks (sold off to developers with the rest of the southern docks in the 1980s) and make my way towards the biggest and most modern of the active northern docks, the Royal Seaforth, which happens to stand just half a mile from my old home in Litherland.

Having spent three freewheeling, colour-drenched years between the ages of nine and eleven living in Malaysia and Hong Kong, in early September 1961 I turned up for my first day at secondary school in Liverpool in a suffocating tie, a preposterous peaked cap and a blazer with a badge emblazoned with the Latin motto *Ad Astra* ('To the Stars'). The coldly monochrome Waterloo Grammar School, with its gowned teachers and smell of cabbage, was a shock after the warmth of the extended family at Minden Row Primary. Finding myself in this drab city at a drab, conservative grammar school, knowing absolutely no one, felt as though I'd slipped from heaven to the lower rungs of hell.

I never did get to like secondary school (I went to three) and quit at sixteen, but in hindsight my time in Liverpool was easily the best. My brother and sister were still living at home, I worked every night on my A-Z gazetteer of Mersey Beat groups (The Denisons, The Undertakers and The Mojos were my favourites) and I also discovered girls in the flesh instead of merely in my dreams.

Finding the way back to my childhood home proves more difficult than raking over my memories. There's no Proustian tickling of the olfactory memory – the nearby Richmond Sausage Works (where my mum worked) has gone, as has the sweet shop I visited twice a day on Litherland lift bridge. The bridge has gone too. The Stella cinema – famously trashed by Britain's first teenagers when it showed Bill Haley's *Rock Around the Clock* – has vanished and the bowling alley that replaced it has gone the same way. Most of Litherland seems to have been flattened to create the major traffic intersection leading to Royal Seaforth Docks.

Miraculously, however, six small brick-and-pebbledash semis marooned between the wasteland and St Winifred's Catholic School (which, I note, has requisitioned the rec where we used to have our huge 5 November bonfire) has been spared by the bulldozers.

The mesh fencing into which my learner-driver brother drove Dad's Bedford van is still there, my father's small vegetable garden is now grass, and the houses have been chi-chied with pastel colours, porch extensions and even garages. The road has also finally found a proper identity – Rimmers Close – after years of being known simply as MQ (married quarters), off Hawthorn Road. As I knock at number 6, I can almost smell the boiling sprouts and see my brother's face as he opens the door. Unfortunately no one is home. I'm a little relieved in a way. I like the idea of our forty-year-old ghosts still occupying the place.

Just three minutes' walk away, the new flyover that replaced the Litherland lift bridge has several plastic-wrapped bouquets of flowers attached to it. Beneath it, in the still, murky waters of the Leeds and Liverpool Canal, I can make out the skeleton of a bike. I ask a small middle-aged man in blue cap and checked waistcoat (on which is emblazoned 'Anfield Academy') if he knows when the lift bridge went. 'Don't know, pal,' he replies in the stringy voice of a lifelong Scouser, 'but they've got a picture of it on the dustbin outside the library.'

The library I used to borrow books from occasionally is still there. Inside a librarian tells me that Richmond Sausage Works disappeared in 1987 and the site is now a children's day nursery. She points me to a local history section, where I thumb through *Litherland – an Outline History* by Jennifer E Stanistreet (published by Sefton Libraries in 1987). Apparently the lift bridge opened in 1933, closed in 1974 and was demolished the following year. I also discover that the name 'Litherland' derives from 10th-century Old Norse meaning 'The land on a slope'.

The dock traffic that once hammered over the lift bridge now takes the flyover. I follow them past police officers on duty at the Royal Seaforth Docks gates, who seem unconcerned that I am the only motorhome in a long line of large container trucks.

I slip into the aluminium city of Liverpool Freeport Docks. Today there are no noisy cranes and swearing dockers unloading old cargo ships that used to spend two or three weeks in port. Now container ships couple briefly with container lorries without foreplay. Modern slick efficiency has also taken the fun out of the age–old sideline in pilfering (now it has to be a whole container that goes missing, and that's a little difficult to fit down your trousers). Everything is clean as a whistle.

As I have made no appointment, I park the tank in two of the visitors' bays at the administrative offices and ask the receptionist if there's anyone around who worked the docks in the old days who'd be willing to chat with me. 'I'm writing a book about the English coast and used to play round the corner at Potter's Bar.' I explain. Fortunately she doesn't relegate me to the category of 'saddo' and send me packing. Instead she smiles warmly and makes a call. Five minutes later Eric Leatherbarrow, head of corporate affairs, appears and takes me off to an empty office of chrome, glass and secretive blinds. Eric dials a number and places his hand over the mouthpiece to whisper, 'I'll see if Terry Kelly is around and willing to talk. He's worked in the docks since they opened centuries ago.'

I immediately pick up on the 'if he's willing to talk'. The bitter industrial disputes in the final quarter of the last century that culminated in the acrimonious picketing outside the Royal Seaforth Docks in 1995, and eventual sackings, has left everybody jumpy and suspicious. Members of families caught on both sides of the industrial divide still don't speak.

Eric provides the employers' perspective. 'In the early eighties it was obvious the port could not survive any longer in its current state. It was handling nine million tons of cargo and losing money. Today it handles thirty million tons – more than ever in its history – with about the same number of staff.' Marketing speak.

'What about the dockers?' I ask.

'There are far less of them today, true. But why does everyone always beat on about the negatives? It's incredible the transformation in the place. According to a survey carried out recently by Liverpool University's Microeconomics Unit, ten per cent of Merseyside jobs are now dependent on the docks.' Apparently the success has also been felt all the way from Medway to Mombasa, Dublin to Maputo, and Belfast to San Nicholas in Argentina, as the Mersey Docks and Harbour Company owns docks there too.

The door of the office cracks open and the smiling face of Terry Kelly, safety and environment manager, appears. Terry, aged sixty, has worked all his life at Liverpool Docks, starting off as a docker. Eric pulls out a chair and Terry sits and shakes my hand as Eric fills him in on what we've been discussing.

Eric confirms the bitter aftertaste of the dispute: 'It was the worst period of my life and I still feel sick thinking about it. Seeing the jobs disappear and the general decline in shipping was hard enough to take in the seventies and eighties. But we got accused of all sorts during the unofficial action in 1995 and that was the worst. It became known as the Big Dispute and was actually against union advice but good people got browbeaten by militants into taking strike action.' Terry lets out a huge sigh before settling back in his chair and repeating. 'A lot of really good men were misled by a handful of militants.'

Terry badly misses the sense of community, the humour and camaraderie of the old days. Today workers are as streamlined and efficient as the dock itself (which, apart from being Britain's largest grain terminal, also handles everything from forest products to metals). The scrummage of pubs round the docks have all closed – workers eat in canteens and prefer to live in suburbs.

'Between 1967 and 1978 there was always great craic to be had. I remember one docker 6ft 4in tall who had the tiniest feet you ever saw. But he still wore size twelves and made a dozen trips in and out of the docks a day carrying stuff to sell in the pubs! Then there was the tanker carrying rum to Africa that was discovered to be full of water on arrival.'

Terry grew up in Bootle at a time when virtually all the male members of his extended family went to sea – just as his grandfather (John Kelly) had and his great-grandfather (Joseph Kelly) before him. His father, also named John Kelly, first sailed to Newfoundland at the age of fifteen. Terry shakes his head. 'Imagine it, going from Bootle to Newfoundland at fifteen! That was in 1913. He must have done "The Pier Head Jump" to get on that trip so young.'

I raise an eyebrow, seeking enlightenment.

'Underage boys would wait at Pier Head and if a ship was light, they'd take you on last minute. He travelled round the world half a dozen times and eventually retired at the end of World War I as an able seaman.' Like everyone else working at sea, John Kelly brought back stories and gifts – records, exotic bananas and even a monkey ('within a matter of days it had wrecked the house and mysteriously disappeared'). Terry laughs at the memory before the cloud of a fatherless childhood settles on him. 'I hardly knew him really. That's how you grew up then. One-parent families were the norm with the men away so long. But we also had crews pouring into the port from all over. That made it exciting. And they'd usually stay two or three weeks and would mix in with the local community. Many settled. Nowadays the container ships are in for eight hours and the skeleton crew never leave the boat.'

Terry shows me the Seaman's Book belonging to his father that he still keeps in a drawer in his office. Inside it there are stamps from all over the world. It gets John talking about other family members. One uncle, now 91, worked in a New York bakery after the boat he was on got torpedoed on the wrong side of the pond. Then there was his grandfather, who died in 1914 when the *Empress of Ireland* was hit by a Norwegian coal carrier on the St Lawrence Seaway. 'He went down with more than a thousand others – a much bigger disaster than the *Titanic* but it happened the year war was declared and there wasn't newspaper space for other tragedies.'

Conversation somehow turns to music and the American imports that sailors brought in that shaped both Terry's and my own formative adolescent years. Terry's father was a big fan of Hank Williams records. I tell Terry of my own discovery of the blues, aged twelve, walking through Lime Street Station. At the time, an unknown group had released 'Love Me Do' and as my mum was working with the drummer's fiancée at Richmond Sausage Works, I decided to give the group a hand by donating my pocket money – well, they were almost family. But then I walked across Lime Street Station and suddenly, from across the concourse, a wail like a wolf caught in a trap froze me in my tracks. The wolf was Howlin' Wolf, the man who raised the howl to an art form. I left with my first import and my first blues album, *Blues Volume 2*, instead of 'Love Me Do'. I had lost my musical virginity but kept it secret from my parents, knowing that anything that powerful could not possibly be approved of.

Two minutes after leaving Terry, I'm driving beside the lagoon and bowling greens of Potter's Bar. It was here I'd come occasionally as a pre-teenager with school friends during lunch breaks, to snigger at the old codgers bowling. We'd then move on to play endless games of 'Who Falls the Best'. This involved pretending to be shot at the top of a sand dune and then, as theatrically as possible, rolling to the bottom in body-twitching death throes. Points would be awarded for style and whoever 'fell the best' would then judge the next performance. It was also in Potter's Bar that I spotted a used condom for the first time, floating forlornly across a puddle.

The gardens and freshwater lagoon across which swans are today gliding were built by a Mr Potter (who was also responsible for the nearby cathedral-sized church that he had built for his own private use). Liverpool made a late entry into the triangular trade of shipping cheap goods to Africa, slaves to the American and West Indian sugar plantations, and then sugar, rum and tobacco back home. Late but successful – the port dominated the slave trade until its abolition in 1807 and it was from its despicable commerce that Potter made his fortune.

A short walk from the gardens, I discover that Waterloo Grammar School is still standing but former pupils' memories have been swept from the hallways and replaced by those of mature students attending the South Sefton Adult Education Centre.

I return to the car and drive north across the Sefton coast's arable flatlands flanked by desert dunes and flat golden beaches. At Waterloo Grammar School playground lore had it that Southport was where you went to have your final game of bowls. True, some marginally younger biddies, like our mums, did visit the annual flower show and come back alive, but most ended 6ft under, pushing up their own daisies. Blackpool was where those with blood moving through veins headed, not Southport.

When, at the age of twelve with a group of school friends, I did finally hop on the Northern Line from Litherland, trundling past dunes stubbled with marram grass, to investigate the outsized nursing home, I found a funfair, a pier, teeth-crunching rock, amusement arcades and – best of all – a huge open-air seawater bathing lake filled with exciting, and excitable, girls. In the days of The Beatles, Bessie Braddock, Screaming Lord Sutch and Everton's Golden Vision, it was another life-changing moment on a par with my Lime Street Station apotheosis.

As a young St Helens girl, my mother-in-law, Joan Abse, also used to holiday in Southport, thirty years before me. In those days, however, men and women were corralled at opposite ends of the lake and any man caught sliding down a strap on his bathers to bronze a shoulder would get a flick from the ever-watchful attendant employed not to save lives but to uphold decorum.

The best pool in the world has gone, of course. The greatest crime the resort has committed was replacing it with a £30 million leisure retail development.

Fortunately Lord Street is still there – in my book the most elegant shopping street of any English resort. Prince Louis Napoleon (who inexplicably rented a home in Southport for several months in 1838 before becoming Emperor Napoleon III) clearly felt pretty much the same way, as he reputedly designed the layout of Paris' boulevards on the Lord Street model. Believe that and you'll believe anything.

The daily promenade along its broad avenue today is the English equivalent to the *paseo* along Barcelona's *Ramblas*. Only the Southport version is enacted by those still able to walk wheeling those unable to, along a leafy central avenue dotted with alfresco cafés, converted gas lamps, fountains, gardens and Corinthian columns.

Down on Red Rum's old cantering ground, the sands stretch in either direction for seven miles. In fact, they've got so much of the stuff that the town has been selling it to Saudi Arabia since the late 1980s (apparently Southport sand is particularly good for construction work). Somehow the beach has even managed to be awarded three blue flags too – despite the fact the sea rarely does more than tickle its toes (it's out there if you look hard, halfway to Ireland). On a previous visit a former lifeguard, Verdi Goodwin, confessed to me rather sheepishly that he'd never recorded a single fatality in the forty years he'd patrolled the beach. The Irish Sea, notwithstanding the occasional inundation, is as well behaved as the town's visitors. Even the amusement arcades, gathered between Lord Street and the prom, whisper out of respect for its middle-class clientele. In Southport, upturned mushy peas or dropped ice creams are considered hanging offences.

On the prom I pass the Floral Hall, where as a pimply Mod in 1966 I side shuffled à la James Brown across the dancefloor with a line of immaculate two-tone-suited soul boys to the sounds of The Four Tops and Temptations. Today a poster announces the exciting return of The Bachelors, no doubt in their bathchairs. The action these days mostly takes place in the town centre in big breezy bars where Sol is de rigueur, drunk from the bottle with a lime stuffed in the top. One hundred and fifty years back, Sandgrounders (the nickname for those hailing from Southport) drank their ale out of pot mugs and their greeting – 'Come in and I'll mug tha' – would have been a more tempting offer than today.

Apart from selling sand to Saudi and providing the blueprint for Parisian boulevards, the resort has been a pioneer on two other fronts. When the cable tramway opened in 1865 – the first constructed for passenger traffic in the world – it was an instant success, though one letter in a newspaper did complain, 'The turnstiles are extremely inconvenient, for elderly ladies especially, the amplitude of dress rendering it impossible to pass through them without much unpleasantness.' Its other claim to fame is its pier – England's second longest – which, at its opening on 2 August 1860, became the world's first iron pleasure pier.

The advent of fast and reliable steam passenger boats in the early 19th century meant increasing numbers for nascent resorts on the south coast such as Margate and Weymouth and simple piers sprang up to provide dry landing for them. With the arrival of railways, more people flooded in seeking entertainment and the piers grew ever fancier with pavilions and illuminations (the fanciest of all was probably at Hastings with its kiosks and oriental pavilion that could seat two thousand). Southport Pier was one of the earliest of the 'entertainment' piers and stretched 4,380ft. Today it has shrunk to 3,633ft, but the herringbone decking, cambered wood, delicate curving ironwork and lattice girders have all been restored in a recent £7 million refurbishment.

As I step out on to it today, the orchestral strings from the introduction to 'A Summer Place' cascade from a speaker and tug at my heart strings. I am instantly transported to Hong Kong and a 'Teen-To-Twenty Disc Club' outing aboard a junk from Aberdeen harbour where local kids dived for coins we threw from the deck. To get on the trip – and to get the free crate of Pepsi that came with membership – I had lied and said I was thirteen (I was actually ten). 'A Summer Place' was played endlessly as we sank dozens of Pepsis each and disembarked high as kites.

At the end of the 1km-long pier, a new arcade has been constructed whose vintage amusements work only if lubricated by old penny coins you get from the cashier for 10p each. Inflation. Musical clowns, Peerless Pics (high-kicking dancing girls), the Personality Tester (mine read 'Dragon Slayer'), and a Novomat classic fruit-machine keep me occupied for the next half-hour.

Corralled in the far corner of the arcade is an exhibition on the pier divers who once entertained the huge crowds that gathered: Professor Osborne, who rode a bike off the pier; Sid Smith (aka Dare Devil Tootzer), who dived from a moving train; and Professor Gadsby (a former champion swimmer before he lost a leg), who plunged from the pier one-legged into a circle of fire. And while these miraculous feats were being performed, the White Viennese Band played on.

The cereal and vegetable belt of the West Lancashire flatlands leads me through a procession of redbrick villages. After the relentless bucolic romp and sunshine of the Southwest, I'm really enjoying the change in pace and landscape and even the dull skies. Not much more than an hour after departing Southport, and for probably the tenth time in my life, I arrive in Britain's most famous resort.

There are those who hate Blackpool and have no time for its saucy tat, its Fylde sludge, its sick-in-the-streets. But they're just dumb. The seafront has changed little since our family used to tailgate from Litherland for the Illuminations. The dirty postcards, greasy spoons, oyster sellers and guesthouses called 'Aloha' are all still there. On the pier Billy J Kramer still crackles over the speaker pleading with his lover not to be 'Bad to Me'. Seagulls hang on the wind against the bruised sky while Scottish holiday-makers in 'I Love Glasgow' baseball hats pose for pictures in the pier cut-outs and then walk off, leaving trails of onions from steaming hotdogs that would have Walt Disney apoplectic.

Blackpool has always been unabashedly brash and vulgar ('Kong-sized male pouches – £1 a throw', 'sexy lace tassels £1'). While many other British coastal resorts are seemingly locked in an irreversible spiral of increasing age and decreasing profit, Blackpool remains forever young by two stratagems: firstly by continuing to attract succeeding generations of 18 to 30-year-olds in their millions; and secondly by getting divorced as soon as things get boring.

In March 2003 Blackpool sat proudly at the top of Britain's divorce league (interestingly, seven of the others in the top ten were also English seaside towns) with 17,578 of its residents having divorced or separated from their partners. Perhaps it has something to do with the 2,900 hotel and guesthouses in town whose owners have to put up with living with strangers and working eighteen-hour days over the summer. Wives get up early to do the breakfasts and husbands stay late with guests at the bar. Or vice versa. It's not all roses living by the seaside.

Trains first started pulling into the village of Blackpool in 1840. In 1862 the Blackpool Pier Company began building the North Pier. And by 1871, as workers from the East Lancs milltowns flooded in with the advent of bank holidays (paid annual holidays were not to arrive until the 1930s), the village was already a town. To keep the punters returning, the resort added a 518ft replica Eiffel Tower in 1890, and an extra pier, and the Illuminations . . .

One hundred years on Blackpool continues neatly to side-step the eclipse of the family bucket-and-spade fortnight with conference breaks, white-knuckle breaks, and staggering-stag-and-hen breaks. It remains, by a long shot, the most popular resort in the country. And it is now on the cusp of reinventing itself yet again as Britain's answer to Las Vegas with more than £150 million worth of new casinos.

On my last visit to town, I'd stayed at the small Coach House guest-house, where owner Mark Smith, a third-generation Blackpool hotelier, had ruefully commented on the far more rigorous expectations of guests these days. 'My gran, who had a hotel of her own in town, would be turning in her grave if she could see us providing tea for guests for nothing, not to mention quality furnishings, personal TVs and private bathrooms. In the 1960s her guests had to bring their own cruets or hire them for 6d!' Mark's wife Claire had also witnessed the rapid changes first hand. 'When I started out as a schoolgirl chambermaid, the landlord charged 50p for a sink plug and guests queued each morning on the landing for the only bathroom.'

Today I start my visit, as usual, with a trip to Roberts Oyster Bar, where I slurp my way through a dozen Anglesey oysters for £8.80 that in 1876 could have been washed down with a cocktail of stout and champagne for the princely sum of a shilling.

Further along the prom I duck beneath a 20ft pirate's skull guarding Coral Island amusement arcade. Inside, a posse of veteran one-armed bandits with battle fatigue are being removed to be replaced by yet more psychotic video arcade games. In 2003 only the 'Camel Derby' and the fifty-year-old 'Cash Falls' – where tumbling pennies attempt to topple a mountain of coins – now operate without an electronic drip.

Some things never change. In a small room abutting Coral Island, I draw back a curtain concealing a crystal-ball-and-tarot-card boudoir and am disappointed to find Leah Petulengro behind, not her daughter Lena who had promised me several years earlier that I would soon sign a book contract worth a fortune. I'm keen to track her down and ask what's taking so long.

I have to make do with Leah. Having had her palm lined with silver, Leah stares into my face as if trying to read an A-Z with bad eyesight. She wrinkles her nose. 'I can see that you're going to become more and more successful the older you get.' A smile quickly follows to signal Leah is done but it rapidly vanishes as she picks up my own singly unimpressed expression. She tries again. 'In two months' time you'll make a major decision. But don't worry, whatever you decide will be the right course.' If only life were like that – no wrong turnings.

Leah has been applying happy balm to Blackpool prom visitors for half a century. And like horses that occasionally romp home at a hundred to one, sometimes she even gets it right. When Karen Kay worked a season as an impressionist on the front in the seventies, Leah predicted that her tiny son would become massively rich and famous. Jay Kay now heads Jamiroquai. Leah also told Johnny Ball his young daughter Zoë (a local girl) would enjoy similar success.

Round the corner, inside the venerable Blackpool Tower, locked bodies glide across the buffed dancefloor as Phil Kelsall rises with his Wurlitzer from the underworld, as he has done most days these past 26 years (and as Reginald Dixon did before him for forty years). I have slipped inside a French Renaissance jewellery box. Decorating the lid of the Tower Ballroom are angelic cherubs clinging to the scalloped ceiling that nubile caryatids are attempting to lift open. Frank Matcham's masterpiece is considered one of the three finest ballrooms in the land (though I can't imagine for the life of me what else could run him close).

The last time I was here, I'd been mesmerised by a septuagenarian with a Shirley Temple ribbon in her hair who was gamely attempting several high kicks of the *paso doble*, while her partner clattered his feet round her like castanets. This time my attention is immediately drawn to a diminutive, dapper couple, no taller nor heavier than sparrows, who move as if they are parts of a single body. They also appear to be totally smitten with each other. When they finally take a breather, with a drink I sidle over to the table next to them and strike up conversation.

In life some people find God but Dorothy Middleton, aged 66, and Norman Casey, aged 71, found the Blackpool Tower Ballroom early on and never looked back. Both first visited the resort as children: Dorothy from Bradford, Norman from Manchester. They both then returned regularly until they finally, independently, settled in the resort. Norman's wife and original dance partner died of cancer in 1993. Dorothy's husband, stalked by the same killer, followed five years later. Eventually Norman managed to persuade his friend Dorothy to return to the ballroom.

'It was really hard – so many memories. But it helped,' Dorothy remembers. 'Both our marriages were very happy ones and we'd spent a lot of our lives dancing here.'

'There really is no place like the Tower,' Norman adds, nodding his head to confirm the special role that the ballroom has had in their rehabilitation. 'And for Dorothy it's even more important. It's her cathedral. When she was a young girl and her parents asked her where she wanted to go, it was always the Tower. Even though we now live in Blackpool, she still isn't interested in going abroad.'

Dorothy attempts to explain the hold the place has over her. 'It's an oasis. When you go out the building, there's all sorts going on, but inside here nothing fades. Blackpool Tower.' She shakes her head. 'Nothing like it. You'll probably think us mad, but when they decided to replace the old carpet surrounding the dancefloor I asked for a piece and I've framed it and have it up on my wall next to a photograph of the pier.'

The couple remind me of those made-for-each-other Hollywood dancing fantasists Ginger Rogers and Fred Astaire. I can resist the question no longer. 'So are you . . .' I stumble for words that will convey my question but not in so indelicate a manner as to embarrass them . . . 'romantically connected now?'

Dorothy smiles as innocently as Doris Day. 'We are . . .' she too seeks the right words, '. . . very close friends.'

'But we do spend virtually all our time together now,' Norman adds, muddying the water a little.

Whether they are intimate or not, they clearly have itchy feet. They excuse themselves and join their friends Mike and Jean, who are having a whale of a time, theatrically high-kicking their way through a rumba. Dorothy's left hand clasps Norman's right, while the latter's left hand slinks round her back and she in turn rests her left hand lightly on Norman's shoulder. They float off across the dancefloor, a single unit once more.

I wander off through the booming corridors and stairways. When it opened on Whit Monday 1894, the Blackpool Tower signalled a revolution in entertainment, providing between its four spindly legs an aquarium, bars and cafés, a Grand Pavilion (later the Ballroom), a menagerie and a circus, as well as the thrill ride to the top. It was as exotic as anything under Fylde's slate-grey skies could ever possibly get.

Today, inside the extravagant Tower Circus, a new show is being rehearsed, without an animal in sight. I ask an attendant when the quadrupeds will be joining the rehearsals. 'Never. We're not allowed to use animals no more.' He shrugs his shoulders expansively, indicating he's long given up trying to understand the world he inhabits.

The animals, it transpires, are the victim (like the dwarves in the Grand Theatre who used to serve drinks from a matchbox-sized bar in the rafters) of a political-correctness cull. In the old days you could see elephants taking their morning constitutionals along the beach. Now the only animals – Bactrian camels, orangutans, gorillas, elephants, flamingos, sea lions, red pandas and reindeers – live out at the zoo

Back on the bracing front, I can wait no longer. It is time for Blackpool's crown jewels, the Pleasure Beach. I start, as always, with a limber up on the Grand National. To the roller-coaster cognoscenti, the Grand National – though a pensioner 68 years of age – is the finest wooden roller coaster on the planet (and one of its only two duelling woodies). People have recited their marriage vows while riding the shuddering leviathan and devotees travel from all over the world to pay homage. Its greatness lies in the fact that it is not one but two roller coasters that race each other with wooden boards shuddering and metal tracks slapping as riders clatter and gallop and scream across at the opposing carriage.

At the other end of the park, and the roller-coaster spectrum, stands the Big One, a hulking steel monster dwarfing everything else around. Queues are light at the tallest and finest ride in Europe and within ten minutes I'm fumbling with my seat belt. I think back to the first time I rode it. For what seemed like an eternity Max and I were cranked up its

235ft, foot by foot. It was dusk. The Irish Sea's iron corrugations lay to our left, the mayhem of the park to our right and, directly below, certain death. As we hovered expectantly, I told Max, who must have been ten at the time, to close his eyes and count slowly to four. Everything but our terror seemed to get left behind as we hurtled vertically, twisting midway in our plummet. I opened my own eyes too early and saw the ground rushing towards me before we were suddenly scooped up and propelled through the corkscrewing switchback.

This time the experience is just wild, rather than terrifying – though a tad less exciting because I'm on my own and excitement, like fear, needs to be shared. Having completed one crazed circuit, with the queues so slight I immediately return for a second spin and this time manage to nab the front carriage to roar myself through several more minutes of pure adrenaline.

At the unveiling of each new ride, the first person to bag the front seat is usually Mrs Doris Thompson who celebrated her 100th birthday on 12 January 2003. Mrs Thompson is the chairman of the Pleasure Beach and Queen Mother of Blackpool. The previous year she'd ridden the latest nasty to be unveiled, the Spin Doctor, and immediately demanded to go on it again. Mrs Thompson has granted me an interview and when I am shown into her deco walnut-panelled rooms beside the White Tower restaurant, she tells me, 'The art of riding a roller coaster is going with the ride, not fighting it. Then you get all the sensations without the terror.' She also tells me her favourite ride of all was the inaugural Ice Blast in 1996 'with those nice boys from Boyzone'.

Doris Thompson could remember when electricity was first put into her Blackpool home. 'Now we have multi-million-pound rides operated by a bank of computers!' She laughs quietly, her voice – like her hearing – not what it once was, and goes on to provide me with a thumbnail history. 'The park opened in very modest form in 1898, five years before I was born. My father was the second son and not favoured but somehow he got sufficient money together for a passage to America where he worked for the Philadelphia Toboggan Company and learnt all about the rides and amusement parks that were starting up in America.

'When we settled in Blackpool, it was just sand here. My father bought it off a farmer who had no use for it. Father could see the potential. He started with just a roundabout and we shared the sands with gypsies who used to come up and greet me when I was out walking and then bring me back to my mother for a reward, saying they'd found me lost.'

Our chat is brief as Mrs Thompson is feeling tired today. But later I strike up conversation with a forty-year-old employee with a monkey wrench outside the Big Dipper who provides more anecdotes from his 24 years working the Pleasure Beach. Lydon Starr first came as a toddler when he used to help his mother thread needles before zipping round the monorail track on his scooter. His mother worked 23 years as wardrobe mistress for the Ice Show and still comes back for reunions in her eighties. And eighty years is the length in total that the family has been involved with the Pleasure Beach, as Lydon's gran did the wardrobe before her ('She originally came as a snake charmer in the Indian Theatre'). Lydon's daughter left school recently and, according to him, she loves the place as much as he does. 'Who knows, we may have another Starr working here soon.'

Lyndon hurries off with his monkey wrench to apply some elbow grease to the hundred-year-old Flying Machines. As a ride engineer, he has to be as proficient with spanners when fixing manual ratcheted tram controllers as he is with a laptop operating the Big One's four computers and bank of control panels 10ft tall and 30ft long.

I move on to the next ride on my check list – the Big Dipper. It was the Pleasure Beach, incidentally, that invented the name, as well as that of the Ghost Train – in America the latter had been known as the Pretzel, but the Blackpool name proved far more popular. Like the Grand National, the Big Dipper is right up there in the hagiology of Britain's three main coaster clubs: the Roller Coaster Club of Great Britain founded by Andy Hine (who recently successfully identified all 32 of the leading worldwide coaster rides just by hearing the sound of the pull-up chains dragging the carriages up the initial incline); the European Coaster Club set up by Justin Garvanovic when he and Andy fell out; and the 235 Club (named after the height of the Big One – 235ft), chaired by Andy Slevin.

A number of coaster fans are so obsessive that they belong to all three clubs. Richard Rodriguez, however, isn't a member of any. He rather distances himself from fans and fanatics. For Rodriguez, roller coasters are more of a mission: he trains on them, watches his diet and exercises for them – he's a pro going to the office. And then he breaks another record.

Now aged 44, the wiry unmarried city boy who works as an English classroom assistant somewhere in America first got into the record books in 1979 by riding the Pleasure Beach's Big Dipper for 140 hours. In 1980 he upped it to 205 hours. In 1994 he did 549 hours then stepped straight off the Big Dipper on to the inaugural ride on the Big One. In 1998 he did one thousand hours and in 2000, you guessed it, two thousand – that's three months being banged about in a roller-coaster carriage (admittedly padded and with the armrest removed and a neat little canopy added to keep the rain out). On his marathon he was permitted a five-minute break every hour for toilet stops and to take insulin shots for his diabetes. Once Rodriguez had completed his two-thousand-hour marathon, he duly phoned his record in to the *Guinness Book of Records* only to find new regulations concerning roller-coaster endurance records were being introduced and he'd have to do it again.

The new guidelines have now been drawn up and so in 2004 he will bed down again in his carriage, back on his lonely road, filling the long recess between school terms, part of the Pleasure Beach family and with everyone's attention on him – the perfect place for the outsider.

Blackpool is not a place for brass rubbing. And with nothing dating further back than Victoria, there is nowt of architectural interest to delay visitors like me either (apart from the rococo romp of the Tower Ballroom and the Grand Theatre). But windswept Blackpool, with its Fylde sludge, saucy postcards, false ears, willie warmers and jellied eels, is as English as England gets. And it's never more itself than when visitors are dribbling ice creams, whatever the time or weather, on their way to the next clattering white-knuckle ride (an estimated 1 million ice creams a year are licked in Blackpool, and 2.5 million portions of chips consumed).

By now, however, I'm feeling a little white-knuckled out and decidedly peckish so I call in at the White Tower restaurant, an Art-Deco building with the sleek lines of a cruise ship. As I stare out through the broad curving windows along the seafront, headlights of lonely cars search out company. By the time I'm back outside, waiting for a tram to take me back to where I've left the van, the fog has rolled in off the Irish Sea and the cars have been swallowed. Upstairs on the tram it's like the *Marie Celeste*. With nothing inside or outside to look at, I conjure up memories of my last visit when, on another packed tram clanging its way along the seafront, instead of fog, steam billowed from chip packets and an impromptu sing-along broke out, led by a hirsute conductor.

*

The next morning, with the town still yawning, only the fishermen at the end of the pier have forgotten to go home. I look around at a resort many people only ever see on TV at party conference time. It may be bleak but Blackpool has an architectural beauty all of its own – the silver bauble of the world's largest mirrorball (part of a new promenade sculpture trail), the blue arching vertebrae of the Big One, the meandering concrete sea wall, and Poseidon's trident of piers jutting into the sea beneath the ice-cream cone of the Tower. As I walk the pier's wooden boards, gulls swearing overhead at the unbending wind, I have the delicious feeling of being the world's last tourist. On the sands a couple of men are digging their way along the beach, seeking tasty lug worms for fishing bait. Three boys attempt to play football but the wind is too strong and they end up chasing the ball halfway to Lytham.

As is often the case on this exposed coast, it is cold and blustery and I'm grateful to be joining the crowd checking in to the George Formby weekend at the Winter Gardens, escaping the weather and the past sixty years. As Martin Harrison launches into 'Little Ukelele in My Hand', with a suitably cheeky-chappy vocal, a grin and a Gatling-gun ukelele style, I feel myself swooping through the loft of childhood. Cigarette cards flicker, brilliantly coloured marbles roll, and a trail of Imperial Leather and Brylcreem leads me back to Saturday night teatime kippers and Dad spinning his treasured collection of 78s.

It must have been much the same for George Harrison (no relation), who checked into a similar convention a couple of years back with his son. George apparently told Martin that as a young boy growing up in Liverpool, as soon as he finished his Saturday morning butcher's delivery, he'd scoot down to the local flicks to spend his hard-earned cash watching another Formby film. The ex-Beatle knew better than most that before the Liverpool Sound there reigned the Formby Sound.

Blackpool was Formby's spiritual home (although he actually lived in posher Lytham St Anne's). It may not be quite the same Blackpool that Formby loved – these days you can buy his Little Stick of Blackpool Rock with Arabic and Chinese letters running through it – but the little man remains its sauciest postcard.

The Formby Society, founded in 1961 (the year Formby died), hosts four Blackpool weekend gatherings a year that are all open to the public.

Many of the 250 attending today have ukes tucked under their arms. Some have come to buy and sell instruments, others to wallow in nostalgia, but the vast majority are simply here to play. As they drift into the Theatre Bar, they add their names to a list that ensures each will get to play two Formby songs of their choice over the weekend.

Martin Harrison is the first up, already a ukelele legend in his mid-twenties and with a Formby grin to match. Martin is followed on stage by a father-and-son team, Andy and Will Parker, who hurtle through 'Mr Wu's a Window Cleaner Now'.

The enthusiastic audience are casually smart and there is not a cloth cap in sight. Ages, geographical spread and backgrounds are comfortingly broad – Andy himself is a surgeon from Matlock in Derbyshire. Younger players like Heidi, sixteen, from Burton-on-Trent – who also plays clarinet, cornet and piano – and Adam Smith, twenty, who hails from Derby, speak of Formby as if he is a close personal friend rather than someone who died before they were born. Older members like Jack Jones, aged 81 and now confined to a wheelchair, can still recall the precise moment he first heard the master's voice. 'I were a young lad in hospital and a nurse had taken a special shine to me and brought me fish and chips each night. One night she brought a radio too. First song I ever heard of George's was "Little Ukelele in My Hand" – 13 December 1935. Unforgettable. I were 'ooked.'

Ukeleles glisten exotically in the audience beneath chandeliers, as Frances Terry, aged 72, fidgets with her specially made outfit and approaches the stage. Later she confesses to me, 'I don't really know why I do it. It's like the dentist's for me every time.' But do it she does, in her riding boots, red hunting jacket, striped satin waistcoat and top hat. She forgets the lines of 'Bunkum's Travelling Show', stumbles over chords and still gets one of the biggest cheers. Over the nine years she's been a Society member, she hasn't missed one of the 36 gatherings (she even attended with bronchitis once).

As soon as the next act starts cantering through 'Bunty's Such A Big Girl Now' ('Bunty's such a big girl now, a boat was tattooed on her hip. Bunty's such a big girl now, it's turned into a battleship'), Frances slumps back in her chair exhausted from the nervous excitement and starts worrying over which songs she'll learn for the next bash and which costumes she should make to accompany them.

Members continue to hurtle breathlessly through more innuendo in two Formby minutes than Benny Hill and Frankie Howerd managed in their lifetimes. No one notices as I slip out of the door. They're having too good a time.

Over in the church of St Stephen-on-the-Cliffs, the marble reredos depicts David carrying the Ark of the Covenant into Jerusalem pursued by a troupe of music hall stars led by Gracie Fields. It suddenly dawns on me that what the high drama of the Anglican liturgy at St Stephen's shares with the entertainment at the Tower Ballroom, the seasonal shows on the prom, and the Formby Society concerts, is an old-fashioned notion of participation. Blackpool itself is just an extension of the extended family sing-along in the parlour, ageless and classless.

Sid and I say goodbye to the lapwings and great crested grebe out on the reed fringe of Marton Mere where we've been camped and head north through more coastal flatlands. We make a pretty good team by now. The shame that accompanied driving the tank down the Southwest's pre-posterously narrow lanes is just a bad memory. The Northwest has sensible roads where nobody gets stuck between hedgerows or stone walling. I've grown, too, to appreciate the deep sighs and relieved grumbles of cooling metal when the ignition is finally switched off and Sid cosies down for the night. Hooking up on site takes me no more than two minutes and everything inside the motorhome is a breeze as I slip effortlessly between the oceanic rear bed, bathroom, kitchen and cockpit. It is, in short, home.

After sedate Southport and bubbling Blackpool, Morecambe looks as if it has suffered a recent terrorist attack. The downtrodden boarded-up wino wreck of the Art Deco Midland Hotel, down on the beach and down on its luck, appears emblematic of the town's destitute state.

Along the prom I keep my eyes glued above the bland shop-window displays. Morecambe has maybe a half-dozen large buildings in the Deco style, twenty or thirty shops and probably a thousand private semi-detached homes with features such as porthole windows in doors, stained glass and even the occasional ziggurat design built into brick-work. Woolworth's is a fine example, but Hitchens, next door, is even better – Egyptian styled with black guttering fanning into lotus flowers, stepped ziggurats, columns, arcs and triangles.

The town's crowning glory, Europe's largest open-air pool, which opened at the time of the Berlin Olympics and was the annual setting for the Miss Great Britain beauty pageants, was knocked down in 1972. Notwithstanding this, there's enough still standing to put Morecambe on the art-safari weekend map. It may not be quite in the league of Miami's South Beach yet – though a splash of orange, pale pink and pastel blue would go a long way towards creating that illusion – but the fact that Urban Splash (who were major players in the regeneration of Manchester) recently bought the Midland Hotel is an unmistakable sign that things are finally on the move. Other indications of life are the £1.2 million restoration of the exterior of the Victoria Pavilion (all that's left of the Winter Gardens) and a new sculpture trail that's doing its bit to battle the depression that has settled on a town suffering massive unemployment and decades of underfunding.

Morecambe is a punch-drunk-getting-up-slowly-one-more-time sort of place. AJ's Double Burger, Fred's Public Bar, Charlie's Karaoke, Huey's Bar and Yankee Burger may rule the foreshore at the moment but last weekend The Damned (an inspired choice if ever there was one) played in the gardens to a large and affluent middle-aged punk audience. And if the Midland manages to open with a great restaurant and dreamy rooms to stare out of over the bay, who knows? They may yet turn the tide.

Today a few canted shrimping boats wait for a less life-changing tide to turn. Mr Edmondson continues to shrimp daily for his wet-fish shop in town, and Baxter's is still under appointment to the Queen (the Queen Mother was apparently particularly partial to Morecambe Bay shrimps).

The tide is already creeping in when I arrive at the neighbouring village of Heysham where bijoux cottages have been bedecked in bunting in preparation for the weekend 1940s fete. Outside one of the cottages, two decorators sit expansively on a dustsheet-covered armchair and sofa. As the pair tuck into their Desperate Dan lunch boxes, one of the men lifts his mug of tea as greeting. I return his greeting and his partner, Vernon Walker, immediately picks up on my effete southerly accent.

'And what, may I ask, brings you to our northerly sunny climes?' he opens grandiloquently. 'By the sound of your voice, I would guess you hail from somewhere south of Birmingham.'

Duly cowed, I tell him about my journey and the book.

'All right for some. Call that work? So where are you heading next?'

'Cumbria.'

Vernon wastes no time in informing me that he has lived most of his life across the border in Cumbria. 'Different breed up there. Fight you 'cos they're bored. Any Cumbrian woman would make mincemeat of a Heysham man.'

I point out that Cumbria is only a matter of a couple of miles north but Vernon chooses to ignore my protest. 'Hope you've got a foreign dictionary with you, 'cos you won't understand a word up there. – "yans" and "taws" instead of "ones" and "twos". They're as foreign as Timbuktu.'

Keith Porter, who turned to decorating after thirty years in the Manchester Fire Service, informs me that the Cumbrian resort of Silloth, with its orderly grid of broad tree-lined streets, was originally planned as the Brighton of the north. 'Don't know what happened to that idea. Brighton it certainly isn't. If you think Morecambe's in a state, wait till you get to Barrow-in-Furness and Workington. When the ironmining and shipbuilding died, they built Sellafield and now that's going too. Another four thousand jobs went recently.'

I leave Keith and Vernon to their pork pies and pop into a deli on their recommendation to buy the local specialities – potted shrimps and nettle beer (which tastes pleasantly like ginger beer but sadly is just as non-alcoholic). As I emerge a wiry man named Jake Edmondson, who's 82 but looks twice that, calls out from across the street, encouraging me to pay 10p to be weighed on his Avery 120-year-old brass beam scale. According to the scales I have put on 3 kilos since leaving home.

I move on to ancient St Peter's church to ask the saint if he can perform a new miracle by psychically liposuctioning the excess. On the floor of the nave lies a Viking chieftain's 5ft-long hogback stone, which was discovered in the cemetery. Out in the graveyard today, all the tombstones avert their eyes from the rushing waters of the Bay. Behind black railings I find a family tomb and a plaque commemorating Harriet Agnes, aged eighteen, and her younger sister, Mabel, fourteen, daughters of the well-to-do Wright family who had their own private gallery in the church. The obituary is as succinct as it is poignant. 'Dearly loved daughters who were drowned while bathing in Morecambe Bay on 24th June 1895 in sight of their home.' The girls' brief battle against the rushing sea was apparently witnessed by congregation members standing in the churchyard.

As I stare out over mud flats gunnelled with streams, I realise it is only a matter of probably half an hour before the estuary is once more in spate. Cut into the rock on the final outcrop of the wild headland, a number of repositories for bones, shaped in the human form, are still flooded from the last inundation – literal watery graves.

I drive back through Morecambe – where many of the inhabitants are just as trapped by impoverishment as Harriet and Mabel Wright were by the tide and then slowly edge round the coast and along the flats to Holgates Caravan Park on the shoulder of Silverdale.

It is an inspired choice of overnight stop, with indoor pool, bar, shop, lots of activities for kids if I had any, and views out over Morecambe Bay. I use a camp's walks leaflet to plot my way to the Woodlands pub that Vernon and Keith had recommended ('Hell to find but more hilarious than Fawlty Towers'). Map in hand I quit the site by a rear stile at about 7 p.m. and disappear into an ancient woodland (Eaves Wood) owned by the National Trust. My Heysham decorator friends had certainly got it right about the pub being hell to find. Eventually I discover it at the end of a concealed track where the village of Silverdale disappears into woods.

An ostentatious crenellated porch leads me into a deserted lobby with an ugly chandelier and several doors leading off that are all closed. I follow the staircase upstairs to the first-floor landing where more doors lead off. This time I find one that does open. It takes me into an ante-chamber where three men are playing pool. Beyond it I arrive at a pocket-sized bar that's heaving. Dave, the barman, is attempting to serve in an area you couldn't swing a cat in. Above him the ceiling has been covered in gaudy red plastic tiles that perfectly offset the sludge-coloured flock wallpaper. It is like drinking in an elderly relative's parlour and almost as cheap, with Abbots and Woody's draught beer selling at £1.80 a pint. Dave took over the pub nine months earlier, when the previous owner had a nervous breakdown. He has just the one room – the rest of the former publican's home remains off limits.

A man listing badly next to me stabs his finger several times at something in the air as if trying to skewer words he is finding difficult to assemble. 'We come a long way for this pub.' He touches his nose and nearly misses.

'Where do you live, then?' I ask.

'Arndale. But it's worth the journey.'

Arndale is, in fact, the next village.

'Don't mind him –' the man returns to stabbing his finger, this time in the direction of a man similarly swaying on his other flank. 'He's the local drunk.'

'Can you pass the water,' his companion asks and I duly pass the jug. 'I don't like to drink whisky neat,' he explains and then ignores the jug completely before staggering off with his tumbler of whisky. An hour later, when I leave the pub, I find him tottering down a street, tumbler still in hand. As I overtake him he asks if I'm all right. Despite the fact that we are both on foot, he then enquires if I have a dog in my car.

I follow a ridge back towards the campsite. It is 10.15 p.m. In the failing light the water in the bay looks like ruffled satin. Large stone houses nuzzle into the wooded hills. Fifteen children squeal their way down a steep wooded incline in single file and then scramble back up again to do it again. The stillness on the campsite is the closest I've got to wild camping in a while.

In the field opposite the campsite exit, parents are setting up stalls for a school fete. Sid refuses to stop and climbs with the lane and the nibbled drystone walls to a crest. In the distance I can see the featureless Lakeland hills. A couple of miles further, I drop down into Arndale, park beside the Fighting Cocks pub and stride out through the village seeking the starting point of the Cross Morecambe Bay Walk that I've booked myself on to.

Outside the Albion pub I'm astonished to discover several hundred people milling about with day packs on their backs. They are dressed, for the most part, in shorts, fleeces and trainers. A party atmosphere prevails.

Behind the gathering gabled attics in three-storey Victorians stare haughtily down at the hubbub. Hemming us in on the opposite flank is a narrow river sprinting for the sea through the broad muddied bay. Considering we're about to embark on a three- or four-hour walk, I'm surprised by the number of children in attendance, several of whom I notice are writing their names in the mud with their fingers.

A middle-aged American male 10ft from me is boring his walking partner with a potted history of his career. 'After McGill I did a polar expedition sampling plant toxins. Then it was back to lakeland chemistry – phosphorus, stuff like that. Then deforestation – my first move from the water.' His friend starts to yawn and then quickly muffles it. Perhaps it's his boss.

The kids, meanwhile, have upped the stakes and smeared mud on their knees and faces. Finding no one admonishing them, they naturally take matters a step further, lobbing great congealed clumps at each other. An older teenager sends a picture of himself on his mobile with the bay as backdrop. A late arrival, in his early forties, calls out to a friend, 'Where's the wife?'

'Had an argument with her last night, as usual, and she wouldn't come,' comes the reply, accompanied by a grin as broad as the bay.

The children have now bored of mud and are scooping water from the channel and hurling it at each other. They're probably starting to think walks aren't so bad after all.

Finally our leader arrives, striding out with his staff and halo of silver hair. Dressed in a blue crew-neck sweater, blue jeans and trainers, it's clear Cedric Robinson is one of those chiefs who give advice but never take it themselves – 'Dress in shorts and sandals that can easily be removed as you WILL get wet' had been the tip regarding the walk he'd provided for tourist board literature.

Cedric, who bears an uncanny resemblance to Robert Graves (or at least the portrait of him by John Arlidge that's on display in the National Gallery) blows a whistle and the 8-mile Cross Bay Walk commences. With the size of the crowd, we do not step out as one but instead stagger our start, the rear mobilising several minutes after the *avant guard*. Initially we track the bank of the River Kent in the direction of the sea. Three different rivers exit into the bay but when the tide is out they are little more than streams in a great plain. When I manage to get through the pack and take up pole position alongside our leader, he tells me he'd spent much of the previous day checking the route.

'Forty years' fishing and walking the bay helps but the river is always changing its course and you have to prepare meticulously.' He sweeps a hand through his full head of hair without breaking stride. 'So I planted the laurel bushes – we call them brobs – to mark the way. They're the best bushes to use because the leaves don't drop off even when they're dead and they usually withstand the tide for a couple of days.'

The route we are taking was the main thoroughfare across the bay before the arrival of the railways and, according to Cedric, has been trodden for centuries. Despite this, it remains a treacherous place for the inexperienced. Seven months after our summer walk across the sands, twenty Chinese illegal immigrants working for slave-labour wages would be drowned by the in-rushing tide while collecting cockles out in the bay.

'There's a tidal range of 10m during the neaps. I don't know anyone that tall,' Cedric portentously tells me. 'Even with a normal tide, in mist and rain, you'd be lost in minutes. The tide comes in faster than a horse can gallop and apart from the risk of drowning – and plenty have – there's also quicksand to contend with. You should see it during spring tide when we get the tidal bore rushing up the estuary, hammering at the sea walls at Arndale and Grange-over-Sands. You have to know what you're about.'

The danger is greatest when suddenly reaching softer sands. 'Walkers don't know what to do and they stop dead. It's the worst thing you can do. You should keep on walking or your legs just might disappear.'

I notice that Cedric's eyes never leave the ground in front of him as he talks. 'Don't know if everyone here today's up to the walk . . . there's usually a few that don't make it. So I've got my nephew out on the sands with a tractor in case they have to be ferried back.'

Cedric is the 25th Queen's Guide appointed to the Sands (the first record of a guide is one Edmonstone in 1501, described as 'Carter upon Kent Sands') and has been leading Cross Bay Walks since 1963. The original appointment, dating from 1536, is still made by the Queen in her guise as the Duchy of Lancaster. When Cedric started the walks forty years earlier, only a handful turned up. Today there are 350 and sometimes twice that number.

For the honour of popularising the walks, Cedric is paid the princely sum of £15 per year (plus rent-free accommodation in a 700-year-old house). Apart from voluntary donations and the souvenir maps his wife sells on the twice-weekly summer walks, it is the only money he brings in now that he has retired from fishing.

The group is already well spread along the bank as we crocodile through a caravan site, duck into blackthorn scrub and emerge on to a pebble beach that leads on to marshland. 'It's all right being spread out now,' Cedric informs the advance party, 'but once we're on softer sands, or if the river is narrow, then it can be a problem. Remember: the narrower the river, the deeper and faster it is.' Cedric pauses before adding, either as an afterthought or to underscore an important message, 'Wide is good.'

What he doesn't tell us is how long you have to wait for the stragglers. We have been walking no more than twenty minutes and have to wait at least half that for the last to arrive. Eventually we are all once more assembled and ready to bisect the 120-square-mile expanse of sand. I resume my pole position alongside Cedric.

'When I was a lad, we used to set nets for oystercatchers,' he tells me. 'Skin them like rabbits. Tasty. In those days we used horse and cart to fish, not tractors like today – some of the lads these days even use quad bikes. If it's your livelihood you fish whatever the weather and you go out when the tide's right whether it's three in the morning or not.

'Sometimes the horses had to go up to their necks in the water and once we lost three of them. We'd all hauled at a sensible place but a couple of the newer lads went trawling further than they should – we could see danger and had warned them but kids don't listen. Anyway, they went into one of the mellgraves – large scoured holes whose depth is hidden by the outgoing tide – and got stuck in the quicksand. The lads managed to scramble off to safety but the horses were going down. It was so sad for the owner to watch. We tried everything. He was going to bang them over the head with a spade, he was that upset: put them out of their misery. But while he was fretting whether to or not, the tide rushed in and under they went. We thought that's that. But then suddenly they bobbed up again.' Cedric shakes his head, still amazed at the happy outcome. 'The water saturated the sands and loosened it and they popped up like corks. That's what we use for rescuing sometimes – waterjets – so it liquefies the sand.'

After traipsing across our own saturated sands for half an hour, there's another wait for stragglers. The line stretches back probably half a mile and it takes the best part of twenty minutes for everyone to arrive. Once the flock has been finally assembled, the shepherd fans his flock out along the river bank in the middle of the bay and gives us final instructions.

'Once you start walking, don't stop. Keep spread out and maintain a steady pace until you get to the other side.'

Moses leads us into the river with his staff. I almost expect the water to part. It is a scene straight from *The Ten Commandments* apart from the shorts, fleeces and yapping dogs. Although the water only comes up to my thighs, for the legion of hounds in attendance the choice is swim or drown as the river twists and flashes like salmon. The symphony of slapping water, the arching pale blue sky and the vast belly of sand become one, and burn into my bank of indelible memories. Somewhere midstream we cross from Lancashire into Cumbria. Behind us, amid the wave-sculpted crests and troughs, are millions of baby periwinkles; on the far bank, between scattered shells and the spaghetti mountains of lugworms, stands one of Cedric's laurel sprigs redolent of the bedraggled Tree of Life in *Waiting for Godot*.

Mike Carter, one of Cedric's helpers, points to a collapsed mud bank in the distance and warns, 'It's brack where the river cut under it. That's where you'll get the quicksand. Dangerous and best kept clear of.'

Mike is as sturdy as an oak tree and I take to him straight away. He has a ginger beard, gentle eyes, an uninhibited laugh and there's a refreshing openness to him. He points in a northeasterly direction, to what appears to be a shimmering mirage of wooden stakes in the midst of the mud desert. 'They're me nets. Set me first at the age of ten and 48 years later I'm still at it. They're rolled up today as I knew I wouldn't have time this weekend to check them but I'll have 'em down next Friday as we've got no walks.'

'Is that what you do for a living?'

'Is it 'eck. I'm a pest controller. I'll drop the nets down after work next Friday and come back the Saturday morning and hope I've caught more than the jellyfish I got last week. Nothing like it, walking out at 4.30 in mornin' with day breaking out over Ingleborough.'

Some veteran walkers in our party believe Mike will take over the walks when Cedric (now seventy) retires but Mike scoffs at the idea when I put it to him. 'No way. Cedric's older than me but I plan on retiring before 'im.'

Apart from assisting Cedric, Mike is also a volunteer for the Independent Sand Rescue service, which uses both hovercraft and a sixteen-wheel agrocart to patrol the marshes. Dressed in shorts, T-shirt and baseball cap, he has a pronounced limp but uses his staff only for checking sand consistency rather than support. He got the injury when the dumper truck he was driving at Grange-over-Sands was hit by a steam train. 'Ended up half a mile down the track. They didn't let my family leave hospital the first couple of days 'cos they were pretty sure I weren't going to make it. Six months' traction. Shattered pelvis. It weren't good. Said I'd never be able to go walking in the Fells again. Ended up doing ten years' Mountain Rescue after that.' Mike's great defiant belly laugh bellows across the empty sands.

When it finally abates I ask why Grange is Grange-over-Sands when it should be Grange-over-Spartina Grass. 'The river's always moving but one night in the winter of 1982 people went to bed and the next day they woke up and it'd moved four miles to the other side of the bay to the Silverdale and Carnforth marshes. That were a bit unusual!' Again the belly laugh. 'It got silted up and the grass took root.'

'What's the major occupation in Grange?'

'Retirement!' The bellow returns. 'There's not much work anywhere. Grange gets plenty of visitors, but Barrow's got little shipbuilding now; the power station employs less. The only thing there's more of round here is less.'

Mike has never married and lives in his venerable family cottage with his brother, who's also single. 'Too independent!' he explains before I even ask. He has travelled abroad only once. 'To Rome with some friends. I loved it.'

Mike switches tack and points to the headland at the mouth of the estuary. 'That's Humphrey Head. That's where the last wolf in England were killed three hundred year back.'

We finally reach the far bank and the tour breaks up. Walkers collect their certificates and throw coins in the plastic bucket for Cedric. I wish there were a bucket for Mike too. Some of the group return to cars and others to the railway station.

I walk a mile alongside the railway track that Mike had his accident on and squeeze through a picket gate with a board attached demanding that we 'Stop Look Listen'. The trail passes pretty wisteria-clad cottages and then drops to long public gardens fronting the town. On the spartina marshland sheep are grazing and one lamb is throwing a tantrum because it thinks it's been abandoned. I swear it's calling

'Maaam, Maaam.' Suddenly it spots its black woolly mother in the distance and makes a dash. The pair rub noses like Eskimos and then lamby gets down to lunch.

My own lunch – a roasted ham sandwich, slice of fruit cake and a pot of tea – I have at a table beside a sign warning 'Caution Fast Rising Tides Hidden Channels Quicksand'.

The Barley Lane Pier built by the Morecambe Bay Steamboat Co. is long gone and the only pleasure steamers are of the ghostly ilk. Worst of all, the open-air pool is closed. Notwithstanding these setbacks, Grange is a prosperous resort that grandly calls itself the Lakeland's Riviera. The houses are well cared for and all the upmarket shops – a crystal engraver, Posselthwaite's Housewares, Ainsworth fine cheeses, spirits and gourmet food – seem to be doing good business (I count twenty people queuing patiently outside Higginsons Quality Meats). A fine legacy of the much-maligned Victorians are the town's oriental gardens, the mile-and-a-half traffic-free prom and the picture-book railway station, where I hop on board the 2 p.m. back to Arndale, passing oystercatchers picking their way across the sands.

Sid is only too pleased to see me and itching to be off. Together we skirt Morecambe Bay, this time in a more circumlocutory fashion, and doff our caps to a sign welcoming us to the Lake District National Park. With each twist in the road, new vistas open up: a pond skirted by a raggedy stone wall, a horse flicking its tail and curtseying backwards, and curtain hills topped by a bubbling cauldron of cloud. At Ulverston (birthplace of Stan Laurel, the Quaker movement, pole vaulting, Hartley's beer and the seventy-mile Cumbria Way) a lighthouse appears on a hill and shortly afterwards two rhinos – a new tourist attraction – graze a field. Well, why not? Sid breasts a final pass and we gallop down to the jungle of cranes, gallumping electricity pylons, aluminium warehouses and 'To Let' signs of Barrow-in-Furness.

The Heysham decorators have prepared me well for Barrow and a friend who knows the area well had also warned me of the deprivation of the urban Cumbrian coast. In his introduction to the area in the Greenpeace book *Coastline*, Hunter Davies talks of 'Cumbrian towns where labour is lost, industry worn out, spirits sagging'. It's almost as if everything that's grand is granted admission to the interior Lake District National Park (the word 'paradise' comes from ancient Persian and means 'green place') and the rest gets swept to fester on the coast. There will be exceptions. But Barrow isn't one of them. The town has been abandoned for the convenient ugliness of the port-side shopping centre with its dribble of McDonald's, Halfords, Tesco Extra, Iceland and Blockbuster.

I park beside hulking dock warehouses and take the harbour path to the Dock Museum, a spacious building constructed over the old graving dock (where ships' hulls were cleaned). The multi-media exhibits tell the story of the town from its village beginnings and a population of twenty or thirty at the turn of the 19th century. This number rose to three hundred when the railway arrived in 1843, 35,000 were living here by the early 1870s (when the docks were built) and the number had doubled by 1900.

The reason for the explosion was the abundance of Europe's best-quality hematite (the chief source of iron), which resulted – for a short period in the 1870s – in Barrow becoming the largest steelworks in the world as pig iron was processed on site to furnish its own shipbuilding industry and to build the railroads criss-crossing the subcontinents of America and India. In its heyday in 1916, the shipyard employed 31,000. Now it's down to three thousand working on Astute-class nuclear hunter-killer subs for the Royal Navy.

I decide to visit a small island in the bay that has no bridge link. Unfortunately my plan is dashed when I discover the ferry is not operating today. Piel Island has had its own king since 1487 – basically, whoever is landlord of the Ship Inn takes the crown and the title. The current incumbent is Rod Scarr, whose family happen to be the only permanent residents on the island. There is no mains gas or electricity and communication is by ship-to-shore radio. Although I cannot visit, I can make out the large ruins of a castle that was once owned by Savignac monks who were said to have been active in the smuggling business.

On my way to Barrow, I'd taken the speediest, inland route, intent on seeing the town's attractions before they were locked away for the night. I shouldn't have bothered. Now, with a spectacular sunset in prospect, I drive back towards Ulverston but this time taking the leisurely coast road.

It's a good decision. The late sun is gilding everything in its path and the sinuous Cumbrian Morecambe Bay Coast Road is an absolute peach.

The road was constructed during the recession that followed World War I, when 60 per cent of shipyard workers (and 44 per cent of the town's total workforce) were laid off. Sid cruises alongside the sea wall from the mouth of the wild, denuded estuary to progressively gentler folds of grazing pasture tucked into wooded valleys. Eventually I pull off the road near Bardsea and camp for the night before resuming my journey the next morning, this time following the A595 around the estuary known as Duddon Sands.

The coastal vista is mostly treeless and exposed. Drystone walls are overrun with undergrowth and white caps of cloud sweep across the serrated peaks of Black Coombe. Signs warn to watch out for rogue cows and sheep on the road. I encounter both. And goats. Stone farmhouses slumber in valleys, smoking heavily despite both society's disapproval and the fact that we are now into July. I criss-cross the railway probably ten times, pass through occasional hamlets hunkering in valleys beside streams, and have several snatched conversations in shops, cafés and at confusing crossroads.

Above the mud flats of Millom, where locals are digging for lugworms, I strike up conversation with a middle-aged woman walking her dog. 'Best lugworm in England you'll find down on the flats here,' she boasts. 'And I should know. My husband spends half his time down there finding bait and the other half fishing with it.' She laughs in a manner that her Scotty dog clearly finds irritating and it launches into a paroxysm of barking.

The woman's husband is from Millom but she hails from Manchester, which is where the pair met when he moved for work with his four sons after the Millom iron foundry closed in 1968. Once retired, they moved back to Millom so he could fish and cycle. With a final 'He's happy now,' the woman completes her story.

The A595 continues to corkscrew along the wild west coast between familiar Lakeland rumpled hills and long-forgotten red telephone boxes. At MOD Eskmeals firing range, a sign discourages beachcombers from touching 'Shells, bombs, missiles or strange objects'.

My next stop is 12th-century Muncaster Castle, fortified against marauding Scots. In the Himalayan Garden migrant rhododendron, groves of bamboo, primulas, irises and anemones remind me of the treks that I've enjoyed in Nepal (whence the plants were transported in the 19th and 20th centuries). From the garden terrace there are views out over the Esk valley and the line of fells – described by Ruskin as the 'gateway to paradise'.

Outside the castle, an old boy in checked sports jacket and brown corduroy trousers greets me cheerily. 'Hello. Thanks for coming.' It's almost as if he's been waiting for me. Except that he's greeting everybody else the same way. He seems genuinely pleased to see us all. I am the third person I hear asked where they come from. My reply ('London, but I've been travelling right round the English coast') clearly takes the fancy of Patrick Gordon Duff Pennington, and he promptly invites me for tea in the family apartments.

Patrick leads the way through a dark labyrinth with even darker pools off it where forgotten rooms slumber through the afternoon. Some are piled high with junk, others seem to be occupied solely by ancient chairs sagging from supporting the aristocracy for centuries. We settle. Tea is forgotten. Patrick apologises that his wife Phyllida, the most recent Ramsden to occupy the castle the family have owned for eight hundred years, is not here to greet me. 'She had a nasty fall this morning and is recovering in bed.' I commiserate and thank him for showing me his inner sanctum.

'Well, it's not really *my* inner sanctum. It's home, but not my spiritual home. I wasn't born here; I married into the family. I'm really a farming Scot. My father-in-law announced to me in 1982, "Patrick, I've been losing £50,000 a year for the past five years. It's your turn."' Patrick laughs and scratches his head as if being faced with the dilemma for the first time. 'I've been here ever since. Slowly we got rid of the debt. I had already experienced bad debt and didn't like it one bit – in 1959 I owned a Scottish farm that nearly bankrupted me. It was a lesson. I've never owed a penny since.'

I look around. It is dark and difficult to make things out. It is a room taken for granted rather than celebrated: curtains that may never have been pushed right back, unreplaced expired light bulbs, musty furniture. The classic unselfconscious aristocratic pile.

I ask Patrick whether it concerns him to live so close to Sellafield (formerly known as Calder Hall and Windscale), which in 1956 became

Britain's first nuclear-powered station to generate electricity on a commercial scale.

'No. Everybody seems to live to a good age here. Must be good for you. The gamekeeper died at 106 and rode a bike till he was 103.'

'What about the Sellafield "accidents"?'

'People got careless. It's been tightened up massively now. We had more problems from Chernobyl when they dumped on us. Let's face it, every couple of years something is sent to try us. The Cumbrian coast has only known hard times for a very long time now.'

I am reluctant to give up on the Sellafield scandal. 'There was a big rumpus about safety in the eighties, wasn't there?'

'That was '83. The beach incident. Effluent discharged on to the beach was found to be above the legal limit.'

'What happened?'

'A woman in Ravenglass, Mrs Merlin – a fine name, don't you think? – wanted to sell her house and so sent the contents of her Hoover off to the United States for analysis. As you do. It was found to have higher-than-permissible levels. The newspapers naturally made a splash under gaudy headlines such as "Radioactive House".'

'Was that all that happened?'

'No. The BBC landed a helicopter on the beach and told everyone they should leave straight away. The local people surrounded the helicopter and told *them* to leave instead. They then superglued the door to Mrs Merlin's shop.' Patrick smiles warmly at the memory. 'It was a pretty clear message. They don't like outside interference and they had lost too many jobs already when mining ended. Sellafield is the biggest employer by a mile, even today, despite gearing up for decommissioning. Anyway, Mrs Merlin sold up and left. She didn't get much for her house, though.' Again the smile.

Patrick kindly agrees to accompany me on my house tour. 'I never bore of it. Often I'll take two or three tours in a day.' As we walk through room after room, rather like stumbling into a set of Russian dolls, our conversation continues to be punctuated by Patrick greeting every passing guest. He invariably has a story for each too, be it about Thailand, Newcastle or America. He also stops for a chat with every passing employee (the 77-acre estate employs seventy of them). Everybody working here seems to love the man.

It becomes increasingly obvious that Patrick's eccentric mind works like a scatter gun and you have to be on your toes to catch the segueing from one subject to another. 'My daughter and her husband run Muncaster now. Magnificently, it has to be said. We packed her off to boarding school at thirteen and she hated it. She wrote to the minister for education saying her educators knew nothing about farming, that she'd be much better off at home with the animals, and could he grant her permission? He refused, so she wrote to the Queen. She's terrifying. We gave up and brought her home. She's 42 now. One of our four daughters. When she finished her education, she went off to Australia to dress bulls in Queensland for shows. Her husband's a vet. They're marvellous.'

Before I can comment, Patrick's off on a new tack. 'We have people come from every corner of the globe. Among my favourites are a party of Russians who stayed and we sang a wonderful song about a man being met by Lady Death out on a lonely road. The man graciously resigns himself to his fate, requesting only that they have a drink together to mark the pact. Naturally he leaves her drunk as a skunk in the ditch.'

Looking down over the gardens from the leaded windows of an upstairs room, I notice owls entertaining a crowd in the garden. Beyond it is a maze. Patrick follows my gaze. 'That's the Meadow Vole Maze, where children learn about the interdependency of life – the owls eat the voles and they need long grass so we cut our meadows late so everybody's happy.' The Vole Maze is a microcosm of Muncaster Castle itself. 'The meadow is where my mother-in-law used to keep her bears. Personally I don't like animals in captivity.'

Patrick promptly starts loudly declaiming a self-penned poem, oblivious to the visitors' incredulous stares. It is the first of several poems that he recites as we continue our tour. This particular one ends something like 'imprisoned in a gilded cage in Muncaster I know how the caged animal feels'.

I'm about to ask him why he doesn't return to the Scotland he loves now that his daughter and son-in-law are so expertly running Muncaster. Unfortunately I take too long and Patrick is once more off on another apposite tangent.

'Too many politicians haven't seen life and death in a lambing field. They don't feel the weight of their influence. And they cannot create the landscape they want without funding. I'm politically agnostic. At Oxford I wanted to be foreign secretary but my tutor in economic history, Tony Crossland, did it instead.'

I'm finding it difficult to keep up. We are now in the Ancestors Room, a forbidding gallery of the Ramsdens (Patrick's wife's family). Here the floodgates really open.

'That's the Protector Somerset who was beheaded in 1550.' Patrick's finger moves several degrees left to settle on a rather plain woman. 'Frances Ramsden. She was Charles II's mistress though heaven knows what he saw in her. Having said that, we did have her cleaned recently and she's looking more attractive these days.'

The finger is travelling again. 'John Charles Ramsden. He introduced the Reform Bill that put an end to slavery. And he was a friend of Wilberforce. He was kicked out of Harrow, I think for fighting a duel over a girl. Joshua Reynolds painted three or four of them . . .' Does he mean portraits of John Charles, of the Ramsdens, or simply paintings hanging in the house? I stop fighting and give in to being mesmerised.

'That's my mother-in-law. I didn't get on with her. And the gentleman beside her is my father-in-law. He came second in the Grand National on a one-eyed horse in 1927.'

Patrick's attention is next snared by the statue of a stag. 'When I was deer commissioner in Scotland, my staff gave me that as a leaving gift.' On its base I read, 'To Patrick for annoying those who needed it.'

'What does the reference concern?' I ask.

'I have been known to get under skins. At different times I've joined picket lines in Scottish docks and badgered the odd MP about rural depopulation. Did you know that 40 per cent of the inhabitants of the Western Isles are English?'

I didn't. As Patrick whips me through a library bristling with more than six thousand fanned spines as threadbare as the edging to his jacket, I ask if I can take a picture of him. 'Best outside. Where you get the grandeur of the setting.'

And so we head outside and Patrick positions himself in front of a large magnolia tree with Scafell Pike (England's tallest peak at 3,210ft) as a backdrop. 'When the magnolia candles are out and there's snow up on the peak, it is the most beautiful place on earth. Well, outside Scotland anyway. From the top of the Himalayan Garden, you can see the Isle of Man.'

After the picture a group of eight Asians arrive. Patrick asks where they're from. 'Taiwan,' one replies.

'Taiwan. Really? Wonderful. Marvellous. You must see the portrait . . .' And he's off with them, throwing a glance over his shoulder to provide me with a courteous farewell. 'Very nice meeting you, Paul. You must come again. Bring your wife. Bring your children. They'll love it.'

Back in the van I fill Sid in on my latest encounters and we drive a few short miles down into the village of Ravenglass, where the national park reaches the sea and travels with it for 10 miles. Once the second-largest Roman port in England (behind Chester), it sits in an antler-shaped estuary fed by the Rivers Esk, Irt and Mite. Its handsome 18th- and 19th-century cottages sit on a medieval street that narrows like a bottle to reduce the likelihood of livestock escaping on market day.

There's no market today but there is a mean wind whistling through from the shore. In one particularly pretty front garden, an old petrol pump (National Premium 1/5) has been planted beside the flower tubs and gnomes. The old butcher's shop is now a gift and craft centre, the post office still somehow manages to pay its way, and there's also a tea shop and a pub. First stop is the tea shop for cream tea. I then move seamlessly to the pub for a pint of Ruddles, which I transport to a bench on a grassy knoll overlooking the bay. On the beach beneath me, a jellyfish the size of a dinner plate has been washed up. The protected bay glitters like gneiss.

Done for the day, I slip past the exotic-looking cooling towers of Sellafield and then take the wrong turning. I reverse into a bank and mash the rear of the van a little more. Double done for the day, I find a wild headland to park on above the sublimely rural (and abandoned) Netherton railway station. I sit out on a flat patch of clover overlooking the station and the sea, eating honeycomb that Max had left behind. According to the wrapper, it's now called 'cinder toffee', not honeycomb. Perhaps the owner decided that a rebranding along the lines of Nick Howell's pilchard-sardine conversion was called for. Since Max left I have found a tideline from his visit: unwanted apple turnovers, a half-eaten box of Frosties, a dog bone. Down below me waders are trawling their own tideline on the beach. Gulls skim the sea. It's 10.30 p.m.

Suddenly, out of the silence, two trail bikes tear up the peace and the hillside. I hear them approaching from below and when the row reaches a crescendo, they appear in the twilight in plumes of expended diesel. One is driven by a man, probably in his thirties, dressed in overalls. The second is ridden by a boy no older than eight. The father-and-son team stand on their footrests, legs fully extended, bums out of saddles. They drive as slowly as possible, veering in and out of the grass verge, constantly correcting steering to avoid falling over. The father is teaching his son about control. When the lesson is over and they finally vanish back inside the house, I'm left with the deafening silence and the sun's final broadside along the horizon. Whitecaps gather in a hem that runs all the way along to the towering cliffs at St Bees Head. The light thickens. The tide retreats, exposing more dark rocks. It's time to return to the dark caves of sleep.

The harbour at Whitehaven would seem to have had regeneration money thrown at it of late if the useless wavelike canopy drifting whimsically over the jetty is anything to go by. Old creaking cranes, strumming halyards and squawking gulls provide the wake-up call to late risers. On Lowther Street I discover Michael Moon's second-hand bookshop, a legend in the Northwest. The window display serves as an eclectic introduction to what lies inside: *The Most Dangerous Pit in the Kingdom* by Ray Devlin and Harry Fancy (a history of the nearby William pit); a biography of Wainwright, whose coast-to-coast walk starts in nearby St Bees; *The Forgotten Trade* by Nigel Tuttersfield (with a chapter on Whitehaven's role in the slave trade); Twiggy's autobiography; *Flora of the Fells*; and Adolf Hitler's *Mein Kampf*. Oh, and there's also a facsimile on view of *Lloyds Evening Post* dated 27 April 1778 reporting on a failed attempt to take the port by local lad, privateer and founder of the American navy, John Paul Jones during the American War of Independence. With an American crew of thirty, Jones stole into the harbour, set fire to a ship 'and committed other Outrages'. It's the kind of bookshop you can easily lose several hours in, especially on a drizzly day like today.

By 11 a.m. I am quitting Whitehaven's rainy terraces as grim as its black-toothed graveyard and pass by another boil on the arse of the Lake District National Park, the Victorian steel town of Workington. This time, however, I slip through without touching the sides. If you ever happen to be up this way, I suggest you do the same, for the town rightly earns its billing – 'Nowt worse than a wet weekend in Workington.' This is a town where regeneration plans have been a way of life for half a century.

Siddick is little better. The sign announcing the town has had the 'Sid-' prefix sensibly removed by local hoolies who wished to rechristen it with a more apt name. A car has been partially crushed by a lorry beside the Iggesund Paperboard factory. Beyond them wind turbines wave maniacally as if trying to sort out the traffic. As I inch past I notice the lorry bears the slogan 'Caring for the environment' beside the company name United Utilities, and the broken promise 'No hazardous products'.

Maryport is an improvement. I park by the harbour, built by the Senhouse family to serve the Cumbrian coal trade, and largely resurrected over the past couple of decades by national funding (the harbour walls have been replaced, the silt removed and paved walkways introduced). The Maritime Museum recounts the now-familiar dirge of eclipse. At the turn of the 19th century, the population of three thousand was spoilt for choice – whether to seek employment in the glassworks, the iron furnaces, collieries, pottery, brewery, paper mill, cotton mill, shipbuilding industry, or the fleet of ninety ships. But by June 1931 unemployment stood at 80 per cent.

Upstairs my mood lifts amid the ship models and an exhibition on the romantic tale of the Mutiny on the Bounty. The hero, or antihero, was a man named Fletcher Christian, a local lad who fell in love with a chieftain's daughter in Tahiti and listened to his heart rather than his boss when his commander, Captain Bligh, ordered the crew to pack for home. Once at sea, Christian dumped Bligh in a boat, requisitioned the ship and sailed back where the weather is kind, the women gorgeous and the life good.

Inside an old Victorian gun deck on the hill overlooking the town is another museum, this time charting the Roman occupation. Unlike Fletcher and his mutineers, the Roman legionaries were far less happy immigrants, according to the evidence in the Senhouse Roman Museum. Rather than willingly embracing the local tribe, as inscriptions on altar stones record, they offered the prayers and supplications to Jupiter for hasty and safe returns from the barbarian northern lands to homelands in Croatia and Spain.

The first of the altar stones were found on Senhouse family land during Elizabeth I's reign. Further generations added to it (the finest being the seventeen sandstone Roman altars in virtually mint condition that were discovered in August 1870), making it the largest collection of Roman altars from a single site in Britain.

Both the maritime and Roman museums operate on donations. Just about every car park I've used in Cumbria has also been free. It's hugely commendable but can't be helping the local economy.

Sid continues his gallop northwards with 10 miles of sand to our left and banks of gorse and wild roses to our right. Halfway to Silloth the wind begins to howl and Sid starts leaping about the road as if stung by the snaking sand. What few trees there are arch like topiary. The sky turns white and rain comes down in stair rods. I shelter in the van beside the post office at Allonby and wait for the storm to abate, distracting myself by reading the post office noticeboard 3ft from my passenger window. Someone has a cast-iron radiator for sale at £35. A 17ft fishing boat 40 HP outboard £1,000 ono. Paintball at Bigrigg. Quiche salad lunch at village hall £3 only. Dominoes at the village hall only 50p.

The rain slackens . . . slightly. Inside the post office racks of sweets have been weighed, wrapped and priced. I ask for stamps and the lady points me to the rear of the shop. By the time I get there, she has beaten me to it and is waiting on the other side of the glass. Having bought two books of stamps, I wave a litre bottle of milk at her. She points back into the main shop and again beats me to the till. While she's getting my change for the milk, I notice there's yet another counter behind her where she sells the fish and chips she fries daily. Juggling balls is what we all do today to earn a living. In a matter of a couple of decades, we have moved from a career for life, to three or four over a lifetime, to several simultaneously.

Across the street the white limewash is coming in handy keeping the rain out at the Ship Hotel and the black mascara round its windows is not yet running. The wooden sign, however, is threatening to fly off in the storm. The homes are strung out in short clusters along the road, the wind whipping through the gaps. People out walking – and there are several – don't use brollies. They prefer to be drowned rather than risk ending up in Northumberland. Allonby is a real Wild West, one-horse – or rather one-woman – town with no trees to protect it and the Irish Sea just a surge away from storming its doors.

*

By the time I reach Silloth, the rain has moved on and the handsome homes, flanking an orderly grid of cobbled streets, are basking in the sunshine. The municipal gardens fronting the beach are spacious and fringed by mature pines. There is a feeling of New England about the place, right down to a street called Eden. But in Maine at 4.30 on a Monday afternoon you wouldn't find the Tourist Information Centre (TIC) closed, the Blue Dolphin Discovery Centre closed, the fishmonger's closed. Susanna's Pantry ('Traditional Meals Served All Day') closed, Peter Josef Hair Design closed, Baguette-Set-And-Go closed, Fine Line Body Art closed, Joan's Home Baking closed, and Thompson Roddick & Laurie Estate Agents closed. I ask a local, 'Have you got an Indian here?' Enigmatically he replies, 'We're working on it.' They're weird in Cumbria.

Roya's Pizza (I wonder where he's from? I bet it's not Cumbria) is open but I don't like pizza much. The smell of hops in the air from the Derwent independent brewery makes me turn to thinking of pubs and I pop in for a quickie in the Balmoral (ugly as sin) before walking the dunes, where I discover a pair of discarded women's panties. The frisson of sex. It's been a while.

I walk back into town from my campsite later in the evening, strolling the promenade with the greensward to my left and the galloping not-quite-emerald-green of the Irish Sea to my right. The sea lashes the stepped storm walls; unperturbed, the sun snoozes, cradled in the rolling hammock that stretches from the horizon. Crows drop mussels noisily beside me like cap-bombs, smashing the shells to get at the meat. Every house staring out to sea from the coast road is different in colour, style and shape from its neighbour. Eventually I arrive at an elegant terrace and slip into the Golf Hotel, where I'm served a pretty traditional lamb and two veg dish by a Spanish waitress, surrounded by puke floral wallpaper that seems to be moving of its own accord. It makes me wonder whether my drink has been spiked with hallucinogens.

As I return homewards, in the penumbra, Scotland is in touching distance across the Solway Firth, the fundamental geological divide of the British Isles. Southern Galloway is as close now as the fells of the Lake District. Once Scotland was even closer; in fact, it was briefly here when Silloth was a Scots town. Inland, darkly, loom the Lakeland mountains, created when the Scottish continent decided to join with the continent of England. I realise with a shock that this is the last time I'll see the sun setting over the sea. Tomorrow I track the dotted line I remember from my school atlas that joins the Northwest with the Northeast and holds the Scots back from storming the border.

'England, where men and the sea interpenetrate . . .'
Joseph Conrad, *Youth* (1902)

'John Bull, like the snail, loves to carry his native shell with
him, irrespective of changes of climate or habits of
different conditions and necessities.'
Richard Ford, *A Handbook for Travellers in Spain* (1855)

Chapter Four: The Northeast

The Sainted Coast

To my right, beyond the A1 and the Mexican wave of wheat fields, the metallic belly of the North Sea stretches across the bay to Berwick-upon-Tweed, Bamburgh Castle and Lindisfarne. A mile north lies Scotland. Having bisected the country and refound the sea, I have pulled into Conundrum Farm, a family business that has replaced typical farming misanthropy with an all-dancing, multi-faceted family-friendly attraction.

For visitors like me – and there are many today – Conundrum offers a smorgasbord of opportunity: farm trail, fishing lake, pony rides, pet barn, pedal tractors, lambs, spotty pigs and, naturally, a shop and café. Unfortunately nobody on site has an answer to my question regarding how the farm came by its weird name. I guess when you've swapped hands thirteen times between Scotland and England – the last time in 1623, admittedly – it must be a bit of a conundrum as to who or what you are.

I make a wide arc through the estate's fields, passing yearling heifers fattening themselves up for Sunday roasts in the restaurant, and an Aberdeen Angus bull patrolling a herd of suckling cows. Beyond a snowdrift of peas, I finally arrive at a boundary wall where an elderly man, stripped to his waist despite the chill wind, is breaking up stones with a 16lb hammer.

John Brassington is repairing a section of the dry dyke that the bull damaged when it was trying to get at bonnier Scottish cows. The grass is always greener. I ask if bulls ever give him trouble when he's working.

'Not up here they don't. I can hop across the fence if one charges. But I was over at Jack Higgins' mushrooming not long back and the bull was angry with me. I got over the wall but he still bashed me in. Oooh, you get bad ones all right.' The dyker sucks in air and blows long and hard before repeating, 'Ooohhh, you do. That's right.'

At first I think John is of German stock but once he's having a run at sentences, I'm able to identify the Irish foundation beneath the battered wall of his language. John Brassington was orphaned in Dublin and moved to Berwick-upon-Tweed via Donegal as a young boy. With an impressive head of hair and well-defined muscles, he wields his bludgeon easily despite being in his seventies and having only recently survived a quadruple by-pass. There is something elemental about this man, stripped to the waist, lumping a hammer at a boundary wall separating Scotland from England. When I tell him I'm planning to stay on Holy Island in a couple of nights, he explodes with joy, leaping about the wall like a mountain goat.

'Ooh, now you'll see the wall I built there for a lady. One hundred yards long right round the house. Beautiful. As you cross the causeway, by the car park, look up on the left and you'll see it. You check that wall at the Snook. I bought the stone off Billy Flanagan. Looks lovely round her house. You check it out.'

Back at the farm shop I buy cured bacon, and basil and sundried-tomato sausages. I then skim a local guidebook over coffee in the café and discover that Berwick-upon-Tweed, where I'm bound next, has a number of conundrums of its own:

1. Salmon caught and smoked in Spittal, on the southern side of the Tweed, has to be sold as *Scottish* smoked salmon, as the river (on which the town of Berwick sits) is classified as Scottish.
2. The mayor's robes are purple instead of scarlet, as Berwick used to be a royal Scottish borough.
3. Berwick has the only English football team playing in the Scottish league.
4. People from Berwick call themselves Berwickers rather than English or Scottish.

5. The King's Own Scottish Borderers was formed in Berwick; their
headquarters is Berwick but they're barracked near Edinburgh.

In town I park beside Britain's best-preserved Elizabethan town walls
and even manage to find a bay large enough to take Sid's bulk. I start my
tour at the Berwick parish church, the only church Cromwell ever had
built for public prayer. Naturally he made it as plain as his personality –
no bells, no spires, no stained glass, no statuary.

Outside the vicarage the far-from-austere Alan Hughes, aged 57 and
dressed in a dapper pale blue shirt with white dog-collar, is ferrying tea
to workmen. He is just back from giving a bereaved family a spin in his
130mph Westfield and keen to tell the workers all about it. Having
sidled into the scrum, I duly inveigle my way further by fawningly
congratulating the vicar on his car. He doesn't bat an eyelid on finding a
newcomer in his audience.

Apart from fast cars, I discover that Alan also likes parachuting. So,
apparently, does his wife, who once had one minute's freefall from
12,000ft with the Red Devils. Having dispensed mugs all round, Alan
stares at my cupless state and offers to brew me one up. I readily accept
and follow him into his home.

Off the hall, the door to his den is wide open. On the wall there is a
picture of the Coldstream Guards in which he served. Catching me
peeking, Alan encourages me to explore inside. The den looks as if it has
recently been under military attack. Piles of paper litter the floor and
perch on every available and not-available surface. On walls and in nooks
and crannies are hunting horns, hats, a photograph of Alan parachuting
out of a Chinook, medals, toy cars, a stuffed owl and a photograph of
Queen Elizabeth signed 'Super BBQ Love Lillibet.'

'Tea's ready,' Alan calls down the hallway.

He welcomes me into the kitchen with a mug. 'It's been a busy
morning. I had a memorial service for the three Driscoll boys
drowned in January 1951. Then we went for the blow in the
Westfield. Sandwich?'

Without waiting for an answer, Alan slices Yorkshire ham from the
bone, heats it up and serves it with a buttered roll. We sit at the kitchen
table and Alan provides me with a rapid-fire CV. 'I ran away from home
at seventeen to join up with the Coldstream Guards and worked my way
up from guardsman to sergeant. I'm actually a major now, but that's with

Operation Telic. In fact, I'm on call right now.' Alan swivels a hip to reveal a pager in his belt.

'What's Telic?'

' "Tell Everyone Leave Is Cancelled". It's a volunteer group. I counsel bereaved families or injured soldiers from the Iraq conflict.'

Alan has been the parish vicar for eight years. 'Did you know Edwin Lutyens made the reredos for the church when he was working at Lindisfarne Castle? We've got John Knox's pulpit too – he was exiled here for two years. A lot of history. But we've also had the safe chiselled open three times now and have had to install cameras and alarms. At least we're still open seven days a week.'

I ask Alan about the schizophrenia that comes with living in a town that has changed hands so frequently.

'Long ago Lord Grey, a former governor, having written to London requesting financial aid during one of the town's low points, received the reply, "Berwick is in the realm, but not of it." It pretty much sums things up. Occasionally, when I've sent letters to Downing Street or Westminster banging on about something or another, they forward it to the Scottish parliament – they don't even know Berwick is in England.' Alan pauses and then repeats, 'In the realm, but not of it.'

Adjacent to the vicarage, the church graveyard doubles up as the town ledger with occupations and histories of the dead listed alongside their names and dates. There are shipwrights and joiners, soldiers and vicars, a flowery tribute to a retired Sunday school teacher, a doctor who fought a duel, and even the skull and crossbones of a plague victim.

Behind the harbour on Bridge Street, I discover another Berwick conundrum. The Original Berwick Cockle Shop (1801) doesn't sell crustaceans and never did. True, it formerly sold Berwick Cockles, but these happened to be a peppermint boiled sweet. Unfortunately the shop stopped making them four years ago so I'll never know if they were any good.

The main window display consists of a pack of two hundred El Rey Economy Cigarillos and an empty box that once contained a Rizla roller. Two of the other three windows are empty. I step over the 'Players Please' doormat and into the shop. Inside, beneath harsh strip lighting, the wooden shelves on either side of the Craven A electric clock are sparsely populated with Swan Vesta matches, a jar of HP sauce, Condor tobacco, Rennies, Tate & Lyle Golden Syrup, Heinz Tomato Soup, Whiskas and a bottle of ginger beer.

Like the clock, time in the Berwick Cockle Shop has stopped. William Cowe, who has run the business for forty of the 117 years it has been in his family, is also marking time. 'I retire in three years,' he tells me without a flicker of emotion. 'I've lasted longer than most in the street. It's the way of life.'

There is something of the mad professor about Mr Cowe in his threadbare tweeds, specs and stained trousers. 'I put it down to the motor car. People drive to the supermarkets out of town these days. The fish-monger went. That's now a hairdresser's. The baker and the dairy followed soon afterwards. Everything is hairdressers or sunbeds these days.'

There is no self-pity or even anger in the voice. His litany is meant merely as an historical record, like the tombstones up in the parish church graveyard. William Cowe is a man who dutifully lived a life he inherited. But no one else will. The family line stops here.

William is right about the hairdressing salons and sunbeds. But Bridge Street, which has retained its traditional shop fronts and hanging baskets, seems to be on the cusp of something of a renaissance. William's brother, across the street, certainly appears to have a little more meat on his bones, his wholesale shop having adapted to bulk discount purchasing.

The roads in Berwick all run like rivers and streams to the harbour. Scattered round the quay today twenty or so art students are sketching as a woman in a wet suit and scuba tank descends into the Tweed from a boat. Beyond her I can see the last two high-prowed cobles (small single-masted, flat-bottomed boats) that fish for salmon on the river, their absent owners employing a traditional and idiosyncratic method that entails describing a semi-circle with a net before hauling in hand over hand from the bank and then bludgeoning the fish over the head.

There is no commercial fishing left in Berwick today and not even a wet-fish shop. The catch that the fish van turns up with on market day has all been landed across the border in Eyemouth.

Having checked into a campsite, I stretch my legs in the balmy evening with a walk back into town via the Royal Tweed Bridge. The arches of the parallel pink stone Jacobean bridge (built 1627) form fifteen perfect circles in the still water and my high vantage point offers uninterrupted views across the Georgian roofscape and out along the estuary to sea.

Down at the quayside the chattering of the students has been replaced by the loud slurpings of hundreds of snow-white mute – a misnomer if ever there was one – swans hoovering up kelp for supper. I make my way up on to the town walls, which swell out to accommodate the occasional serpent bench, gun placement or barracks.

The Berwick fortification was the Star Wars defence system of its day and just as revolutionary. Instead of unscalable height, 50ft-deep ramparts of earth soaked up as many cannonballs as the enemy chose to throw at it. Arrow-headed bastions provided a wide angle for the military's own guns and behind them more cannon awaited the enemy if it managed to land and bridge the 150ft-wide water-filled trench. The fortification cost Queen Elizabeth more than the entire defence of the realm against the Spanish Armada and was the single most expensive enterprise of her entire reign. It wasn't just the Scots she feared but the five-hundred-strong French army camped nine miles up the road in Eyemouth.

My two-hour stroll naturally leaves me thirsty so I pop into the Free Trade, the grungiest unreconstructed bar I can find. The entrance is via a three-quarter saloon door that gives way to a sheep pen whose beer-coloured wood panelling and ceiling is given a sickly sheen by strip lighting. My comfortable blue plastic banquette is fashionably, though naturally, distressed. The table I rest my pint on is hammered tin. Four men sit at the bar laughing and chatting, mostly about kitchen conversions and the advantages of gas cookers over electric. What is happening to the world?

At 10 p.m., as I head homewards, the crimson and purple sky over Stephenson's exquisitely articulated railway bridge is as fine a nightcap as a glass of claret after a meal. Some towns have so little but they never stop trumpeting themselves. Berwick council somehow manages the reverse, hiding its plenitude of charms under a bushel.

The journey from Berwick to Lindisfarne (also known as Holy Island) takes no more than half an hour and I time my arrival to coincide with the tide peeling back like a curtain on Britain's holiest offshore retreat. For centuries monks have trod the causeway seeking isolation. Within a century, as a result of rising sea levels, the island will almost certainly be cut adrift and cars will no longer scuttle crablike across the causeway as they do today.

Virtually every month someone doesn't time things well enough and, imagining their car can outrun the in-rushing sea, misguidedly makes a dash for the island. That's why there is a ladder halfway across the causeway to shin up. By the time it's safe to come back down from the eyrie, the occupant is minus a car. Somewhere out at sea there must be an impressive underwater car park of Mercs, Rovers, BMWs and the rest.

There is a great deal of excitement at the Lindisfarne Heritage Centre today. At first I wonder if someone has won the lottery or there has been news of a birth. In fact, the delirium is down to the recent donation by the British Library of a new perfect facsimile of the 8th-century Lindisfarne Book of the Gospels. Gerald of Wales summed up the achievement of the earliest surviving translation of the Gospels into the English language (housed in the British Library) thus: 'If you take the trouble to look very closely, and penetrate with your eyes to the secrets of artistry, you will notice such intricacies so delicate and so subtle, so close together and well-united, so involved and bound together and so fresh still in their colourings that you will not hesitate to declare that all these things must have been the result of the work, not of men, but of angels.'

In the nearby ruins of Lindisfarne Priory, an elderly woman in tam-o'-shanter and kilt is sketching. At her feet is a neatly packed picnic bag with a thermos protruding from it. 'Wanted to get out of the wind,' she explains, with reference to her position up against the priory wall. She comes from just across the border in Eyemouth and is sketching a statue of an ascetic St Aidan, whose hollowed cheeks and gaunt expression stare heavenwards to an empty sky.

Inside the adjacent church of St Mary the Virgin, the similarly ascetic-looking Brother Damien, in cassock and sandals, is poring over a 1950s copy of the Lindisfarne Gospels pointing out cat's whiskers in an illustrated border to schoolchildren. 'You need a microscope really to see them, which just shows what a miracle the book is.' Equally miraculous is the fact that such detailed work was executed in a primitive stone windowless shelter on a wild and unprotected island. Today Lindisfarne can still get pretty wild – that's why it's also known as 'The Windy Island'. Last winter a garage roof was blown away along with a cross from the church spire.

The first small community of Christian monks was founded on the island by St Aidan of Iona in AD 635 on the instructions of King Oswald of

Northumbria, who wanted to convert the pagan population. Under Aidan's successor, St Cuthbert, Lindisfarne became one of the most important Christian centres in Europe. Fast-forward more than thirteen hundred years and when the last parish vicar retired, it was decided it would be a good idea to reintroduce the monastic tradition by bringing in Brother Damien. Damien's teeth resemble the parlous state of the priory, he has a raggedy beard, is all skin and bones, and his parents in naming him Damien possibly didn't envisage a Christian future. And yet despite all these handicaps, the Anglican Franciscan simply fizzes with energy and enthusiasm.

As he walks and talks, the schoolchildren interrupt with a barrage of questions. They are not naturally inquisitive: it's simply that they have a questionnaire to complete and are haring round the church in a typically competitive frenzy trying to beat their classmates. Brother Damien never fails to stop and answer. Similarly, a stream of visitors from all over the globe ply him with questions of their own. At one point he stops to show a group of Filipinos how the organ can be pumped manually in the event of a power cut. They appear totally bemused. Is this the England of microchips and the Sugababes?

'Parts of the building date back to the 9th century,' he explains, attempting to illuminate the timeline he inhabits for the visitors. Above us on one side of the nave are smooth columns and rounded Saxon arches; on the other, octagonal pillars soaring to Gothic arches. On the western wall is a roll-call of the former shepherds of the Lindisfarne flock, starting with St Aidan, followed by the bishops of Lindisfarne, the Benedictine priors, the post-Reformation vicars and ending with Brother Damien.

When Damien qualified as a chartered accountant at the age of 23, his father, a very religious man, said, 'Lay your qualification on the altar of service.' I know what my son would say if I tried that one. Damien was clearly different. From that moment on he found himself increasingly drawn to the church and he took up his Franciscan vows and the celibate life in 1966 at the age of 24.

Damien is still the same man, possessed with a mission to serve and keen to intoxicate others with the godliness of the place. I comment that it must be difficult for the locals to find space in the pews in the peak summer months when they are outnumbered by visitors in the congregation at a ratio of nine to one. 'It is a place', he replies elliptically, 'where salvation can always be found.' Earlier I'd spotted Damien outside the church telling a woman who'd been struggling to tie up her dog, 'Bring him in, bring him in.' Even dogs can enter Damien's gate.

That evening, as I watch a local man collecting winkles and whelks in the primal brightness at the water's edge, church bells break out calling believers, nonbelievers and dogs alike to prayer at St Mary's. I toy with returning but instead follow a track away from the small town.

Tonight the island has a luminosity I can't remember encountering anywhere before: the place simply pulses with life. Man's imprint is clearly visible everywhere, from the cockle-shaped Tudor castle on Beblow Crag to the poetry of the priory ruins and the statue of St Aidan searching the empty sky, brandishing the torch of Christianity. But it is Lindisfarne's natural landscape that simply takes the breath away.

Bathed in a golden light, I walk a straight track past bleating lambs and farm buildings. After a mile, 4ft-tall grasses provide a headdress to the drystone walling. The sun is still high and no shadows are being cast despite the fact that it is now 8 p.m. Purple viper's bugloss and yellow ragwort give way to a carpet of small mauve, pink and purple flowers and flickering butterflies. Arriving at the wildlife haven of the dunes, I notice my trainers are caked in piri-piri burrs. The dunes have been sculpted into peaks and slacks, the tough marram grass providing the glue to the feckless sands and a home to marsh orchids and skylarks. Beyond the sierra of sand lies the rich intertidal zone and a landscape of transcendent beauty: stone platforms, pools, incarnadined rocks, undulating kelp and blinding white sands flanking the bluest of lagoons.

Guillemots beat a path across the sun's furrow while eider ducks frantically slap the water attempting to get airborne. Fifty metres offshore a colony of forty common seals honk, bark and fan their tails. As my sandal loosens the surface scree, stones clatter down the cliff. In concert the entire colony turn as one towards me from the water, a cell of nuns in their wimples.

A 7ft-long bull seal is arched on an outcrop rocking like a paper-weight. The cows – lighter, shorter and speckled – rest, somewhat more demurely, on their own rocks near by.

For an hour I sit on the honeyed rocks, enjoying the aroma of kelp and wild chive and the luminosity of the seascape. Meanwhile the seals track my every move. I am adrift between the high-pitched squawks of terns and the baritone barks of the seals, beneath the cobalt-blue sea and the cobalt-blue sky. A single white cloud provides God's signature. I think back to what Brother Damien had said to me earlier in the church: 'Those who stay overnight on the island have more chance of grasping the ineffable.' There is indeed a numinous quality to the place. A holy place. Holy island.

By 10 p.m. I'm back in the church graveyard staring up with St Aidan at the moon hung high above the dereliction of the priory. The Celtic cross behind his head appears like a halo; his mouth hangs heavy with words as he preaches to the parish of the dead. Once again I hear the familiar eerie hooting of seals, like the sound the wind makes rushing through the priory's gap teeth. I look over a wall to get a view. Offshore lies a tiny island, a discarded shoe thrown into the ocean, on which rests a single wooden cross. Hob's Thrush was where St Cuthbert chose to exile himself before seeking more remoteness on the Farne Islands. Between the cross and the graveyard, three seals lie on their backs honking and barking. The roofs, trees and the horse crossing the field are all silhouettes now, the moon above them shining as brightly as it did on the day it began work with its cohort, the sun.

Sid and I retrace our journey across the causeway at 10.15 the next morning, seven minutes before the tidal curfew. From the A1 I can see the pincer of Guile Point almost touching Holy Island at the southern-most point of the bay. The passenger seat next to me seems to grow in height several inches every day with assorted maps, parking tickets, films for developing, tourist literature and booklets. Fortunately every time I swing round a sharp bend or brake suddenly, the top layer is jettisoned like the calving of eroded coastal cliffs, leaving space for the next batch of new arrivals.

Soon I abandon the A-road for the B1342 coastal route to Bamburgh Castle, which rises on its basalt crag as imperiously as those at Edinburgh or Windsor.

Inside the citadel I discover the usual period furniture, family photographs, gruesome weapons and trinkets left by grateful guests (including a forest of teak donated by the King of Siam that was used to construct the roof of the King's Hall).

The vagaries of fortune provide the predictable contortions of history. The headland was occupied by the 1st century AD before becoming a

Roman garrison and Celtic stronghold. By AD 547 Bamburgh Castle was the royal seat of an Anglo-Saxon king and from the 11th century it served as an impregnable Norman fortress. During its second millennium it continued to see great days but also abandonment. Finally, in the 19th century, it was bought for £60,000 by Lord Armstrong, who then lavished £1.5 million on refurbishing it under the direction of Edwin Lutyens.

The aim of the industrialist and inventor was to create a retreat for his workers. Unfortunately Armstrong died in 1900 before the restoration was completed and, as he had no direct heirs, it passed to a nephew who promptly moved in and changed his surname from Watson to Watson Armstrong so he could also inherit the title of Lord Armstrong. Instead of a castle the workers got a more modest retreat down in the village. There is a picture over a fireplace in one of the castle rooms of an aristocrat playing cards with five aces in his hand – I like to think it is of Watson Armstrong.

The present owner, Lord Armstrong's grandson Francis, didn't inherit the title because he was adopted. Neither does he inhabit the castle, preferring instead to work and live on his nearby farm, Greenhill, with his three children and wife. By all accounts the 37-year-old is a popular, down-to-earth, self-effacing type.

As I stare with the cannon over the parapet along the long blond beach, out of the corner of my eye I notice a group digging at the earth beside the stable block. I lose interest in visiting the castle's Armstrong Museum and instead head their way.

A young woman with short hair and big boots is covering a depression in the ground with a tarpaulin. I ask her what's going on.

'Archeological dig.'

'What are you looking for?'

'Better talk to the project director,' she replies and then screams at the top of her voice, 'Paul! Paul!'

A man dressed all in black with shaved head and colourful beads, raises a hand in acknowledgement and slowly makes his way towards us accompanied by a Rhodesian Ridgeback. His name is Paul Gething, he's from York and I guess he's in his early thirties. Paul informs me that the team working beside the stables are part of a larger ongoing archeological dig. 'There has been a fortress on the site from at least the early 6th century, so there's a lot of history beneath our feet.'

Paul is a founder member of the Bamburgh Research Project, a loose group of like-minded archeologists who give up time to sift the castle grounds. The group first came down in 1996, intrigued initially by a copy of the very first Ordnance Survey Map (dating from around 1860), which indicated a Danish burial ground inside the estate. In 1997 the group started cutting three test pits to the south of the castle and just two hours after starting work, Paul, excavating the lower pit, discovered the first 7th- century cist (box-shaped burial chamber). Over subsequent summer digs several more Saxon graves have been uncovered.

Paul tells me that there are three groups working today and he offers to escort me to the burial site to the south. He believes that in early Saxon times Bamburgh's impregnable stronghold was twinned with a summer royal residence at Yeavering, fifteen miles inland. The fort was established before Lindisfarne was settled and the skeletons that have been found date from the pivotal period spanning from the late 5th century up until the late 7th century. The Ordnance Survey got it partially right: it was a burial ground, but Saxon not Danish.

Jake the Ridgeback barks at something invisible – perhaps a ghost unsettled by the digging. Paul pats the brute's head absently and continues. 'One of the skeletons is of a large-muscled, powerful individual, aged around forty. From his frame we're guessing he's from aristocratic stock. What we do know for sure is that he came from Iona, like King Oswald and St Aidan. Radio carbon dating places the date of his death at around 630, perfect for Oswald's return to Bamburgh.'

King Oswald was born in AD 605 and probably, according to the scholars, at Yeavering. In his mid-childhood an invading army forced him to flee to Scotland, where he was converted to Christianity. When he finally returned to Northumbria, he sent for St Aidan, who set up a mission on Lindisfarne close to Oswald's Royal Court at Bamburgh.

I don't know if my jaw dropped but I do remember a rush of adrenaline. Was Paul suggesting his skeleton was a member of Oswald's entourage? That he might even be Oswald or St Aidan himself?

Jake the Ridgeback barks again, derailing my train of thought and this time managing to distract Paul into a diversion. 'Ridgebacks were trained to hunt lions but you don't get many here.'

We cross a stile and discover a group of students – mostly young women from five different countries – sitting or squatting round a cist containing a recently excavated skeleton. The group is being instructed in the correct procedure for listing and categorising bones. I cannot quite believe what I'm seeing: on the proscenium at Bamburgh are scattered the corpses from some Greek tragedy (only these are 7th-century Saxon). There are four skeletons in all, lying in shallow graves. Two who died in their teenage years lie in identical repose, one leg resting lazily over the other, their heads turned to the side as if burrowing into down pillows in blissful sleep. The only difference between these juveniles and their living counterparts is the lack of flesh, and absence of blood and air coursing through their bodies. Two full sets of teeth grin gruesomely at the students flanking the northern bank of the grave.

Near by other students are kneeling and scraping with teaspoons, delicately manoeuvring leaf trowels or sweeping dust away with fine paint brushes. Two of the skeletons being revealed are female. One had been carrying a flint and shell for fire, and the other had in her possession a primitive set of keys and a bone comb. I chat with several of the students about the significance of their find. Everyone appears infuriatingly nonchalant. They have been living with the dead too long.

One of the living is a very attractive woman in her twenties. She has red highlights in her hair and is wearing a skimpy brown top and matching tight brown trousers. She looks more model than archeologist. Paul catches me ogling. 'That's Tin. She's been coming for the summer digs for the past couple of years – she works in the movie industry in Hollywood.' I subsequently discover that the lovely Tin and the jammy Phil Wood, the project's director of postexcavations, are now an item. Racy things, these archeological digs.

Boyfriend Phil fortunately misses my covetous eyes as he's distracted, taking measurements of the exact positions of the skeletons so they can be returned to the graves and buried after analysis in Durham. Paul informs me that the cist graves were far more prevalent among the British Celts than among Anglo-Saxon graves. 'This leads me to believe they just might be the Christianising link with the Romans – Roman artifacts have also been found on site – before the arrival of the English.'

Phil, eavesdropping, interrupts his measurements to argue the toss. He believes the skeletons are more likely to be those of retainers of the Anglo-Saxon court as they are muscular and tall. I prefer Paul's thesis.

Maybe this was where Christianity first started to stick, having slipped in by the back door after being chased out of the country.

Jake, who has been tied to a post, is starting to get on everyone's nerves with his incessant barking. 'Go on, give him a bone,' I suggest heretically. Paul is the only one to laugh; as there are French, Canadians, Taiwanese and Australians among the group, maybe they don't understand the humour . . . Paul is encouraged to remove the dog and he walks with me back to the van.

As I drive south I feel several more shivers down my spine as I rerun my mental video of the painstaking excavation of lives that ended around fourteen hundred years ago. Why did the boys die so young and yet seemingly so peacefully? What killed the women? I am hugely envious of those spending their summer here discovering the bones of history and romance.

From Bamburgh, Sid and I travel south, tracking long, wild, empty sands. Our next stop is at Seahouses, an unattractive town with a rash of chippies and a Londis. Fortunately I'm not here for the town. I'm here to take a boat out to the Farne Islands, where St Aidan spent long periods meditating and St Cuthbert spent his final years in self-imposed exile (and in his protection of the eider ducks there – subsequently known as Cuddy's ducks – founded the world's first nature reserve). The name Farne, unsurprisingly, derives from the Celtic *Fahren* – place of retreat.

The pair of saints wouldn't have lasted a day nowadays on the guano atolls that simply teem with flapping wings. Not unless they were as fearless as the resident National Trust wardens, who don't seem to notice that the nesting terns are crashing into our heads and crapping all over us. Perhaps they think their white-splattered hats and smocks are fashionable tie-dye.

Inner Farne is the breeding colony for thousands of terns who seem to seek chumminess the way we seek space. Eggs sit beside the path, chicks waddle and demented parents viciously attack anyone who goes near them. The noise is deafening. All around us, packed on to the ledges and cliffs, are colonies of puffins, shags, guillemots and kittiwakes. Clearly you have to be a very particular type of person to see living on one of the most important bird sanctuaries on earth as fun. The Arctic and sandwich terns may be the most graceful seabirds in flight, streamlined and Deco-ish, but they are the nastiest bastards on land.

I express the opinion that they are nasty bastards to Alein Shreeve, the 24-year-old head warden who hails from Derbyshire and has spent 24 months on the islands over the past three years. He politely laughs but I know I have just uttered another heresy. Freckled, unshaven (well, who would you shave for?), he is one of five boys – they look too young to be called men – who put up with the most primitive of conditions just so they can be with the birds and the hundreds of seals we have passed on our journey out.

'We get so close to nature here and everything happens so quickly, from nestbuilding, to courtship displays, to learning to fly. It's a privilege watching it all so close up,' Alein enthuses. Around us are nesting shags, roosting puffins and precariously perched ebony razorbills. 'In autumn we get thousands of thrushes and finches. And the storms can be very dramatic. We had a couple of mink whales pass earlier in the season and a pod of eight dolphins a couple of weeks back.'

When the bird breeding is over, in October and November around a thousand grey seal pups are born (approximately half the world's population of its rarest seal breed around the British coast). The calves start life at 28lb and put on 4lb a day, while their mothers shed 9lb feeding them. The sumo-sized bull seals weigh in at around 700lb.

Across on the other side of the island from the Pele Tower where the wardens live is the lighthouse from which the 22-year-old Grace Darling set out with her father in a flat-bottomed lighthouse coble on 7 September 1838 to save the lives of nine survivors of the wrecked steamship *Forfarshore*. The florid Victorian hacks duly made her a heroine: 'Surely, imagination in its loftiest creations never invested the female character with such a degree of fortitude as had been evinced by Miss Grace Horsley Darling on this occasion. Is there in the whole field of history, or of fiction even, one instance of female heroism to compare for one moment with this?'

Grace reaped rich rewards, including a gift of £50 from Queen Victoria. She continued to live on Longstone Light with her parents but when visiting her sister ashore at Bamburgh in April 1842, still only in her mid-twenties, she caught the flu and died.

I overnight at a site on the shoulder of Seahouses. The seashore stages another riotous sunset, the late sun rusting ponds that are tenebrous bird sanctuaries in their own right. Looking northwards, Bamburgh Castle stands as dominant and indomitable as ever. I hope Paul, Phil and Tin have remembered to put a blanket over the Saxon children.

The next morning I continue down the Heritage coastline of long fields and huge skies. Sid gallops with the white caps beneath broken clouds that look like dinner plates thrown across the sky.

I park in Craster car park and take a stroll along the grass headland towards the 14th-century fortress, Dunstanburgh Castle, rounded and smoothed like a pebble in the surf. A gang of cows have made their way down on to the rocky beach seeking a little kelp to supplement the boring grass diet.

At Craster's small harbour an image flashes into my consciousness of a hirsute fisherman in wellies and sea captain's peaked cap, striding out with his sheep dog. I recognise it as the photograph I took last time I was here that appeared alongside an article of mine in the *Daily Telegraph*. A week after publication I received a letter from a lady who asked for a copy of the picture, saying how shocked she'd been to see it. I expected the letter to go on to recount the unravelling of some infidelity but it transpired that this was in fact the very last photograph taken of the old sea captain. He had dropped dead two days later.

Appropriately, the harbour is funereal black, carved out of the same basalt whin sill that provides the dramatic headland settings for the castles at Bamburgh and Dunstanburgh. At L Robson & Sons Ltd, home of the redoubtable Craster kipper, I can hear Eminem's 'Cleaning Out My Closet' playing on the radio. Neil Robson, the owner, is about to ignite several piles of whitewood shavings that will in turn set fire to piles of oak sawdust that will smoke the next batch of kippers. It is the same method, and the same smoking house, used continuously since 1906 by his great-grandfather, his grandfather and then his father. Above the six piles of wooden chips are 120 skewers, each one holding fourteen herrings, and this is the first of three five-hour smokings they'll have before being sold from the shop or by mail order.

I'm disappointed, but hardly surprised, to hear that the herring comes frozen from Iceland. In the mid-1970s there was a complete ban on landing herring from the North Sea, so Neil started getting his catch from Ullapool on Scotland's west coast. Then they banned it there too. He switched to the Clyde but the fleet started using rock-hopping trawlers that churned the sea bed and disturbed the herrings' feed, which resulted in the quality of the catch deteriorating. In the old days trawlers would be out and back the same day landing the catch fresh in the harbour. But now they're out several days with nets that could comfortably contain St Paul's Cathedral. 'The catch is not the best and the fish aren't graded. Which, in a roundabout way, is why I get them frozen from Iceland and transport them up from Grimsby as needed.' Neil smiles the smile of the long-suffering. 'Having said that, I have just had a sample sent down from Scotland by someone who is grading out the larger herring. He sent me 100 kilos and the signs are they're very good. That's the batch I'm smoking now. Then we'll see what they're really like. Hopefully we'll be able to start ordering from Scotland regularly again. Did you know the UK exported 3,410 tons of herring last year and imported 41,000 tons?'

'How many tons do you smoke a year?'

'Three hundred tons.'

'That sounds a huge amount.'

'Last year UK households consumed 5,150 tons of kippers . . . and 21,000 tons of fish fingers!' Neil laughs. Dressed in blue overalls and wellies, he is an open, friendly man with a mop of scruffy hair and smiling eyes. He is also clearly a man who likes statistics as much as he does kippers.

Neil supplies GNER and Waitrose ('They started using us in 1998 and we doubled their kipper sales in a year') but sells just as many over the counter. Jackie Charlton apparently used to pop in while visiting his mum in Ashington. 'And Bobby used to come every summer too in his playing days. He used to fish off the pier.'

I decide an early lunch is in order. Neil points me in the direction of his flamboyant and theatrical mother-in-law Katheline at their adjacent restaurant. I order a terrine of cooked local crab with chargrilled marinated aubergines, peppers, courgette, beef tomato and fresh crab served with a light vinaigrette. Katheline relays the order in Portuguese to two women working in the kitchen.

'Brazilian,' she explains. 'I lived there and like languages. I also used to make wine in France.'

Katheline is considerably younger than her husband and every year drags him off somewhere exotic for two months. 'He loves it,' she says – more for her own reassurance than my information, I feel. I look around the restaurant. The food is as memorable as the views and it strikes me that if Katheline replaced the carpet with fashionable seagrass, got rid of the ugly plastic menus and installed a few blinds and Lloyd Loom chairs, she could well be Northumberland's answer to Rick Stein or at least offer herself as a successor to Jennifer Patterson to Clarissa Dickson Wright.

In Amble a new marina has supplemented the town's regular diet of caravanners with a new, wealthier cordon bleu breed of yachtees splashing money about. Unfortunately one of the biggest attractions from the early 1990s, Freddie the Dolphin, has long departed, leaving the town with a stack of unsold Freddie Biscuits and Freddie T-shirts.

They're clearly big on animals and sentiment in Amble. On a bench in the memorial garden is a plaque that reads: 'Donated by friends and family of Jessie Taylor 1913-1999 recognising a lifelong devotion to the welfare of animals.' On another bench is a commemorative plaque to a Miss Muriel Usher 'Who used to run the chemist shop for so many years.' I ask a woman in the adjacent TIC why Ms Usher is thus remembered and am told, 'Because she was so nice.' Fair enough.

Amble is the only town I've ever visited that's known for 'niceness'. The reputation apparently started with a telegram from a departing liner in 1935. 'Mauretania to Urban Council, Amble, to the last and kindliest port in England, greeting and thanks. Mauretania.'

To the north of Amble, five miles of sandy beach and rocky inlets stretch to Warkworth; to the south, six miles of dune-backed white sands – hauntingly lonely and lovely – stretch in an unbroken crescent round Druridge Bay. The latter marks the end of the AONB that commenced 50km further north at Spittal. Fortunately I still have a few kilometres left to run until the Heritage Coast ends at Cresswell where the hulking towers of Alcan, an aluminium smelter and one of the biggest employers in the area, blots the coastal copy book and signals the start of a grungier, more urban coastline.

Inside the QE II Country Park, I pull in to Woodhorn Colliery, where slagheaps and black air have been Tipp-Exed out and the winding wheels, shafts and lifts that once lowered the Morlocks to their underground hellish kingdom now stand like exhibits in a sculpture park. On the greensward beside the museum stands a bronze statue of a miner and a plaque commemorating the loss of thirteen lives in 1916 during an underground explosion.

It wasn't the worst coalmining tragedy in the area. In 1862, 204 men and children took three days to suffocate when the only shaft in and out of the Hartley Pit became blocked. One-third of the victims were aged eleven to eighteen. But if the accident had happened twenty years earlier the dead would certainly have included five- and six-year-olds, for it wasn't until 1842 that a new law outlawed children under ten working underground (and also limited a shift to a maximum of ten hours). As a result of the disaster, all pits were subsequently required to have two exit shafts.

As the horrors of the Industrial Revolution have become sanitised into heritage wheelchair-friendly museums with pleasant cafés and terraces, it's almost impossible to imagine the grim reality of the life endured by pit communities. At the Woodhorn Colliery, which only closed in 1981 and opened as a museum in 1989, I find myself descending from the heavenly coast of saints to the depths of hell. I stay for just over an hour, unlike the ponies that remained in darkness for up to a dozen years before reemerging to be blinded by the light.

Among the archive material on display is a picture of Jackie Charlton in his pit helmet (his mum Cissie, who died a couple of years ago, provided part of the recorded commentary for the museum). Jackie was trained at Ashington Colliery before moving on to nearby Linton Colliery and hated it so much that he sought any other employment going: the options were the Morpeth police force or Leeds United FC. His more famous brother Bobby never worked the pit but, like Jackie, still sends memorabilia whenever requested for special events in the museum.

On the nearby beach at Newbiggin, where the Charlton boys played, you can still find coal washed up from the undersea seams on the beach. But only one deep pit (with four hundred miners) is still operating in Northumberland and Durham. Ashington continues to be known as the biggest pit village in the world but soon the Ellington colliery workforce will go the way of the others and its pitmen will join the other 8,500 unemployed miners on the Ashington slagheap (the town has some of the highest unemployment figures and indices of deprivation in the country).

What is most miraculous about Ashington is that just as the wild Northumberland coast served as a cradle to Christianity, and the scrapyard of 19th-century industries gave birth to wildlife reserves, so too the hell-hole of the town's mines produced wonderful art, musicians, agriculturalists and major athletes.

In the past century four of Ashington's sons were crowned Footballer of the Year: Jackie Milburn – 'Wor Jackie' – in Ireland playing for Linfield in 1958; Jimmy Adamson for Burnley in 1962; Bobby Charlton for Manchester United in 1966; and Jackie Charlton for Leeds in 1967. Jackie Milburn, the most legendary of the four, worked five years in the Ashington Colliery and for a fair amount of that time played for Newcastle United on a Saturday afternoon before returning to the pit for the night shift. Maybe the fear of a lifetime spent underground spurred these men to dash around like whippets whenever they saw daylight.

Not everyone, of course, can become Footballer of the Year. Many miners found other avenues for their achievements. Ashington regularly hosts the Leek Growing World Championships and one of the photographs on display shows a miner playing a violin to his leeks (like many gardeners, he believed music encourages growth). Iron Man, a pigeon from the North Seaton Colliery next door, won the gold medal at the 1965 Pigeon Olympiad in London. And then there was the Ashington Group, a group of artists also known as the Pitmen Painters, led by Oliver Kilbourn, whose own compelling primitive canvasses depicting the everyday life of the community are on display. The group somehow found the energy to meet after shifts or on Sundays from 1934 until 1984. Only one of its members, Jack Harrison, has not moved permanently underground and he is living out the remainder of his days in a nearby nursing home.

The women had it no easier than the men. A century ago Ashington wives led considerably shorter lives than the national average. Mining families only got to keep their houses as long as men were working down the pits. To bring in a living wage, typically there would be a father and three or four sons working different shifts. The women had to have meals ready for the returning men and be on hand to wash their clothes and clean up after them. They were on call round the clock and like the pit ponies were literally worked to death.

*

Emerging back into daylight, and having made a promise not to moan about anything petty for at least 24 hours, I decide to call it a day and find the nearest campsite. I'm directed to one next to a river on the edge of Ashington. Here I bed Sid down for the night and then stride out seeking life.

Along the riverbank three boys are taking it in turns to swing on a rope over the water. One says something to me that I don't understand and I stride on, ignoring him. He repeats whatever it was he said and as I turn, the words simultaneously compute into, 'Your bag's open.' I swing my rucksack round and indeed find it yawning. Miraculously my camera and other bits have stayed in place. I feel ashamed of my suspicious reaction based purely on unconscious prejudice.

On the opposite bank a mixed gang of eight teenagers are flirting on a huge uprooted tree. One waves. Several people exchange greetings with me as they pass. I head up past fields flanked by cow parsley and rosebay willowherb into a modern estate, which in turn leads into an older estate. For the next twenty minutes, I don't pass a single shop or pub and barely a handful of people. Eventually I come upon the 'Ashington and District Comrades Social Club – The Taste of Tyneside. C.I.U.' and head inside.

No one is behind the desk but a book is open in which members' names have been entered alongside guests and the names of their affiliated clubs or unions. I scribble my name and leave the other columns blank.

Inside the vast main bar, I discover why the streets are empty. I estimate there are around three to four hundred people perched on every available chair. Spread across tables are multiple bingo sheets. A sign at the bar tells customers that we're not to congregate at the counter as space is needed for serving. I pay £1.30 for a pint of Northumberland Smooth and try to strike up conversation with the people at the nearest table.

'What's that for?' I point to something that looks a cross between a pen and Tipp-Ex on the table.

The man nearest me takes a while to locate the accent. 'Jackpots. For marking the housey.' He shows me the numbers he has blanked off from a previous game and then immediately turns away. The women seated with him also look away. My accent is as alienating as Dracula's fangs. I sidle back to the sanctuary of the bar and then remember the sign and end up hovering in no-man's-land. I feel like a giant leek. The women at the table start inclining their heads and whispering. The men steal sidelong glances. Gamely I try another table.

'Do they have bingo every night?'

I should know better than fishing with questions that risk only a 'yes' or 'no'. I need to be the antithesis of Quiz Inquisitor Michael Miles, whose task was to get you to utter those same simple affirmatives and negatives in the shortest possible time. I guess the Ashington and District Comrades Social Club is what is known as a closed shop.

I move into the bar next door where someone is attempting a broadsheet crossword with the barmaid's help. Another couple are playing pool and a fifth solitary male on a stool looks up as I arrive at the bar and order another beer. Again my voice has the same effect as an infectious disease. I swear the man shuffles his stool a good yard from me. I stare at the sign over the bar: 'Rooster Booster – 8 x Smirnoff Vodka. 3 x Red Rooster. Jug £10.' Someone appears at my shoulder to order more drinks and finally I manage a record-breaking conversational sequence.

Me: 'Busy tonight.'

Him: 'Not really.'

Me: 'Is it usually this busy, then?'

Him: 'No, usually quieter.'

Me: 'Friday night I guess.'

Him: 'Be quiet again soon when housey's finished. Then they'll go up the street for more housey.'

And with that my best friend turns his back on me and walks out of my life for ever.

I follow his lead, asking one last customer lurking at the door the way to the nearest chippy. I find it with some difficulty hidden in the middle of an estate. The Kielder Fish & Chip Shop is owned and run by Cypriot Tynesiders. Among the options are chip butty with gravy, curry or peas (£1), bread buns (25p) and made-to-order spam fritters (no price listed). My cod and chips could feed a family for a week. Courageously I manage to polish it off all on my own beside the riverbank.

Inside the weatherboard blue-and-white Watch House of Tyne-mouth Life Brigade and Coastal Rescue (est. 1841), I stare up at two bare-breasted figureheads from the *City of Bristol*, a cloth seductively draped across their nether regions. 'Beautiful women to remind the sailors of what they were missing,' Bill Scott, one of the volunteers, interrupts my fantasy. 'And in between them, that's the Horn of Plenty to remind the sailors of what they weren't getting – plenty of anything!' He laughs expansively before providing the obituary. 'She was wrecked on Battery Point just off the Black Middens.'

Bill points through a thick windowpane to the treacherous wrecking reef where the incident took place. 'It were much more dangerous before the piers were built at the mouth of the Tyne at the end of the 19th century.'

Bill, dressed in blue jeans and a pale blue shirt, looks to be in his early sixties but is in fact 74. He has a stubbled grey beard and the thickest of Tyneside accents. I compliment him on his tan. 'That's not from abroad. That's from standing upstairs with the bloody window open on watch.' He is a small man with a low centre of gravity, a man built to balance in a storm at sea.

Bill shifts my attention to the Stanley Bell, hanging from a rafter. 'Belonged to a passenger steamer heading from Aberdeen for London that was wrecked in a storm along with the schooner *Friendship* on 24 November 1864.

Thirty-two died on the Black Middens that night, including a party of female opera singers bound for Covent Garden. And two lifeboat men were killed too when their lifeboat, *Constance*, was pitched over the Stanley and on to the schooner.'

Bill shakes his head. He has had a lifetime's practice.

After the Stanley went down, the first trained Coastal Rescue station in the country was established at Tynemouth and a hundred men immediately volunteered for service.

I ask Bill about another object on display, which looks like a baby bouncer. 'Breeches Buoy – that's what was used right round the country. Before that, they used the Mamby Mortar.'

'What's a Mamby Mortar?'

'A cannonball with a hook on it and rope attached that they shot from a cannon over the ship.'

'What if they hit it?'

'Too bloody bad.' Bill cups his ear and leans forward for effect in a simulated rescue. 'The volunteers'd listen to the shoutin' and hollerin' from the crew an' if they were bloody Cantonese, Greek or Hindustani, our men would take out the instructions in their language written on a bloody block and winch it over so the crew knew what to do. But after the Stanley, all the men were trained to use the Breeches Buoy.'

Bill has served twenty years as a volunteer. Before that he spent forty years as a watchkeeper in the merchant navy. 'Twenty-two years of it in Australia on boats and a year manning the lighthouse up at Booby Island in the Torres Strait. Saved a toddler's life once too out there on the Bass Trader ferry to Tasmania. We was coming into port and the skipper, Mr McCallam, was waving down to his wife and she let go her toddler's hand to wave back at him. The kid just stepped off the quay and went down as the boat was coming in. I jumped in and bloody grazed all me side on the quay and ended up in hospital. Went under three times before I found little Alistair. Mr and Mrs McCallam sent me Christmas cards every year until seven year back, when they stopped for some reason. I got the ship's bell as a thank-you with "To William Scott for Bravery" engraved on it.'

Back in Tynemouth life has been quieter for Bill, apart from the occasional rescue. 'Been home now twenty years just sittin' here and gain' up to the club. Tynemouth Social Club, £1.20 a pint. Can't beat it.'

I ask how many other volunteers take their turns manning the upstairs lookout.

'Sixteen plus maybe another fifty of us old buggers. But we're not active. We just look. Young man's game.' As Bill leads the way upstairs, I ask him about the rescues he's been involved in.

'Funniest one didn't involve a ship. The man were right round the bend, though. Took all his clothes off and was standing on the cliffs out there.' Bill points through the window to people sunning themselves on cliff-edge benches. 'Said he was gonna jump.'

Bill switches voice for dramatic effect and hops about from one foot to the other. ' "I'm ganna do it . . . I'm ganna do it." He was yellin' his head off. I started talking to him, asking why he wanted to jump. He grabbed hold of me hand and wouldn't let go. A policewoman grabbed hold of me belt. It was a tug of war. "I'm takin' you too, I'm takin you with me," he was screamin' and yellin'. He stank of drink.

"Have you had a drink?" I asked him.

"Might have."

"Why not come down me club, man? It's cheaper."

"How much cheaper?"

"£1.20."

"All right then."

'And that was it. He let go of me and the ambulances came in and took him away.'

On our way back downstairs, Bill shows me a full-size snooker table. 'A hundred and twenty years old, that is. Nearly as old as me. We play it all the time when there's nothing happening.'

'Couldn't you miss something – like a shipwreck – leant over the table all day,' I ask provocatively.

'Oh bugger the boats. I've swallowed enough sea. I want peace. I've done me whack.'

I leave through the back door, skirting a monumental statue of Lord Collingwood, Nelson's second-in-command who, according to Bill, 'Did all the fighting and got none of the credit.' In my opinion it should be Bill up there.

As I return to Sid, I pass three men with identical Zapata moustaches accompanied by three children aged four to six all dressed in identical Newcastle United tops.

Tynemouth is an elegant, expansive resort with long, sweeping sands. And over recent years it appears to have had something of a makeover. Smart Victorian railings and bollards, reinstalled old-fashioned lamp posts and new seafront walkways will be the rule rather than the exception as I continue down the eastern seaboard. New money is clearly filtering through from Europe and the lottery targeted for regeneration. Hopefully it is being used for more than titillation.

My journey through North Shields to the tunnel under the Tyne is along a greenish corridor that similarly appears to have had plenty of dosh lavished on it from the evidence of the cycleways and the slew of smart new roads and retail parks. In Seaham I find more new Victorian lamp posts and railings, as well as a sprinkling of the red-and-white-striped football shirts of Sunderland in among the more dominant black-and-white forest of Newcastle United.

I skip Sunderland (it looks pleasant enough) and Hartlepool (a tall ship in the historic port is not a big-enough incentive to stop) and pass a fiery furnace of flames, smoke and steam on the northern bank of the Tees where the whole of England's industry appears to have relocated after the rest of the country got fed up with it. Seeking more big open skies, I similarly put my foot down through Middlesbrough. Making a journey and writing a book, you can sometimes feel driven rather than driving. Not today. I am whipping through like an American tourist seeing Europe in three days. Somewhere on my journey I passed into and out of the County of Durham. Whoops.

I get a takeaway curry in Marske-by-the-Sea (not a highlight) and park for the night on a brow overlooking the beach with views all the way to the towering sandstone Huncliffe Headland beyond Saltburn-by-the-Sea. In the opposite direction, beyond Redcar, the fabulous inferno continues burning along the banks of the Tees (there is a point when industrial ugliness becomes sublime: the fantastical compositions on the Teeside skyline tonight are such a point). Down on the beach the late sun is mixing familiarly with the sea that stayed late and got left behind in pools. House lights start to sparkle in Marske-by-the-Sea and a fat moon rises over them like an air balloon.

As I drift off to sleep, I hear the crunch of rubber on gravel as a car pulls up. I peer out of the window from my bed and spot the occupants already relocated to the back seat going hammer and tongs in the age-old Saturday night ritual of car sex. Heavenly visions. Around 3 a.m. I'm woken by the sound of other cars racing along the straight coast road behind me. A little later a beery crew spill out from their charabanc and litter the car park with their good mood and laughter before taking a communal pee and bundling back into the car with the stereo still pounding.

By morning the stereos and squealing rubber have been replaced by the keening of gulls. I slip on my shorts and sandals and am walking the beach by 7.15 a.m. beneath a swirl of terns on a feeding frenzy above a fish-rich channel. A man, his toddler and two mongrels appear on the beach. As the boy waddles I feel a pang of loss. Where did my little ones go so fast? The sea is already nibbling at his footprints and rivulets in the cracked wet sands are streaming seaward.

I get back behind the wheel and Sid and I sing along to John Martyn's *London Conversation*.

Saltburn-by-the-Sea is a well-maintained resort with most of its character located round the railway station (where the bakery, butcher and Barbour Traditional Outfitters are camped) and on the clifftop promenade, which is decorated by a requisitioned coble bursting with pretty flowers. People sit at benches reading the Sunday papers and sipping from cartons of fresh coffee. Beyond them a man in a hard hat is whistling as he slowly works his way up the steep incline of a hydraulic lift, squirting oil into cable rollers as he goes. His name is Ken Fellows and he's been the lift engineer for sixteen years. 'Do it every morning before the first passenger takes a ride,' Ken informs me.

'Scarborough's is older, but they switched to electric. Ours was installed in 1884 to ferry visitors down to the pier and beach and it's the oldest in the country still operating on hydraulic power. Since we had the new roof put on the hut and replaced the rickety wooden fence, it looks better than ever.' A proud man. The lift, like the stubbed pier below, has been the recent recipient of lottery money.

From the A174 coast road, I take an unmarked road through a plunging valley and stop to ask a large woman taking a dog and a pony for a walk if I'm on the right road for Skinningrove. 'This is Skinningrove, luv,' she replies. I park in the only available space, just before a bridge fording an iron-rusted stream. Beyond it there's a scatter of lobster pots and a herd of tractors waiting to drag Yorkshire fishing cobles in or out of the sea. The village consists of a sea-facing terrace of pebbledash and net curtains, flanked by a couple of more modern brick terraces. And that's it; a working town by the sea, rather than a resort.

Up among the colourful allotments and pigeon lofts on the hill, I chat with a father-and-son team sorting out pigeon feed.

'Had a big race yesterday,' the crop-headed, unshaven father informs me. 'Real good 'un, except our birds were rubbish. Dodgy chocks over France.' Mike Prokopowicz catches my quizzical expression and provides elucidation for the foreigner.

'Bad chocks can be down to a change in the weather – it definitely is different these days. Or it might be that the birds get liberated different, in two lots rather than staggered in groups. Whatever the reason, our birds did bad. The best came in five minutes after the winner – on a short 126-mile race that's a long way. Sometimes we race all the way from Bourges in France – 540 miles. Ours keep coming back messed up. Bad chocks.'

After 25 years as a security guard at British Steel, Mike is enjoying retirement with his birds. His son Lee recently lost his job with the same employer (though by this time British Steel was known as Corus). He originally trained as a slaughterman but found there was no call when slaughter became automated.

Having failed to spot a single shop on my way through town, I ask if there's anywhere I can buy milk.

'No shops really. Well, just Sheila's at the old post office. And there's one pub – Tim's Coffee House. We had a working club but that closed.'

I leave Mike and Lee to their pigeon pep talk after their charges' dismal weekend display, and follow a signpost pointing almost vertically up the cliff. 'Cleveland Way. Staithes 5m.' I don't go all the way but I do walk for an hour. Tall grasses dotted with thistle and cow parsley rustle in the breeze, the sun beats down, cabbage whites flitter and a kestrel hovers. Inland, the North York Moors National Park broods. A little bit of heaven in Yorkshire.

The views are similarly pretty dreamy as I resume my journey south-wards through rolling cereal fields, pine forests and a blaze of purple moorland heather. My next brief detour is for coffee in the headland garden of the Cliffemount Hotel overlooking Runswick Bay, where I also make a phone call to Rex Greenwood before I continue into Whitby.

When I first met Rex on a visit to the town almost a decade earlier, he was struggling with a coffin on the 98th step of the 199 that lead up to St Mary's Church. He had slicked-back hair, outsized protruding fangs, and was dressed in a generous cape. Pausing, Rex and his band of Japanese tourist pallbearers stared out over the town that stretches up both flanks from the harbour. Once sufficiently rested, Rex summoned up a spooky voice to tell his group of visitors, 'It was in the churchyard of St Mary's that Dracula tucked into Lucy, after the Russian schooner the *Demeter* ran aground on East Cliff. The dead body of the captain still stood at the helm, his hands and a crucifix lashed to the wheel, a huge black dog leaped from the ship into the night . . . Count Dracula of Transylvania had arrived in Whitby.'

Later that day I discovered Rex in a café poring over a book. I introduced myself and mentioned I'd spotted him earlier with the

Japanese tourists. 'Ah yes. That was fun,' Rex smiled. Thankfully he had removed his fangs. Apparently the tour was based on three of the chapters from the Bram Stoker novel that were set in Whitby. But Rex didn't always do Dracula. Sometimes he wore a powdered wig and transferred himself into Captain Cook, who served his apprenticeship as a young merchant seaman in Whitby. Now, however, Ray was poring over a book by Dylan Thomas, preparing an evening's entertainment for the town councillors. 'I think Dylan Thomas' "Welsh Vampire" might be appropriate. What do you think? Do you know the one?' I shook my head.

> 'Councillors' jugulars suck I with glee
> Oh! Oh! For the taste of a scrumptious JP
> Tremble ye alderman!
> Town clerk beware!
> As I hoover the veins
> Of your succulent mayor.'

That first encounter with Rex had taken place eight years earlier. Today, when I get through on the phone, Rex fortunately remembers our meeting (probably because I subsequently wrote about it). He immediately invites me over despite the fact he's just got out of hospital.

I follow Rex's directions and when I get to where I think his home must roughly be, park and walk thirty yards along an avenue. Beyond a hedge Rex stands waiting for me in his Captain Cook hat. He looks considerably frailer than the last time we met. Rex shakes my hand and leads me through the gate, simultaneously apologising for his unshaven state. 'Just had another cancer lump out,' he explains, pulling the top of his V-neck sweater down to reveal a zipper of metal staples across his left thorax. 'Twenty years they've been chopping bits of cancer out. It's a surprise there's anything left.' He smiles cheerily and pulls up a chair for me in the shaded lee of the house, simultaneously explaining, 'The surgeon told me to keep out of the sun at the moment.'

In front of Rex on a table are two neatly cut ham sandwiches and a mug of tea. Rex's wife appears with a mug for me and some biscuits and Rex switches from cancer to a happier subject. 'Since you were last here, I've taken Dracula to America and Madeira. Very popular.'

In preparation for my visit, Rex has assembled some photographs from the trip. One is of a couple of American Goths posing with him. 'They loved me. Said I was The Boss.'

Rex claims to have first played Dracula at the age of nine, after seeing Bela Lugosi perform on stage in Barnsley. In his adult years, having spent the day earning his living working winding gear in the Boulby potash pit, occasionally in the evenings or at weekends he'd don his cape and fangs and do a performance for charity. It was during this period that he added Captain Cook and the Town Crier to his repertoire.

Since retiring from the pit, his thespian leanings have been given free rein but he still refuses to take a penny for his performances. When I last visited Rex, he used to park his car in the street and keep his coffin in the garage ('At least my children won't have to splash out on one when I pop my clogs'). In the intervening years he'd moved homes and he now keeps the props, all his cuttings, and letters from round the world up in the attic. 'Nothing's really changed, though. I still use the same fangs as I did at seventeen!'

Slowly he leads me up into the loft, which has a tidy disorder to it and is stiflingly hot. I sit on the coffin while Rex pads round the carpeted coop, sweating. Alongside his various outfits there are photo albums, cuttings and letters. One is from a girl in Transylvania who used to write regularly to Rex until her father discovered a letter from Dracula and stopped her. 'She said she was fascinated by the cruelty. Some of them go a bit over the top. I had a Canadian who had his teeth taken out and fangs put in and he told me he was going to kill a cow and drink its blood. He did too.'

I can see Rex is tiring and so move on into town. From the new bridge I look out along the estuary. Whitby is drenched in sunshine and heaving. Above the moored boats stands the squat tower of St Mary's, which in turn is overlooked by the skeletal beauty of the Abbey ruins on East Cliff. On the opposite bank the Kyber Pass winds up the hill past a line of guesthouses to the Captain Cook monument and the Whalebone Arch (which recalls the town's former preeminence as a whaling port – a local skipper, Captain William Scoresby, caught 533 whales out of Whitby and also invented the 'crow's nest').

Down in the harbour fishermen are unloading their catch as a bell clangs, warning that the swing bridge connecting the two sides of town is about to be lifted for a departing Scandinavian freighter. On my last visit the local newspaper ran a story about a sixty-year-old woman living on West Cliff who that week had crossed the river to East Cliff for the very first time in her life.

The long, arching beach is as packed as the town. Naturally I head for the water. As I swim and splash about, an aquatic neighbour informs me that it is the hottest day of the year so far. He also tells me that Whitby is one of the few English resorts where you can see the sun both rising and setting over the sea. A marine anorak.

I make my way up to St Mary's, a church as eccentric as Rex himself. The stained glass of the 12th-century chancery, the Elizabethan communion table and pre-Reformation altar are impressive but the pièce de résistance is the triple-tiered pulpit, complete with ear trumpets and rubber tubes installed by a 19th-century vicar determined that his deaf wife, sitting beneath him, should hear every word of his sermon. He may well have also been responsible for the alignment of the family box pews built from shipwrecks (and some still displaying Jacobean graffiti), which face the pulpit rather than the altar.

On my way back to Sid, I swing past the railway station from which Dracula left on the 9.30 goods train to London in one of fifty boxes of common earth he'd brought with him from Transylvania. It reminds me of Rex's parting shot today. 'I'll be alive in another hundred years, me. I'm Dracula!'

Just five miles from Whitby, I pull into Robin Hood's Bay and park next to the village hall. Adjacent to the car park, bowling club members (eschewing whites for civvies) are out playing the game the northern crown green way: checking that the coast is clear and no rogue balls likely to impede progress from the flanks, they aim their balls corner to corner, diagonally across the green. The fundamental differences between crown green and flat green bowling seem to me to encapsulate the North-South divide. Southerners like to keep to orderly, space-efficient polite lanes and wear the club whites and tie; northerners congregate socially in whatever they're wearing and if there's a barney with the balls in the middle, all the better.

Robin Hood Old Bay, Grade II-listed from top to bottom, is to Yorkshire what Clovelly is to Devon but not so self-consciously prissy and you don't have to pay for the privilege of walking through it. The pretty pantiled stone homes, clinging like limpets to the hillside, may be every amateur watercolourist's dream but in the old town you can buy Indian waistcoats or kid's fishing nets and eat at seafood stalls or bistros. Alongside the tea rooms, guesthouses and rampaging flower boxes, a couple of abandoned, padlocked shops still even display plastic goods from the seventies in the windows as if the owners suddenly had to flee impending disaster. Maybe it was the influx of second homers they simply couldn't take any more.

Inside the local history museum, I find volunteer June Hunter battling with a bluebottle that won't vacate the premises. She tells me that the number of homes occupied by someone born and bred in the old town can be counted on one hand. She herself has been resident for forty years. June paints the usual modern coastal evolutionary migrant picture.

'When I first came we could buy shoes or get them repaired, go to the hairdresser's and shop at the grocer's, butcher's and baker's. Now all the shops are for the tourists.'

The first display that grabs my attention is of jumpers. Next door to the museum stands a mortuary that has provided plenty of redundant clothing over the years. When a fisherman was washed ashore in the past, you could often tell where he was from just from his jersey, or 'gansey'. The ones made in Robin Hood's Bay were knitted in the round on five double-pointed needles . . . seamless. Each port had its own distinctive pattern.

Another exhibit charts the town's long history in the import of human urine from London – which, mixed with the alum shales from the Cleveland escarpment, produced aluminium sulphate to be used in the fixing of textile dyes. Apparently the people of Robin Hood's Bay simply could not provide enough urine of their own. I imagine the relish with which London football crowds would embrace the tale as the basis of some new pissing-on-them slur for visiting fans from the North to supplement the perennial favourite: 'In your Liverpool/Manchester/Newcastle slums . . . In your Liverpool/Manchester/Newcastle slums . . . You look in the dustbin for something to eat . . . You find a dead cat and you think it's a treat . . . In your Liverpool/Manchester/Newcastle slums.'

Most of the urine-heavy boats pulled into the more substantial and protected harbour of Whitby rather than risking an accident in Robin Hood's Bay. Another tale recounts how in January 1881 the Whitby lifeboat was called to assist a brig, *The Visitor*, after it ran aground in Robin Hood's Bay. The storm was so severe that the brig could not get round the headland and so it was dragged six miles through 7ft snow-drifts on a road rising 500ft. Two hundred men cleared the way ahead and eighteen horses heaved the towlines. Meanwhile, men from Robin Hood's Bay were clearing the route from the other direction. The lifeboat arrived two hours after leaving Whitby and the entire crew was saved.

Today, thankfully, there is no snow and no angry seas. The crowd that has congregated outside the Bay Hotel are enjoying the sunshine, eating their fish and chips and watching waves crash up the jetty. A man in a kilt is berating a group of southerners for living in the wrong part of England. 'Yorkshire is God's country,' he tells them but doesn't explain the kilt and the accent from considerably further north. Above him on the wall of the Wainwright Bar is a plaque commemorating the end of the Coast to Coast Walk that started in Cumbria at St Bees 192 miles away. There's also a sign pointing coastal walkers south along the cliffs of the Cleveland Way. I make a mental note to do one or the other sometime soon.

From Robin Hood's Bay I briefly cross the blaze of purple heather in the moorland national park. My campsite is one of the best yet, the merci-fully small Lowfield Campsite, nestling in rolling forested hills a short walk from the coast. Paul, the helpful site owner, shows me a map of the area on the reception wall and plots me a 'perfect route for a perfect evening'. He assures me the outward stroll along a forest stream will take just twenty minutes. Once I reach the sea, I am instructed to stop for a couple of pints in the pub (apparently the only building there) and return along the disused railway cinder track. It does indeed sound perfect.

I set out on my walk about 7 p.m., waving to a couple sitting outside a small shed in the middle of a field, before disappearing into a forest. Cooing pigeons lead the way and I wonder if they might be some stragglers from Mike and Lee Prokopowicz's brood, dazed and confused from more bad chocks.

I never do make it to the pub. The dark forested trail by the tumbling beck is enchanting and, stupidly, I take no notice of my route because I expect to be coming back a different way. The stream leads me to a waterfall cascading into a freshwater pool on the boulder-scattered shore.

There is no pub. I retrace my steps half a mile and find a waymarked trail leading off that takes me into the National Trust's Hayburn Wyke. Still no pub. Burrowing back into the woods, I find tracks leading off in every direction. I spend two more hours trying to find my way out and am just about ready to bed down for the night as it has grown dark and continuing could be dangerous, when I recognise a high track above another stream. When I finally get back to the campsite, Sid is strumming his fingers and looking like thunder.

The contrast between the sylvan wilderness of the evening walk and the worker-drones tailgating into Scarborough the next morning could not be more marked. It provides me with plenty of time to look around as I sit in traffic. The sign proclaiming 'Britain's First Resort' recalls the discovery of natural springs in 1626 by a Mrs Farrow who proclaimed the waters a 'most Sovereign remedy against Hypondriack, Melancholly and Windiness'. She then got a little carried away, also claiming it 'cleanses the stomach, opens the lungs, cures asthma and scurvy, purifies the blood, cures jaunders, both yellow and black, and the Leprosie'. Understandably the quiet ancient borough was inundated and Scarborough indeed became Britain's very first planned resort.

The approach, alongside mature trees, parks and lawns, is through classic Georgian and Victorian resort hinterland. The high street, on the other hand, is the usual 21st-century wallpaper of M&S, Next and other ubiquitous stores. I try to keep my eyes fixed above the bland shop fronts on the medley of bowed Victorians, leaded and half-timber mock-Tudor, and assorted Georgian upper stories. A tide of shoppers washes up and down the tipping street. I slip off the main drag into the Victorian Market Hall. In the upstairs gallery there are four butchers, a fish shop and a greengrocer's. Down in the Vaults things are more interesting. One shop sells solely tin boxes and another only stamps. There's a herbalist, a jeweller's, second-hand clothes and fine art. Best of all, however, is the shop selling collectible toys, the owner of which left college three years back, raided his bedroom of all the toys he'd amassed since he became a collector at the age of eight, and opened his market store.

With cropped hair and long, pointy sideburns, Daks sits behind his desk relishing telling me where he bought his first Action Man and the History of the Human Fly, Power Rangers, X-Men, Buffy, Six Million Dollar Man, Captain Scarlet and the Legendary Zoids. He pays £30 a week rent for his base and just about makes ends meet. Like Sam next door, who sells second-hand clothes, he bemoans the lack of shoppers. It is indeed hard to understand how the high street can be teeming with consumers stocking up on pap while only a handful rattle round in the market.

Descending Eastborough I can see that Scarborough, like many of the northern coastal towns, has been pulling itself up by the lottery or European financial bootstraps: there's the ubiquitous retro Victorian bollards and lamp posts, far more trendy cafés than when I last visited, and even a couple of decent small hotels. Fortunately the town also still retains its tattoo parlours, angling supplies and shops offering fifteen sticks of rock for £1.

From the harbour jetty the *Hispaniola* (replica *Golden Hind*) is taking punters out and the *Grand Turk Pirate Ship* is preparing to do the same. Stretching along the front is a line of amusement arcades faced by a gauntlet of cockle and crab stalls. Where the foreshore ends Roy Orbison's 'Pretty Woman' plays to visitors queuing for dinner-plate-sized Yorkshire puddings filled with gravy.

On the deep cuticle of beach, holiday-makers are disappearing in a fine mist as the wet sand is steam-dried by the sun. A man suddenly emerges from behind the mist curtain chasing a tennis ball. He trips and falls. I can hear his children roaring with laughter as darkly as ghosts from behind the veil.

In these lazy, hazy days, few bother walking the kilometre round the bay to the five leaded cupolas of the Victorian Spa beneath which the Spa Orchestra is playing to an audience of mostly empty candy-striped deckchairs. Those humans still breathing tap fingers on the wooden armrests. There is no chance of miraculous resurrections from the spa water today for the dead, poorly and infirm. By the time the Brontë sisters took the waters here in 1849 (Anne subsequently died and was buried inside St Mary's church), the fashion was already on the wane. It has waned ever since, except in smart country hotels.

A little way out of town, I pass a sweep of white beach at Cayton Bay and beyond it a sign welcomes me to the East Riding of Yorkshire. I immediately quit the busy A165 for the largely ignored coastal B1229 that takes me to the RSPB Bempton Cliffs Nature Reserve.

The sandstone is now behind me and for the next three-and-a-half miles around Flamborough Head, the coastal path skirts 400ft blinding-white sheer chalk cliffs. Two hundred thousand seabirds breed on the white duvet of the Yorkshire Wold over the summer months. Razorbills and kittiwakes are making one hell of a din today as the path through the reserve finally leads me out on to the cliffs. My binoculars fail to spot one of the peregrines that are regularly seen here hunting for feral pigeons. I am equally unsuccessful clocking one of the cliff-dwelling foxes that scavenge for eggs, chicks and dead seabirds. The puffins too are invisible, playing at hermits in their caves. But it really doesn't matter: guillemots comically face inwards on ledges as if scared of heights; fulmars glide imperiously overhead; England's only mainland nesting gannets plummet into the sea as if shot; and a gang of kittiwakes loaf on the waves, shooting the breeze.

Seabirds are to England what big game is to the African bush. Our reserves are our most significant contribution to biodiversity and nowhere else on earth – apart from the Pacific Northwest and New Zealand – can match the volume and richness of our breeding seabird population. At the TIC I ask one of the volunteers, Tony Mayman, what it is about Bempton Cliff Nature Reserve that makes him want to spend all his free time out here.

'I work as a technician in an oil refinery in Hull. That means twelve-hour shifts and it's very hot at the moment in a factory, I can tell you. Coming to Bempton is stepping off that planet.'

A couple of miles down the road, I park Sid next to the new lighthouse at Flamborough Head and stroll across the SSSI. It's early evening and the headland is bathed in sunshine. I follow a path due east along a grass carpet patterned with clover and bird's-foot trefoil. In adjacent fields cattle graze and wheat ripens; out at sea I can hear a plangent bell tolling as if from a drowned church. Eventually the concertina folds of the northwesterly facing cliffs come into view. Smooth white Cappadocian caves ring with squawking kittiwakes; stub-winged razorbills pump like crazy to keep above the swirling waves; and puffins stand around in DJs beside pillars and arches like guests at a ball.

As day thickens to night and I bed down in the car park ('No overnight parking') the sea continues a mantra that has been my constant companion for seven weeks now.

The next morning, the mood is buoyant inside the van as Sid and I sing along to JJ Cale's *Troubadour*. All the music I've brought with me on my journey has been selected for driving or to complement moods or to shift them. Miles Davis covers all these categories; JJ Cale is for driving, like Van Morrison, Vincent Gallo and The Pogues; The White Stripes, Gillian Walsh and Albert King are for campsites.

By the time we reach the end of the album, we're in Bridlington, where my senses are assaulted by what is euphemistically called 'an old-fashioned seaside resort'. Never having visited before, I had built up an image of a more sedate version of Scarborough. In fact, it's the other way round and there is no relief to be had from the grotty shops, grotty front, grotty everything. Thankfully a kind of apartheid operates in Bridlington: everything worth seeing is corralled into a few streets out in the old wool town (originally called Burlington), and all the grot (apart from the impressive beaches sweeping a mile either side of the quay) spills itself across the main resort where gangs of youth with plastic hammers vie for territory with crazed motorised wheelchair owners.

The most impressive feat I witness in Grotsville is an eighteen- or nineteen-year-old male ordering the £3.50 Pint of Seven-Flavour Ice Cream with Syrup, Chocolate, Rainbow Dips, Nuts, Chocolate Wafer, Flake and Fresh Cream and polishing the whole lot off without assistance.

I don't like Bridlington and am glad to get the hell out of it. The Old Town, one mile from its messy sprawl, is altogether different, however. Its Georgian terraced high street is occupied by a sewing machine repairer, a cobbler, a butcher and a string of pubs and restaurants. There are leaded windows, fancy door knockers, prettily painted lintels and bulging bays. In short, it's what all good resorts could do with for when you tire of beach – a quiet shaded corner to wander into and take tea in. I take mine at the Georgian Rooms, where tea is served in fine china cups and a whole pot costs just 80p. I forgo the £2.50 banana split for a fine scone, raspberry jam and a huge dollop of whipped cream for £1.10.

*

Fortified, I hit the road once more. At Lissett I slip on to the B1242, which takes me as close to the Holderness coast as I can get without resorting to my feet. More than thirty villages have been lost since Roman times along this coast that you settle at your peril (it has the dubious distinction of being Europe's most rapidly eroding coastline).

Dylan's *New Morning* accompanies me as the empty road cuts through gaping country and whispering fields of salaaming wheat. I meet five tractors and probably not many more cars.

On the Holderness coast there is a feeling of having slipped off the map. Entering Aldbrough I follow a road until it staggers drunkenly off the cliffs. A few cottages back from the severed tarmac, in the front garden of number 347, a white-haired lady is mowing her lawn, seemingly oblivious to her fate. I can't help asking if she's worried about disappearing over the edge one night.

'Not at my age. *I'll* be disappearing soon enough anyway,' she replies cheerily.

The next house to be called by the Great Bingo Caller in the Sky will be number 343 (does that mean 341 has already gone?). The cane shutters are down, shielding eyes from the inevitable.

To compound the nightmare, where the road vanishes a sign warns, 'Unexploded ordnance on this beach beyond this point. It may explode and kill you. MOD.' The sea washes up unexploded shells as well as an occasional body from submerged churchyards. Once discovered, the shells have to be cordoned off and then exploded, and the bodies have to be reinterred. Neither is conducive to a stress-free retirement stroll with the pooch along the beach.

The cottage owners at the edge of the world have created pretty gardens and kept their picket fences freshly painted and hedgerows trim in classic denial. Gingerly I peer over the severed cliff edge to see a recent raw landslip. I count out the paces from number 343. Twenty. I think I'd start packing.

On the shoulder of Easington, I park beside another road that vanishes into thin air. Standing on the tongue of tarmac is a man in his twenties dressed in an England football shirt, shorts and sockless trainers. He is staring out to sea and behind him is a wicker basket, which I initially assume is a picnic hamper he is waiting to share with friends. Instead of quiche and pigeon pie, however, inside Jason Yeoman's wicker hamper there are live juvenile pigeons and they're here with their L-plates on to see if they can find their way back to their loft in Hull.

Jason tells me that it's quite common to lose a couple of the brood on early training flights. Probably those chocks again. Tonight he is planning to open the basket at five past five. It is now two minutes to.

'Why five past?' I ask.

'Give 'em time to get their bearings.'

I decide to give up on that one and switch to training methods – what sort of pigeons are used, where he gets them, that sort of thing. The answers are equally vague.

'All sorts of pigeon. Buy them from all sorts, all over. Just let 'em go and 'ope they come back.'

Eventually Jason's minute hand reaches five past and he slips behind the basket and loosens the wooden pegs. With a flourish he whips back the lid and, abracadabra, twenty pigeons flutter into the sky, arching en masse one way, then the other. As soon as Jason grows confident that they've finally settled on a route, doubt sets in and they return once more to circle uncertainly overhead.

'Tryin' to get their bearings and then they'll be off,' Jason comments. A few more minutes elapse. 'Do seem to be takin' their time today, though.'

Eventually something clicks for one of the brood, or perhaps there's a collective decision. Anyway, they fly off in the direction of Hull and Jason relaxes. He packs his wicker basket in the boot and climbs back into the passenger's seat next to his mother who has sat unmoving throughout the operation. Just before she turns on the ignition, I hear her ask her son, 'What did 'e want?' She nods her head in my direction. Jason's reply is swallowed by the growling car.

I sit in the front seat of the van, watching waves churning the sand, creeping ever closer to our cliff perch 10ft above the beach. It is a surreal place, this Holderness coast: a La Mancha of rich arable land (with brash broom fields and waving windmills), parts of which keep dropping off into the sea. Equally surreally, halfway between Easington and Kilnsea, I notice a fortysomething male, miles from anywhere, driving down the middle of the road in a motorised wheelchair. He is clearly enjoying being alone, driving through countryside that he perhaps once rode on a motorbike.

I reach Spurn Head, which dangles like bait in the mouth of the River Humber, via a 3½-mile single track from Kilnsea. Miraculously, for the time being, sea and sky remain separated by this fragile strip formed by the southerly drift of sand and shingle from eroded cliffs further north. Each new storm, however, threatens to punch a hole right through the National Nature Reserve. As I creep southwestwards shifting sands slither like snakes across the single-track road. To my right curlews hunt grubs on the gun-metal mud flats. And 20ft to my left, waves are crashing and leaping in the air. It wouldn't take much to transform the bird-and-butterfly stopover into a marine habitat.

Back in Kilnsea I call in at the Crown and Anchor and sit at an outdoor bench, blowing on scorching salmon cakes and new potatoes. Beneath a forest-fire sunset over the Humber, an argument breaks out between the landlady and a couple of customers. The dispute is over the drink being consumed by a large woman in a motorised wheelchair (they really are everywhere) and her even larger husband, whose gut is resting on a plate on the adjacent table.

Landlady: 'I'd appreciate it if you didn't bring your own ale to drink on our premises.'

Large Man (eyes agog, all innocence): 'What d'you mean?'

Landlady: 'The cans in front of you that you're using to fill our pint pot with. I wouldn't bring my dinner into your fish and chip shop, would I?'

Woman in Zippy Wheelchair: 'Don't have a fish and chip shop.'

Large Man: 'On fuckin 'oliday, aren't we?'

Landlady: 'Yes, and this is my business.'

Woman in Zippy: 'Well, you should stock barley wine. We like that.'

Landlady: 'It doesn't sell.'

Large Man: 'Well, it would if you stocked it.'

Landlady: 'I used to but it didn't sell.'

Large Man: 'Well, if you cut the price it would. Then we'd get it cheap and we wouldn't have to bring our own.'

A brief intermission follows while a tractor rumbles by pulling a boat with a family of four who are standing in it, waving.

Landlady: 'That doesn't alter the fact you can't drink your own beer on our premises.'

Woman in Zippy: 'Well, you should charge less then.'

The landlady gives up. I spend the rest of the night camped back where I'd watched the pigeons being released, overlooking the sea at Easington. In the middle of the night, I'm woken by Sid having a nightmare. Either that, or the earth is moving for him. Maybe I parked too close to the edge. I can hear the sea crashing at our toes and a strong wind is giving us a royal buffeting. I turn over and head back to the land of nod.

At 8 a.m. the next morning, I take a deep breath and burrow into the dense human concentration that always gathers around estuaries for work and leisure. I cross the Humber Bridge, which for seventeen years – after it opened to traffic in 1981 – was the world's longest single-span suspension bridge at 1,410m. It proves to be aesthetically easy on the eye and offers clear views up and down the estuary.

Once I'm on the southern bank, motorway and dual carriageway carry me to Grimsby and a sign welcoming me to 'Europe's Food Town'. And indeed, the seaport more than deserves such a title, if you happen to count Bird's Eye, Findus, Pizza, KP and the like as food. Perhaps instead of Europe's Food Town they should be more precise in their legend building and put up a longer sign saying 'Europe's Mass-Produced Frozen Food Town'. Or 'Europe's Freezer Food Town' if they want something snappier.

Grimsby still handles more fish than any other port in the country. It just isn't ours. During the late 20th century, fishing went the same way as shipbuilding, mining and agriculture – into the heritage museum. Grimsby has replaced its home-grown fishing industry with refrigerated warehouses and processing and packaging plants for other nations' fishing industries. Nowadays other countries make and we provide the wrappers.

Once in town, I follow signs for the docks and pull up at a security barrier at the fish market. Unfortunately the guard knows the difference between a motorhome and a container lorry, and points a finger to a car park across the street. I lock up and tell Sid I'm leaving him behind.

'You're ashamed of me,' he challenges me.

'It's not that . . . it's just that the security guard didn't like you.'

Snap out of it, Paul.

I return to the guard and ask if I can go inside.

'It's not open to the public.'

'I'm writing a book about . . .'

'You'd better see Carol. Go to the big glass doors. The market's finished anyway. They'll be washin' out by now.'

Inside the office block Carol confirms that the market is indeed over. 'Seven a.m. it starts and it's all over by 9.30, latest. Come tomorrow at 6.45 a.m. and I'll leave you overalls, hat and boots at the barrier with security.'

I thank Carol and leave. No fitting first? Ah well, I'm not as vain as I once was. Grumpy Sid and I decamp to the National Fishing Heritage Centre and park in the adjacent Sainsbury's car park, taking up around fifteen berths.

The Centre opened in 1991, at a time when money was being thrown at museums in failing economies. If you can't have a fishing industry, then have a fishing heritage museum. It's all very experiential and wheelchair-friendly. I learn that the problem of overfishing that led to the introduction of quotas is the direct result of ever-improving technology: the journey from coracles and log boats to late 19th-century engine-driven vessels; the introduction of nylon nets in the 1950s; all the way to the vast £10 million floating cities that suck up the ocean floor today. Once skippers acquired their knowledge learning the life cycles and habits of fish. Now a computer screen shows the shape and size of a shoal and then sets the nets to the appropriate shape and depth and scoops them up like a spoonful of cornflakes. The superefficient pelagic (deep-water) ships can return from a four-day trip with a £1 million catch.

The fleet is just one more example of our drift from the particular and small to the impersonal and vast. Rider Haggard in *Rural England* mentions that in a survey of Feckenham in East Worcestershire in 1591, 63 different owners held some 2,900 acres. By 1900 just six owners had it all and another 3,000 acres on top. For Feckenham, read just about every other village and town in England. Meanwhile container ships replace small freight carriers, villages become city dormitories (their shops replaced by out-of-town hypermarkets), vast anonymous comprehensives replace community schools, and multi-nationals hoover up the world's resources.

I pad through the Centre's The Way It Was, the recreated (though grimeless) back alleys that in the 1950s put the 'grim' into Grimsby. I navigate the icy waters of the Arctic and plot my course 'in search of the catch in the Skipper's Wheelhouse'. I pop into the Freeman's Arms and then queue at the Settling Office for my pay. I watch a film on trawlers at war (1,300 trawlers were at sea during World War II; one-fifth of them – and 11,500 men – were lost to the enemy). And finally I learn about the lot of the fisherman's wife: repairing nets, keeping house, providing food and doing everything but fish (in the 19th century on Scotland's west coast, the women even carried their husbands into the boats so they wouldn't get their boots wet).

As I drive through Grimsby and seamlessly into Cleethorpes, I enter a resort that was to the southern Yorkshire and Lincolnshire holiday what its neighbour was to fishing.

A century ago the world arrived in Cleethorpes in railway carriages and spilled out of a station the size of a town. They then took fifty steps, plonked themselves on to North Beach and didn't budge. Today the majority of visitors come by car rather than train and spend just as much time on South Beach, which in the past decade has spawned a white-knuckle park and one of Europe's largest children's activity centres. Its finest feature, however, remains the Victorian boating lake (rechristened 'Lakeside') on which an elderly couple in a rowing boat are having problems with their steering and keep smashing into a wall. The woman tries to offer tips; the man gets irritated and smashes some more. A bit like life, really. Meanwhile assorted geese – graylag, white-face and bean – bark orders at the pair and then switch their attention to those eating outside the café.

They are not the only food source. Lakeside also boasts a stylish new restaurant, Vue, with a wooden turret, shingle walls and pale decks. Unfortunately for the geese, the contemporary dishy diners here aren't sharing a morsel of their tasty contemporary dishes with anyone. The new venture, along with another couple of stylish cafés, is an attempt by the town to swim to a new economic life raft and a very different crowd. For such targeted visitors, Cleethorpes' crown jewels isn't the white-knuckle park or amusement arcades but the SSSI stretching along the northeast Lincolnshire coast from the freshwater boating lake.

Mike Sleight, the Cleethorpes countryside ranger (hard to believe such a thing exists) is just ending a walk and visitors are snapping

pictures of him standing beside the Greenwich Meridian Line, 0°
longitude, which cuts through the resort at the far end of the lake.

'Cleethorpes is the first town the meridian passes through since
leaving the North Pole. Withernsea says *it's* the first, but the line doesn't
go through the town, it avoids it like the plague.' The Cleethorpes ranger
looks the part with rockerbilly quiff and checked shirt.

Mike's a 'meggy'. In other words, born and bred in town, he has
Cleethorpes running through him like the local rock. His own history
even mirrors that of the resort, a testimony to the coastal credo 'adapt
or perish'. Mike's half-century has experienced chameleon changes
from schoolboy to car mechanic to farm hand to taxi driver and now, at
the tail of his working life, he is finally being paid for pursuing his
lifelong passion for wildlife.

'When my wife took the kids and divorced me, I saw a programme
on telly and a man was talking about an environmental course he'd
just completed. I went and did the same in Lincoln and then applied
for this job. Money's crap but I can't imagine anything I'd rather be
doing. See these?' Mike bends down to a clump of bird's-foot trefoil.
'See the red band where they're opening? Eggs and bacon. The kids
love that.' Mike points to a carpet of sea lavender on the salt marsh.
'Covered twice daily by the tide and doesn't mind a bit.' It's hard to
imagine the tide, presently two miles out in the estuary, ever managing
to reach it.

Mike is galloping again. 'See that?' He's now pointing to a ridge of
emerging dune. 'When it's fully formed we'll have a seawater lagoon
behind it. This is our sea defence and it's all natural – the salt marsh takes
the power out of the sea and the dunes take care of its height.'

Mike gathers up his flock and leads them back to the Lakeside café. I
head in the opposite direction, passing hopping rabbits, thrushes and
starlings. In a matter of fifty yards, I recognise the white trumpets of
bindweed, wild garlic, yellow rattle, lady's bedstraw and white yarrow
(which Mike claimed is better than insect repellent). I have often
imagined myself as a ranger on a stretch of Heritage Coast but would
never in a million years have expected to envy the lot of a ranger in
Cleethorpes. Mike's manor – from the freshwater lake to the dunes, salt
marshes, mud flats, sandbanks and estuary – is a haven for flora and fauna
in the heart of a busy seaside resort.

Having walked a mile or so, I cut inland to the Winter Gardens, which has nothing to do with gardens but does, surprisingly, do more business in winter than summer. The reason for this, I'm told, is the staff parties, professional boxing, live bands and dances that Jimmy Jackson, who's been at the helm since the 1950s, books over the winter season.

Jimmy has witnessed many storms on this exposed northern coast but none like the gale that crashed through when the Sex Pistols played the Gardens in 1976. 'They caused a riot, whipping up the drunks into a frenzy, and would have done even more damage if we hadn't got them off stage fast.' It was a very different experience from when Lulu first performed as a fifteen-year-old and Jimmy had to whip her back to his house so she could watch herself on *Top of the Pops* performing 'Shout!' with the Luvvers. 'The maddest pandemonium, though, was when Bay City Rollers played,' Jimmy tells me. 'We had girls fainting everywhere.'

Today things are calmer. In the main ballroom a tea dance is in swing, maybe sixty clinched bodies gliding stiffly like a scene out of *Invasion of the Body Snatchers*. The dance is a quickstep but it is more step than quick: it is the dance of the dead played to a dirge Hammond organ. No one talks. Concentration is intense.

I leave the dancers, slowly turning like the cakes rotating in the glass display case in the adjacent café.

Walking back along the shore, I pass coloured mooring buoys balanced on the mud flats like abandoned snooker balls. Eventually I make it back to Sid and together we search for a manger for the night. We find it at Peaks Top Farm on the Clitheroe outskirts. A storm lashes down most of the night. On the raised dais of my bed, my head is just 3ft from what sounds like a tapdancing troupe. There is a brief intermission and then the tapdancers are replaced by an army goose-stepping across the roof. Even without the storm I would have slept badly – I always do when I know I have to wake early.

By 6.15 a.m. I'm up and washed and by 6.50 I'm back with my security guard friend at Grimsby's fish market, donning a nifty white Airtex pork-pie hat, white overall and black wellies. The new market only opened in 1996 and cost several lottery wins. At the raised shutters to the loading bay, cruise-liner-sized trucks wait open-mouthed, greedy for breakfast. The vast hangar has a pitched roof and stretches the length of a football field. It is screaming with artificial lighting and fork-lift trucks are whizzing around like bumper cars.

The market is far too big for our numbers today and those of us gathered here are Lilliputians, identikit Lilliputians in white pork-pie hats. Only one woman is present – Carol – and she is wearing a flower in the brim of her hat just so nobody confuses her with a bloke. Her job is to make a note of the average price the fish sell at so the information can be posted on the market website.

Today there are probably a thousand 50-kilo boxes for auction. On Monday, the busiest day of the week, there can be up to eight times the number. A bell rings and the agent who's first on the rota yells out 'Per-laice! Per-laice!' There's not much cod at this time of year but seemingly plenty of plaice and haddock. Most of the fish speak Norwegian, Icelandic and Faroese, sprinkled lightly with a little Dutch, Scottish and Belgian.

The auctioneer starts at the price he'd like to get and takes the first bid working down. Once he's sold his batch, the next agent on the rota takes over. Soon a dozen boxes have been sprinkled with the confetti of merchants' names – Oliver Brothers, Fraser, M & J Seafood, Scot Prime.

Skate stare up from their iced sarcophagi in the next row. The most senior merchants gathered round display their longevity in post by balancing on the edges of the plastic boxes, as they probably once did on the gunwales of trawlers. Their stance says, 'I was doing this before you were born, nipper, and don't you be trying it or the fish will be flying through the air and you'll be on yer arse.'

'Haaaaadock!' screams someone from further down the line and a rugby scrum ensues. One man stands apart from the rest and I naturally gravitate towards him. The small bespectacled fish inspector is a man even more reviled than parliament and Brussels. Along the far wall are a few boxes he has pulled out that are destined to become knock-down fishmeal to fertilise farmers' fields.

He explains his criteria for rejection: 'It can be down to texture, smell, colour, if they're flaking . . . They also tend to turn quickly if the fish have been eating rich food. It's all down to quality control. Some may have been stored in ice for a fortnight before reaching the docks and if they haven't been properly looked after, it's my job to spot them.' I peer into the boxes. They all look fine to me.

I notice an agent standing by a massive halibut, worrying at the broken flesh of a wound, no doubt hoping the inspector won't notice. It sells for £5 per kilo. Younger boys learning the ropes (called 'barrow boys' in the old days) stretch and yawn, still not comfortable with the ungodly hour. Another agent is asking for £1 a kilo for his whiting but settles on 60p. Once it's agreed, the buyer's nametag (known as a 'tally') – Chas Butler - duly floats down into the box. The fish lie there unmoved and unmoving, their mouths gaping in horror or shut tight on life, their bodies shaped into whatever the box has demanded of them.

A man is videoing the still lifes and speaking into a microphone. His name is Carl Oswin and he's been working the market for 25 years. I ask what he's doing. 'Security. I'm filming the boxes and their tallies so no one nicks anything. Had three boxes further up that didn't have their tallies on and anyone could have walked off wi' 'em. Doesn't happen as much as it did, mind.

'When I started, you could start at the beginning of the dock and walk two mile of boats without touching the quay. And the dockside market then would have eight times as much fish for sale.' Carl, like everyone else I talk to, has the same story to tell: once it was us selling to everyone else. In the 1950s Grimsby was the biggest port in the world. Now our fleet's gone and we just fillet and process and pack other countries' fish.

A final insult and irony is that most of the fish don't even come in by boat any more, according to agent Richard Macklan. 'They really should have the market in Birmingham, not here. Most fish is flown in or brought down by lorry from Peterhead. There's nothing left in the North Sea any more anyway – it's all fished out – so what's the point having the market in Grimsby?'

By 7.40 a.m., most of the boxes have been cleared and we're down to the final few. The agents relax. There's time now for the usual badinage and good-humoured mickey-taking that pass for male bonding. Someone attempts to push a colleague into an iced coffin. Another merchant tells me to pretend to take a photo of his friend who happens to be claiming dole but is at that moment bidding for one of the last loads. I do as I'm told. 'There y'ar, smile yer c***, he's from Inland Revenue,' the man taunts his friend and everyone falls about.

It's all very male. The all-purpose f-word peppers conversation no less than agents' tags do the boxes. It appears as a standard verb, phrasal verb, adjective, gerund and variants thereof to avoid tiresome use of superfluous vocabulary: 'fuck about', 'fucked off', 'the fucking business', 'the fuckwit', 'fucking twat', 'don't give a fuck', 'don't give a flying fuck', 'fucker', 'fucked up', 'fuck this, fuck that', 'fuck around', 'fuck my old boots', 'you fuck', 'fuck you' and even 'fuck off'.

Just a couple of boxes remain now for auction. They contain small whiting whose future is fish crumbs or pub meals. A man guarding the boxes tells me one of the tricks of his trade. 'It's easy to get round the regulations restricting the gaps in nets. All you do is slow the trawler so the net sags a bit and then the buggers can't swim out so easy. Or you can do like the foreigners do and use two nets . . . one inside the other . . . that stops them in their tracks no trouble.'

With business done there's also time for fishermen's tall tales. The monster halibut in the box that sold for £5 a kilo I'm assured is a tiddler. 'I once saw one 10ft long,' someone tells me. The male braggadocio is contagious. I just stop myself from telling him about the 150lb black marlin I landed in Kenya's Pemba Channel on my one and only deep-fishing sortie. I've got a photograph to prove it, if you'd like to take a look.

Outside, back in the natural light, I stare up at the towering brick Victorian folly that by rights should inhabit Venice or Istanbul. 'It were used as a hydraulic system for the lockgate,' the security guard tells me. 'When Queen Victoria or her bloke Albert opened it, they 'ad a fockin' lift put in to get 'em to top.'

It's around 8 a.m. now. Time for breakfast. The guard points me in the direction of the Salsbury Café, where white coats are now splayed wide, hats resting on empty chairs and their owners relaxing over cribbage boards or games of cards. I order a standard breakfast: bacon, sausage, toast, baked beans, tomatoes, egg – one of the best yet. As I'm completing my order, an elderly gentleman in the card school asks me to pass him a fresh mug of tea. The woman behind the counter tells me to, 'Let the lazy bastard do it himself.' I pass the tea. 'Good,' the woman commends me. 'At least you didn't put sugar in, so the lazy bugger'll have to get up anyway.' Sitting at the next table is an abandoned book: Philip Roth's *La Touche*. I wonder if it's the French translation of *The Human Stain*. Bizarre. Someone at the other end of the small café waves his *Daily Mirror* in the air to see if anyone else wants a read as he's done with it. I scour it for more news about Chelsea's wonderful pillaging of Europe's top clubs.

Having polished off a truly memorable breakfast, I wander up to the card school. 'As I ferried your tea, can I take your picture?' I ask Lazy Bastard. Someone shouts out from another table: 'That's right, ugly c***s' gallery.' Everyone laughs. 'You couldn't just pass the sugar could you,' Lazy Bastard asks me by way of reply. I comply and am granted dispensation to click away. Lazy Bastard then asks what the pictures are for. I tell him and his four companions about my journey and book.

'You'd better sit down here then,' he instructs and pats the chair next to him. The others in the school mutter words to me about Tommy Rudlands definitely being the man for the job. Patiently I sit and wait for the hand to finish. As I do so, someone at the adjacent table loudly proclaims that Tommy is a 'c***' because he was one of the first to start buying all the cheaper foreign fish and freezing out the local fishermen. Tommy ignores him and focuses on the cards. He is still dressed in the white overall he wore at the market and will continue to wear when he returns to his filleting and packaging room round the back alley.

The man who cast the insult is probably in his late thirties. His name is Len Rogers. All Len's brothers used to fish. 'Now one works in a pub and the other on an oil rig. They both stopped fifteen year back with the decommissioning. Bloody Anthony Crosland's fault. He was our MP and when he was negotiating with Iceland fishing rights and they said we could fish outside the 50-mile zone, he demanded a better deal. "Well then," they said, "Fuck off," and they made the exclusion zone 200 mile. We had gunboats shooting over our bows, nets being holed, boats being boarded and punch-ups going on. They impounded our catches and boats. We were beat. Me brothers came home and sold their boats for scrap. We had lots of immaculate trawlers and nowhere to fish. They knew it were all up.' Len, having said his piece, bids me good luck with my journey and heads back to work.

The card player seated opposite me has finished his hand and tells me a little about Tommy, still sitting alongside me mutely. 'Tommy's 74 and has worked longest on the dock.

'You're in good shape,' I compliment Tommy.

'That's working with c***s like this lot,' Tommy replies. There is no animosity or criticism in the name calling; I have simply encountered a different register for terms of endearment for men who cannot do endearment. There's a little pushing and shoving and shadow boxing too for physical contact as we leave via the back door and Tommy invites me into his nearby workshop. He has large features, a full head of white hair and is still a handsome man who looks considerably younger than his years.

Tommy has left a radio on inside his workplace and Tom Jones is belting out 'It's Not Unusual' as we walk through the rainbow curtain of heavy rubber flaps into the kitchen-sized room he rents. He opens a polystyrene box and empties the contents into a large tub, which he fills with water and then paddles with a wooden spade before starting to slice the plaice like envelopes. Once filleted, he will pack them in a case for one of his regular customers.

As he works he tells me a little of his story. 'My father spent sixty years on the dock as a lumper unloading catch.' Tommy reels off the names of the jetties – Pneumonia Jetty, the West Wall, Chapman's Jetty, Henderson's, Doughty's, Mellish's – that stretched two miles when he started work as a barrow boy at the age of fourteen. 'Over the years I worked myself up a good business – Big T Fishmerchant – employing 150 workers. Then I had a great fall. I was at my height and so was Grimsby – the biggest port in the world then, it were. And the fuckin' bank got cold feet. I'd just spent £100,000 on a first-class freezing factory, taken on more workers and the unions had just come on the job. The bank got the wind up. They didn't like unions. Fuckers reduced me overdraft from £250,000 to £76,000. They pulled the plug on me and I went belly up. Bankruptcy. Now it's just me here. Occasionally I might get someone to help if I'm really busy.' The rain is starting to fall again as Tommy continues his expert filleting and sums up. 'I was strangled by the bank like the fishing industry was strangled by the Government.'

Tommy's expected customer arrives. He takes the box and then suggests they head next door for tea. I think I know who'll be at the counter doing the ordering. I wish Tommy better luck than he's had in recent years as he's disappearing through the door. 'The luck's all gone. There is no more luck,' he replies and is gone.

I quit town on the A16, reflecting on the careless bruising cruelty of this very male society. I have absolutely no doubt that the tight community would be as ruthless with an odd fish as a fish inspector is and that anyone not conforming to the male stereotype would soon be fertiliser in a field.

I have noticed too that these men who work with fish, like farmers, are very clear in their condemnation of those they believe failed them and their industry. Certainly the past is viewed through rose-tinted spectacles, and their perspective on historical errors has the wonderful clarity of hindsight. Nevertheless, they believe the eclipse of the industry could have been avoided if only they, the experts, had been listened to. Their biggest beef is that the momentous decisions concerning their lives have been left to uninformed and inexperienced outsiders.

Eight miles or so further south, I quit the purposeful A16, which takes the straightest Lincolnshire line for Skegness, and turn on to the B1201 coast road that meanders with a dyke through wheat fields and grazing pasture. Occasional farms advertise PYO strawberries, and signs in villages announce upcoming horticultural craft shows and car boot sales. As I drive, I slowly become aware of a stye that has formed on my eye. If I were a fish, I would be destined for the offal box.

There is no sniff of sea until a couple of wind turbines put in an appearance, as streamlined and graceful as terns in flight. The windmills wave me into Mablethorpe, a rock-and-ice-cream-and-amusement-arcade-and-sandy-beach-with-a-blue-flag kind of place, but really it's only a pocket-sized Skeggy. Cleethorpes, Theddlethorpe, Mablethorpe. What is it with these thorpes? I look it up and find that 'thorpe' is Vikingese for village or farm. Other Viking bequests in suffixes along the coast include '-by' (settlement), '-brough' (shelter) and '-ness' (promontory). We name things to understand them. Ever since we visited Holy Island, Sid has been insisting his name is not Sid but Siddhartha.

On the outskirts of Skeggy, a driver in an oncoming motorhome waves to me. It is a moment of truth. When I used to ride a 1000CC Z1R Kawasaki, I used to enjoy the gloved-palm V salutation between biker brethren. But returning the enthusiastic wave of an elderly woman in a mobile home? Do I want to belong to this club? Oh what the hell. It's a watershed moment. A coming-of-age-and-accept-you're-past-it fishmeal moment.

I consider my impending retirement and consignment to a motorised wheelchair. It is clearly to the flatter, open Northeast and Northwest that such veteran drivers head. Trust such a vehicle to the narrow, precipitous lanes of the Southwest and you'd end up either as flattened fauna or sailing into the drink.

Skeggy's liquorice-twisting white-knuckle rides appear on the horizon. Fantasy Island. I like the sound of it as much as its appearance. I decide that next-door's Butlin's trailer park will be our home for the night. First, however, I head for the seafront town itself – and it is a town, not just a resort, complete with butcher's, cycle shop, M&S, Boots and, heaven help us, even a Body Shop. One shop I am particularly interested in is Seacroft Mobility, which I notice is offering 0% finance on its wide range of part-exchange and second-hand motorised wheelchairs.

No resort is more associated with kiss-me-quick hats than Skeggy (though you'll never see one these days, unfortunately), nor more reviled; the snotty butt of yesteryear jibes about poor-quality holidays; the archetype for coach ghettoes, chips on the pavement and steel skies. It's all rubbish. True, you risk being run over by a drunk granny in charge of a demented wheelchair, but it's a healthy, happy place with a necklace of attractions – Natureland Seal Sanctuary, the Water Leisure Park, endless amusement arcades, and a boating lake with bumper boats.

I like Skeggy. I like its jungle of racy neon, its beach donkey rides, its 'mince-and-onions giant Yorkie with veg. and pots'. Look up and there's some fine Victorian architecture gracing the streets, and down below you can still buy 'three quality towels a tenner', '7 lighters or 25 bars of rock for a quid'. Skeggy even has a blue flag.

By evening it is again chucking it down so I skip Fantasy Island and head straight for Butlin's, which is basically Skeggy indoors – or perhaps Skeggy is Butlin's outdoors? Overnighting in the park costs a family of four in a tourer £32 and that includes the electric hook-up and access to the park and attractions. One tourer site in Cleethorpes (Thorpe) quoted me £32 just for Sid and me to overnight (we went to Peaks Top Farm instead and paid a fiver; the most I've paid anywhere is an outrageous £17 at Berwick and usually it's been around a tenner).

As I enter the aluminium-clad amusement arcade at the entrance to the complex, bingo numbers are being called. The noise of fun is deafening. Three boys are aiming guns on the Time Crisis 3 simulator, trying to slaughter as many people as possible. Three girls, meanwhile, go through their steps on Dancing Stage 2 Euromix. There you have it.

The arcade leads into the Skyline Pavilion, one of those ubiquitous white nomadic-type constructions beloved of airport terminals. The Pavilion provides the ultimate grazing experience – entertainment hall, show hall, cinema hall, food hall, crap-weather hall (and it is crap weather tonight). My wife's vision of hell. Max's vision of the promised land. I'm somewhere between the two but nudging closer to Max.

A man in a turban and gold waistcoat is cheering punters on as they maniacally hurl their balls into holes to move their steeds on in the Arabian Derby.

In Noddyland, Benny Hill ('It's Brian Hill really but I've always been called Benny') is overseeing the spinning cups, as he has done for 33 years. He even claims still to enjoy it. 'Boredom wasn't invented when I was a kid,' he offers, by way of explaining the grin on his face. Benny is single and lives in a caravan. His face seems familiar. I trawl the archives and finally realise he's the spitting image of Roger Daltrey, the Pinball Wizard. Visions of redcoat Uncle Ernie Keith Moon immediately roll (naturally followed by the scene in which the voluptuous Ann-Margret slithers in baked beans).

When Britain's first Butlin's opened at Skegness in Easter 1936, the one thousand guests who checked in stood about and shuffled their feet. They didn't know what holidays were and so they waited as they would in a ballroom for the entertainment to start. Norman Bradford was immediately dispatched by Billy Butlin to buy a distinctive jacket in town so he could act as master of ceremonies. He returned with the red jacket that has become the Butlin's hallmark.

One of those original chalets still remains on site to remind guests who might be considering complaining about something of just how lucky they are. Despite being Grade II listed, it is the size of a garden shed and could easily pass for one. Several other Grade II-listed edifices have passed through as redcoats – Charlie Drake, Michael Barrymore, Des O'Connor and Jimmy Tarbuck, for example. It's a good place to learn stage technique and presence in front of an audience of two thousand who are already behind you simply because you're wearing a red coat. Laurel and Hardy played Skeggy and so did Grace Kelly. Oh, and Ringo was playing here with Rory Storm and the Hurricanes (a band I have a soft spot for) when he got the call that The Beatles wanted him.

Billy Butlin was the Richard Branson of his day and never one to miss a promotional opportunity. Having imported the first UK dodgems on to the forefront at Skegness (he had the franchise from America), he bought an unwanted sugar beet field and opened the UK's first fixed-structure holiday camp. In the late 1940s, when parliament was considering making annual holiday a statutory right for workers, Butlin invited every MP to Skegness to try to persuade them of the wisdom of such a revolution. Once the Act was passed, he coined the Butlin slogan 'A week's holiday for a week's pay'. Eventually he owned nine holiday parks, a string of amusement parks, hotels and restaurants; in 1972 he sold Butlin's to the Rank Organisation for £43 million. Over the next two decades, Butlin's fell increasingly out of favour, sites were sold and the business was basically used as a cash cow, with very little ploughed back into improvements. Since 1998, however, £190 million has been pumped into its three remaining sites – Minehead, Bognor and Skegness.

Tonight there are around 6,500 checked into the place and it's buzzing. The accommodation nowadays bears more than a passing resemblance to Disneyland. The water centre (Splash), has two of the best water rides in the country – Master Blaster is a raft roller coaster with a sheer drop at the end, and Space Bowl has a triple vortex twist. Naturally I try them both.

In one of the cafés, I meet Raymond Alli, who's dressed in a West Ham football shirt. Initially I think he's one of the staff as he's clearing a table but I soon discover he is a guest who's been coming every year for 25 years. Raymond usually checks in for around 11 weeks (yes, three months) annually. Anyone who takes three holidays in five years at Butlin's becomes an automatic member of the loyalty club, and entitled to discounts. Raymond is a gold member and has negotiated a special deal whereby instead of welcoming champagne, he receives credits for his mobile phone as well as a 40 per cent discount on the next holiday.

Raymond has a debilitating stutter and at first our conversation is slow. When we discover a common bond, however – Raymond lives in Acton and I used to teach there – he seems to relax more and talk becomes a little more fluid. He always comes by rail, though he is uncertain about how long it takes directly from Acton as he goes via Scotland, because he likes train journeys so much. The self-service cafeteria staff seem to have adopted him and he clearly thinks of them as family, and Butlin's almost perhaps as a second home. Back home, he says, he works as a volunteer for a trust.

Although Raymond isn't typical of a Butlin's guest – surely no one else checks in that often – he is more representative of the clients than the models on the cover of the *Butlin's Breakaways* brochure: two fashionable women and a trendy man in their late twenties laugh excitedly while sucking at straws from the same cocktail glass. They are coiffured, polished, confident: city bankers or media types. Such people are not seen at Butlin's Skegness.

Butlin's redcoats pioneered karaoke before the word was invented and every employee taking to the main stage is applauded enthusiastically and generously just because they have the balls to do it. The girl singing 'It's Raining Men' does a commendable job but the dancers are like figureheads in a storm. The two young men who sing 'Uptown Girl' are just plain awful.

As I walk through the resort, the feelgood factor is palpable. Girls practise their moves in the kids club while simultaneously singing along to Daniel Bedingfield; pre-teens run about excitedly in the late stormy light with new friends; and toddlers queue to be propelled 40ft into the air on rubber bands. Billy Butlin came from a fairground background and was at heart an entertainer. Despite the £190 million pound injection and new technology, it is still this fundamental of the seaside holiday that remains his legacy.

'A large country it is, and full of havens.'
William Camden, *Britain* (1610)

Chapter Five: East Anglia

Creeks and Backwaters

I leave Skeggy early in the hope of avoiding the work traffic streaming into Boston and King's Lynn. Across the endless flatlands of the Fens, great water machines trundle beneath a raking blue sky. A gentle beauty settles. White Mini Veg Packer trucks wait patiently in fields of beet, cabbage and potatoes, their canvas rears splayed revealingly wide. Inside, stacked plastic boxes wait for the workers to arrive and start their back-breaking work.

Having crossed the lift bridge over the silvered Great Ouse into Norfolk, I park on the seafront at Hunstanton (the only coastal town in East Anglia that faces west) and stare out over the agitated Wash. In winter more than three hundred thousand birds similarly park here, including forty thousand pink-footed geese from Iceland, ten thousand oystercatchers from Norway and up to sixty thousand knot from Arctic Canada. The mud flats are simply stuffed with food and a fine winter dawn on the Wash is like nowhere else. The sun rises over the hills in a sky all pastel pinks and blues. The tide rushes in, cornering waders until they're forced to lift off with a clamorous beating of wings. The vast flock arc in the sky, grumbling and cussing, before descending to small shingle islands where, packed tight as sardines, they sit out the tide.

We are only halfway through July and yet some of the early migrants are already winging in for the winter. In Hunstanton, however, there are no mud flats for them to nibble at. The tide is in, licking at the cliffs' sickly layered cake of strawberry, cream and chocolate.

Hunstanton is a resort but not as Devon, Lancashire, Cumbria or Yorkshire know them. Firstly there's the distinctive carrstone homes gracing the tipping village green. Then there's the demure amusement arcade and an equally small, rather sweet funfair. The pier was snatched years ago by the sea, the lighthouse abandoned, and the very elegant grassed Boston Square has been made into a sensory garden with fragrant plants, Braille messages and a wheelchair trail.

Even the rock shop, Dales, is supremely dignified. The owner stands behind the ice-cream boxes, scooping raspberry pavlova flavour, rum and raisin (my favourite) and pina colada to a bevy of polite uniformed secondary schoolgirls. The shop is lined with jars of sweets – clove balls, aniseed twists, rose creams, buttered Brazils – that instantly transport me back to my childhood sweetshop on Litherland lift bridge.

Last winter Barry Dale was admitted to hospital with cancer and his wife Suzanne had to cope in the shop alone. The experience made them take stock and they decided to bring forward their planned retirement. Today is the last day of their working lives. Barry is clearly struggling with the prospect but Suzanne can't wait to bring the curtain down so they can spend time at home and visit Barry's sister in New Mexico.

As Suzanne weighs my cough candy twists, another customer appears at the door. The new arrival is an old friend, Stan Goldman, who coincidentally hails from New Mexico. During World War II Stan served with the RAF at Marham (which he proudly tells me is now the largest Tornado base in the country). Hunstanton was where, in Stan's words, he 'first fell in love with the English people but not as much as I did my future wife, Brenda'. For the past seven years, since Brenda's death, Stan, who claims to be ninety ('I'm in pretty good shape for the shape I'm in'), has been making the transatlantic crossing alone. The three old friends, deep in discussion about the Dales' upcoming New Mexico trip, do not notice the schoolgirls and me exiting with our morning treats.

*

East of Hunstanton hand-painted oak signs introduce a succession of exquisite knapped-flint villages. Fortunately there is a welcome absence of other highway furniture that would detract from the coast's stylish – rather than quaint – old-fashioned feel.

From the seashore at Holme-by-the-Sea, I look for a four-thousand-year-old henge that was revealed by a particularly low tide in 1999. Beneath a tumultuous sky there is nothing to be seen but water. The discovery of the henge – 55 timber posts encircling a large upturned trunk – created an archeological and media frenzy as it was the earliest site discovered where axes were known to have been used by inhabitants.

TV crews and professors descended on Seahenge in droves but so did a number of druids to voice their objection to the planned removal, arguing that as it had survived well enough without our interference for thousands of years, it should be left to its own devices. The druids believed that if the henge was moved, the magic of its circle would be broken.

As professors failed to throw light on its origin and function, a reporter finally tried his luck with one of the activists known as Buster the Druid who was playing a nose flute to the henge and predicting dire consequences if the site was removed. The interviewer told Buster that all the experts were stumped and asked if he had a theory about its origin.

'Well, they're missing the obvious, aren't they?' Buster replied. The interviewer encouraged him to continue. 'Sandringham.' Silence. The interviewer finally remembered his job and asked what Buster meant.

'Royalty stay there, don't they? It's only a dozen miles away. How do you think it got the name? Sand-ring-ham – the hamlet by the ring in the sand.'

Silence.

Like Buster, north Norfolk moves slowly and its tiny conurbations can be passed through in a twinkling if you don't slow yourself down. Thankfully there are no real resorts in the grand sense and very little to do. What doing there is mostly consists of walking and looking.

I pull into the RSPB Wetland Reserve at Titchwell expressly for this purpose. Where the Wash ends and the sea begins, it signals the start of a 47-mile coastal romp to Cromer that has been awarded just about every designation that can be landed apart from gaining UNESCO World Heritage recognition.

Lying in the sea beneath the big blue Norfolk sky, I am the only human sharing the landscape with terns, grazing cattle, skylarks and a pair of abandoned World War II tanks slowly rusting in the sand. From the sea Norfolk is barely visible, a hiccup of land, an intermediary world of shingle spits, dunes, tidal marsh, brackish lagoons and reed beds.

After my dip I walk the blazing white sands, crunching shells underfoot, and then turn inland tracking a boardwalk through marshes dotted with intense purple sea lavender. People sit on memorial benches, their binoculars searching the sky for one of the six pairs of marsh harriers that inhabit the reserve. I pass rustling reed beds and pond-dipping platforms where water scorpions lurk and dragonflies patrol like Huey Cobra choppers. An avocet, its beak shaped like an upturned scimitar, fishes for shrimps in the mud. Along the margins hairy willowherb and bulrushes screen deadly nightshade and the pungent water mint that I crush between my fingers. Skeggy's full-on man-made bombardment of the senses seems a very long way away.

There are, of course, drawbacks to living in this wonderland they call the north Norfolk coast. In Titchwell there are two shops where you can splash out £1,000 on a pair of binoculars but you won't be able to buy a newspaper, bread or a bottle of milk. The upsizing villages have adapted to their new downsizing residents. The village shop in Thornham has just closed and taken temporary refuge in the pub, the pub in Titchwell is now four luxury homes, and the garage in Burnham Deepdale is likely soon to follow the rest in the area into the clutches of property developers.

Less than two miles inland from the coast, the Georgian town of Burnham Market, epicentre of London downshifters, has a hat shop, a fine wine merchant, a wet-fish shop and a deli. Unsurprisingly it is nicknamed Chelsea-on-Sea. Jamie Oliver was spotted in the deli a week ago and on that same day Thierry Henry and his girlfriend were in nearby Wells, Hugh Grant on the links at the Royal West Norfolk Golf Club, and The Stranglers in Hunstanton on a photo shoot for their new album cover. The low-key, slow-time coast of rangers and Range Rovers is popular with celebs.

My overnight base is the campsite at Burnham Deepdale, which has a café, a TIC and thankfully a larger number of younger, alternative campers than I've encountered anywhere else (maybe it has something to do with the adjacent YHA). The place is brimming with kids too as school's finally out for the summer and their whoops and barmy games bring a real sense of holiday, in place of the usual retirees' convention I've found on most sites. It is, however, hilly. The advantage of this is that it creates an attractive shapeliness to the land; the disadvantage is that it's harder to kip at night when all your blood is inhabiting either your head or your feet.

I set out for an evening stroll passing a Fitzcaraldo beached boat. The rippled creeks are quicksilver, the still ponds copper, and the silhouettes of raised outboards imitate the greedy beaks of hungry chicks. Everywhere birds twist, turn and sing in this in-between, demi-land, demi-water world. The track eventually leads me to the first-floor deck of the White Horse, where I watch the sunset blaze over the marshes. I would be more than happy to accept a managed retreat here as I erode.

Those sharing the deck with me tonight are an affluent, confident – should I venture cocky? – lot. The men dress uniformly in chinos, Docksiders and loose-fitting stonewash shirts. The younger women are pristinely casual; their elders dolled up to the nines, as if off to the Royal Opera.

One man takes a photo of himself with the jigsaw of boats, creeks and marshland as backdrop. He sends it via his mobile phone to someone in London. It is about the only time I see anyone actually looking out at a view that is the equal of the Serengeti and Himalayas. Most are here for a spot of weekend sailing or golf and they chatter like skylarks. 'We must lunch, darling,' one air airkisses another as she makes to leave. Their tall tales of holidays round the globe have replaced pub yarns of 10ft-long halibut no less than they have physically replaced the fishermen them-selves in the bijoux cottages.

Yesterday it was the offal box of the pasty and unnourished at Skeggy. Today it is the masters of the universe brimming with health and confidence. True, they must erode too; but as they do, they enjoy a much better diet.

The next morning, crossing the road to explore the parish church with its distinctive flint-knapped circular tower, I'm almost run over by two biddies in a vintage car smiling their way along the coast. An elderly man simultaneously clipping a hedge from a ladder and smoking a pipe smiles and shakes his head. Another world. Outside the BoatYard, which is home to the SailCraft Sea School, Andy Ralli, a member of the coast's most endangered species – indigenous human – is picking up some diesel for his boat. I tell him he's a lucky man to inhabit such a village and how much I enjoyed the view from the deck of the White Horse the night before.

'We call it Cheval Blanc because it's full of bloody foreigners.' Andy's comment stings but is soon ameliorated by a rider that indicates he's well aware that he, like the other handful of locals still living here, relies on the incomers and tourist trade for a living. 'Got nothing against them personally, of course.'

Andy asks me how long I'm holidaying here and the story of my trip and the book emerges. 'Well, you'd better come for a run in the boat with me and Sooty then.' It's more of an instruction than an offer.

Soon his laughter is booming across the harbour at Brancaster Staithe, where kids are getting kitted out for sailing school while adults back cruisers off trailers and unpack the champers and hampers from the 4x4s. Andy stands out like a sore thumb in his unreconstructed thick yellow waterproofs, spectacles with broad side flaps, and flip-flops. His companion, Sooty, a three-year-old Patterdale terrier, immediately replaces Sid in my affections. *Olive Oil*, Andy's battered old boat, makes up the perfect threesome. Like Andy's waterproofs, *Olive*'s wonderful Skeggyness stands out against the fleet of highly varnished 1920s mahogany 'Sharpies' that are practising for an upcoming race (speeding across the bay, they look like very fast coffins).

Olive Oil needs only eight inches of water in the creek to get out, which is pretty much what we've got this morning. With the day spread out as invitingly as the waterscape beneath a cloudless sky, it's hard to imagine the bleakness of the winter months. Andy, predictably and idiosyncratically, puts me right. 'Winter's best, actually, because everyone goes home.'

He quickly warms to his misanthropic theme. 'Anyway, there's no such thing as bad weather, just inappropriate clothes . . . the winds are like the rest of us who live here, lazy – they go through you rather than round.'

Andy sweeps his left hand over the plastic bucket seat adjacent to him in the wheelhouse, brushing Sooty away like crumbs so that I can sit alongside him.

'It can be treacherous at times,' Andy finally concedes. 'But usually when we lose someone it's in summer not winter.'

'Does that happen often?'

'Not often but a lot,' Andy replies perversely. 'It can be from the beach or from a boat. If we don't fish a body out one year and get cocky, we'll lose two or three the next. Four years ago the assistant coxswain turned up his own son. It can happen to any of us, however good we might think we are.'

Andy was born in 1959 in Stanhoe, three miles inland from Brancaster Staithe, and still lives there. He used to be a farmer but now fixes farm engines, rebuilds boats and turns his hand 'to anything that earns a penny'. When he was growing up, there were more than 250 families in Stanhoe and he reckons he knew most of them. There are probably no more than six of those families still around and the four shops in town have gone too. 'Changing sands. Market forces. You have to roll with it. Adapt. That's the hand you're dealt. You play it.' Andy spills the words as if their sheer rush and volume will explain and ameliorate.

According to my skipper, the best career opportunity today is in domestic skivvying. 'House cleaning used to pay £4 an hour but with all the newcomers forcing the locals out to the more affordable homes in King's Lynn, there's no one left to clean up after them and so they're forced into paying £9 an hour.'

I ask Andy if he has children who are likely to avail themselves of the fat fees. 'No, no kids. Preventable nowadays, fortunately.'

Our leisurely pootle is suddenly put on hold for half an hour as Andy goes to the rescue of a sailing instructor and student who are having difficulty righting their boat. The problem is that the breeze is pushing them one way and the tide the other. Andy throws a line and the instructor ties it to the bow and we edge him in to more protected waters. It doesn't help. He removes the sails, hauls back in the anchor that has fallen into the drink and eventually, bouncing lightly on the keel, brings it up. His student, meanwhile, has deserted him, hitching a lift with another boat.

We resume our journey, speeding by caked mud flats and fanning dykes. Yachts float across the bay like feathers. A marsh harrier hitches a ride on the breeze. It was in the nearby marshes, bizarrely, that they shot the opening Korean paddy field sequence in the last Bond film, *Die Another Day*. As we pass the nestscrapes of terns out on a shingle spit, up ahead I can see the Royal West Norfolk Golf Club (where Hugh played last week and Prince Andrew regularly plays). Over the past two decades, the club has spent a fortune on its sea defences. Ironically the adjacent marshland was the location of Norfolk's recent first managed retreat. The golfers now play with water on three sides and the clubhouse looks like an island floating out to sea.

I ask if Andy thinks local people were consulted sufficiently before the recent planned inundation. He is predictably scathing.

'We get consultations about bloody everything. We just don't get listened to!' The same story. 'I know we're a bit slower in Norfolk – that's why we give our villages names like Little Snoring – but we know the effect one thing might have on something seemingly totally unconnected. We've been dealing with life cycles all our lives. What looks like a short-term fix for the terns, for example, may long term be bad for them. It depends.'

Before heading back to shore, Andy squeezes in one final rant against 'bullshit DEFRA and Marine Safety Agency and Environment Agency forms.' They are, apparently, the bane of his life on both land and sea. We snake our way back to harbour along a creek through oozing mud banks on which two men in a small boat are picking samphire. Approached from the seaward side, the land appears to be under siege, the water filtrating every pore, constantly undermining the land's attempt to link up.

From Brancaster Staithe I slip through a succession of knapped-flint villages. The inhabitants of Stiffkey clearly live on a diet of antiques and lamps, for that is all you can buy there. I wonder if the village's name has anything to do with the former defrocked vicar who provided sanctuary for London prostitutes in the hope of saving their souls, but reputedly saved several for himself. Eventually defrocked, he left the village in disgrace, became a lion tamer and was subsequently eaten by one of his charges. How Freudian is that?

In Wells-next-the-Sea, boats are kept in garages instead of cars. Next up comes Cley-next-the-Sea, whose homes look to have been built of oyster shells. Offshore and underwater, meanwhile, the ghosts of sabre-toothed tiger, bear, rhino, hippo, hyena and elephant graze the savannah of tree stumps and peat of the Cromer Forest Bed.

At Cromer I wander the pier, watching crabs futilely clawing to escape their transparent bucket prisons after being lured by bits of bacon on hand lines dangled by local kids. Inside the Pavilion café I share a table with an elderly woman with a mop of white curly hair and a white cardigan fastened over a pretty green floral dress.

Mabel Hunt, who will be 75 in a month's time, has come straight from the Conservative Club, where she cleans three days a week. Born in Cromer, like her father before her, Mabel started work at the age of fourteen and claims never to have been unemployed a single day. The family house she inherited (which got central heating only last year) she shares with her daughter and three grandchildren. Mabel can barely mention her son-in-law, who also shares it with her.

'I have my own part of the house and they have theirs and we have a joint kitchen but if I find him there I just leave. I try not to talk. To hold my tongue. But if my husband had been alive, he would never have let our daughter marry him. At night they leave me with the three girls to look after and then go out drinking till four in the morning. I lock the door when I go to sleep but he just climbs through the window.'

Mabel gathers up her bits. 'I'll be back tonight, and again on Wednesday for the Seaside Special. I come twice a week right over the summer season. We've got the Abba tribute band next week. I've seen them lots and still write to some of the stars who've moved on, like Gordon and Bonnie J. You've heard of them? You *must have* heard of them!'

Cromer is a mainstream, everyman and everywoman resort, restrained by Skeggy standards, no doubt viewed as wild and debauched by the likes of Cley-next-the-Sea. Faded Red Indian chiefs in full headdress waddle on the flabby chests of middle-aged men, kids chuck crabs at each other, and an eccentric throwback strides through town togged up in checked shirt, tie, braces, high-hitched jodhpurs and brogues.

I join the modest crowd divided by groynes on the beach, strip off and swim. Two lily-white boys fresh from being locked up in school until this week, gingerly toe the water and squeal. I float on my back, looking up into the topless sky and then lie out on the warm, dry pebbles, where the sun kneads me into sleep.

A few miles south, at Happisburgh, I stand on a cliff with a jumble of pick-a-sticks scattered beneath me that have crashed with the eroded cliff. In the distance I can see a pod of nine man-made reefs that is preventing the same thing happening at Sea Palling. The shoreline lies low in East Anglia, as if in deference to the sky, and anything that gets above its station is quickly bullied into submission by the sea. The rocks in the most vulnerable corner of the country may be geologically the youngest to have emerged from the sea but they are destined to return soonest after their brief holiday on Britain's driest coastline.

The first mention of a great flood at Sea Palling was recorded by John of Oxenedges, a monk from nearby Ludham, who in December 1287 wrote that the sea, 'agitated by the violence of the wind burst through its accustomed limits occupying town and fields'. The last major flood was in January 1955, when a wall of water breached the dunes, causing major structural damage to the town and the loss of nine lives. The disaster prompted the building of a sea wall and the current, highly expensive raft of reefs was funded by the Environment Agency in 1995.

It could have been worse for Sea Palling: further south at Dunwich in Suffolk – once the chief port of southern England – a succession of storms over the centuries have taken the entire town (the very last gravestone, that of John Easey, tumbled off the cliff in 1990 following the route paved by the churches of St James, St Leonard, St Martin, St Bartholemew, St Michael, St Patrick, St Mary, St John, St Peter, St Nicholas, St Felix and All Saints). And what lies next to Dunwich? Sizewell nuclear power station. If that's not an inspired bit of planning, I don't know what is.

Beyond Palling I pass Horsey Mill Windmill, which is having one of its sails repaired. In the distance its young children, a line of modern wind turbines, wave enthusiastically across fields of beet and corn.

By the time I slip into Caister and am rugby-tackled by an Indian takeaway, I have left the best of Norfolk behind. With a brown paper bag full of sensational-smelling goodies, I check into a campsite 500 yards further down the road and park next to another Sundance motorhome. My neighbours have a more compact four-berth, which cost them around £28,000. They say they're very happy with their new home, apart from the fact that they can't open their front door. 'Someone tried to break in and buggered up the mechanism.' They wince when they see the damage to Sid's rear.

The last and only other time I had visited Caister, five years ago, I had also been on a campsite but on that occasion it was on a static site, attending one of the Caister Soul Weekenders with a photographer friend. We had finally reached the Vauxhall Park Holiday Centre at around 8.30 p.m. after our journey up from London. From a distance the neat rows of massed caravans looked like orderly cemetery lots, but as we got closer I noticed each of the plots was throbbing to a stereo. Some of those queuing for four days of sweet soul music, dance, drink and maybe a dash of sex hadn't even been born when the first Caister Soul Weekender was staged in 1979. Fortunately, I noticed, there were plenty of wrinklies in line, some even older than me.

The atmosphere in the arena that first night was as mellow as at any British event I can remember. As early as 9 p.m. boys out on the floor – many shirtless – were already dripping from their exertions, and as newcomers slowly packed in from work every new track was being greeted with a knowledgeable roar. Some dextrous souls even managed to whoop, dance and balance a drink at the same time, though the trick became more problematic after the third or fourth hit of double vodka and Red Bull. By midnight the dancefloor was toffee and we finally gave up wading at around 4 a.m.

The next morning, at 11 a.m., I was woken by someone clanking a wheelie shopping bag filled with bottles of hooch past my caravan. Heading in the other direction and dancing through the traffic was a conga of bleary-eyed revellers making for hangover fry-ups at Asda. '£2.79 for ten items – you can't beat that,' said Buster Hymen, one of the Morecambe Hatters posse, who encouraged me to join them. I, however, was distracted by a female in male pyjamas inviting me in for a drink at a neighbouring caravan.

Wafting out of the caravan door was the unmistakable whiff of recently consumed baked beans on toast. Roy Ayers was playing on the stereo. Debbie introduced me to her co-habitees Selina, Lisa and Lorna (aged 25 to 28). Two of the group were foreign exchange dealers, one was an accountant and the fourth managed a gym in central London. On recent holidays their passports had seen action on a Caribbean cruise and scuba diving in the Red Sea, and there had also been jaunts to New York, Cyprus, Brazil and Barbados. These were Essex girls with the funds to fly anywhere but who wouldn't dream of exchanging *any* holiday for their twice-a-year Caister jaunts spent cramped in a caravan living on vodka and baked beans and sharing lipstick and the mirror.

Back on the floor that evening, dancing up a storm were bridal veils, bondage gear, wimples, police uniforms and an inflatable sheep attached to a male groin. Their owners were black, white, fat, thin, gorgeous, ugly, young and middle-aged. Each belonged to a family within the Caister family: the AWOL Patrol, the SAS Sisters, Private Parts, Brixton Front Line, Funkmaster Generals, Sax Maniacs. On stage one balding, ageing and overweight DJ took over from another – 'Sean French, ladies and gentlemen, a big hand but don't let him near your chips.' The biggest roar of the weekend, however, was reserved for Chris Hill, the Godfather of British Soul.

'This track and Caister were born here 21 years back.' Chris launched into his set as the first bars of 'Ain't No Stopping Us Now' played. The crowd exploded, united by a common passion for soul music that transcended the fickle fates of jobs, relationships and wealth. Many in the audience had made the 21-year journey with Chris and their oral history was recorded in the back-to-back classics he was spinning. The floor seemingly danced of its own accord. The Caister soul congregation had come seeking miracles, to have its faith reaffirmed, and the high priest of soul was doing his job, his communion cup filled with Red Bull and vodka.

Cynics may sneer at the Vauxhall Park Holiday Centre caravan park and snigger at Essex girls – particularly new-money Essex girls – but the Caister family has too good a time to worry. It is the positive face of modern England, a blueprint of racial cohesion and integration rather than polarisation and distrust. Chris yelled 'We Are Family!' as his congregation sang every word of every song. Instead of 'Land of Hope and Glory' it was 'Joy And Pain' by Maze, Solo's 'Blowing My Mind', Tower of Power's 'It Really Doesn't Matter', and The O'Jays' 'I Love Music'.

There was hardly a dry eye in the place at the end. After four days of too much music, too much dancing, too much laughing, too much junk food, too much drink and not enough sleep, the pilgrims gathered up their possessions and started shuffling back out of the park for Essex, Morecambe and Brixton, shouting to each other as they departed, 'See you at the next Weekender!'

*

This time around there is no Soul Weekender scheduled and nothing to hold me so I slip out of Caister and into Great Yarmouth, a town that Andy, the misanthrope from Brancaster Staithe, had told me was 'a shit-hole'. In fact, I remembered it pretty much the same way from when I visited it in squally weather during my previous Caister trip. Then the decidedly run-down resort cowered under lead skies. Today is different. Firstly it's sunny. Secondly a fair amount of regeneration has gone on. Thirdly it's dead easy to park – a real rarity these days. Fourthly the long, pale sandy beach stretches as far as you can see in either direction. And fifthly the usual quota of beachfront mayhem by way of fairground rides and attractions is backed up by a proper town to wander through.

On the front a strong breeze is whipping the Mr Whippy flags into a frenzy and making the plastic furniture dance like the soul posse. A few holiday-makers sit in a pavilion reading their newspapers while a handful of braver souls lie buffeted on beach sun-loungers. Turn back the clock 120 years and the wind would be playing havoc with those big Victorian skirts that graced the broad-grassed esplanade. A couple of kids are cycling the bikeway behind the dunes and the empty bowling greens beneath a cerulean sky. It's 9.30 a.m.

At the front of the pier, a pony-and-trap driver tells me he has been patiently awaiting punters for sixteen years. 'First came from Leicester at eight on holiday and always wanted to come back. I like animals and I've got room for them here. Got a dog, horses, rabbits.'

'Is this your only job?'

Bad question. Seaside workers live in fear of the tax inspector. If it had been an enclosed trap, the curtain would have come across.

'Can't be talking all day. Got to work.'

I look around and see there is no one within a couple of hundred yards. I take the hint and move on.

Facing the seafront there are some fine buildings such as the Empire with its neoclassical pomp and Doric columns, and the brick-domed Hippodrome where a water circus performs in one of the world's only three sunken circus rings. Other buildings are dressed in plasterwork scrolls, garlands and leaded cupolas. On the seashore side of the street, a knuckleduster of attractions wait for the lazy holiday-makers to rise: the Victorian Winter Gardens (now with a new children's play area), the pier, the Sea Life Centre and the fairground. The street provides a distracting trompe l'oeil to the cripplingly deprived economy that lurks behind – out of 44,000 households in the town, 11,000 reputedly get council tax benefit or home benefit. A Grade II-listed Georgian home in the centre (with planning permission for it to be converted into three residential units with a shop below), recently sold at auction for £16,000. Money, thankfully, is slowly starting its regeneration drip-feed and Great Yarmouth is now off its knees and staggering. A fund of £12 million is to be spent over the next three years on revitalising the seafront and historic town centre buildings.

Considering the gloomy statistics, the old town looks to be in surprisingly good shape. The River Yar, on its final leg from the Broads to the sea (thus Yar-mouth), provides a western border. Skirting it, alongside the container ships moored at South Quay, are a number of museums. Near by too there's an open-air market that has some of the finest chips you're likely to taste (though no fish, as an ancient bylaw prohibits the cooking of fried fish here). But the town's best feature is undoubtedly a pottery that doubles up as a museum, hidden away in Trinity Place beside the most complete section of the medieval walls.

My initial – and, as it turns out, correct – first impression is that The Great Yarmouth Potteries has been built from a shipwreck. The former herring curing works has been largely refashioned by current owners Ernie and Karen Child from the flotsam that washes up on the beaches and in the harbour. The entrance gate is made from a rudder, old masts are used as vertical beams, and the front door is made out of rope. Each has a history that Ernie is keen to recount. A shelf, decorated with a kettle stuffed with flowers, was apparently made from a 200-year-old ship's knee (angled support in the hold for supporting the hull) – 'You know that from the ash pinholes because they weren't using nails yet.'

Ernie, a large man with a ferocious handshake, was born and bred in Great Yarmouth. His family was one of the last to be rehoused from the Rows – the narrow medieval fishermen's alleys that had degenerated into slums. 'One of the alleys was just 27in wide – I swear I never saw the sun for the first five years of my life.'

Ernie, now aged 56, and Karen, 53, opened their pottery in January 1979 and they've been working 364 days a year ever since.

'One year he even had the kiln going on Christmas Day . . .' Karen starts raking over the coals of an old domestic dispute.

'Hang on. That's not fair. I was only trying to help because the cooker packed up and we had my daughter coming home for dinner,' Ernie protests, all innocence.

'He put the turkey in the kiln but the fat off it created a fire so it got incinerated.'

Next door, in the cottage the couple rent out, I'm introduced to a 1.25-ton oak trunk that Ernie found washed up in the harbour already carved into a crown depicting birds, fish, squirrel and cattle. The TV rests on another ship's knee, a diver's air tank has been converted into a lamp complete with dancing figurines, the floor is made from 2in-thick stripped masts, a window is a porthole, the 700-year-old door comes from a prison, and a 20ft rudder rises from the ground and passes through the upper floor to the roof.

Inside the pottery itself a family friend, John, is casting a vase, his trucker looks – swallow tattoo on his upper hand and T-R-U-E L-O-V-E running across the sierra of his knuckles – belying the delicacy of his touch. Ernie, meanwhile, is back painting another of his seascapes (he's a painter as well as a potter). I move on through the labyrinth to the 18th-century herring smoking chamber that Karen has converted into a museum. The smell of fish is overwhelming, despite the fact that the chamber ceased operating 37 years earlier. On the wall are several black-and-white photographs of Scottish girls who came down to do the poorly paid work of gutting the fish. 'They could do sixty herrings in a minute,' Karen informs me, full of admiration. Also on display are the tooth and hip bone of a mammoth, a whale head and Tudor rigging. All the exhibits were brought up in nets and donated by local fishermen or found on the beach by Ernie.

Karen and Ernie's home and workplace has the feel of having been created by the tide over centuries. The successive periods of the town – from the medieval walls that run at the rear of the pottery to the Georgian homes and Victorian and Edwardian seafront – are timelines too, no less than the rings on the requisitioned oak tree in the cottage.

A few miles south of Great Yarmouth, as I pass from Norfolk into Suffolk, a sign declares London to be 120 miles away. I head down the A12 and on to the B1127 to a campsite nestling behind dunes alongside the River Blyth in Southwold. To a north London boy it is familiar territory. A quick occasional dash at weekends has brought me here several times (and to Walberswick across the estuary).

I start my evening walk in the unreconstructed harbour, strolling beside the tar-black fishermen's sheds, wooden jetties and red-flagged marker buoys on the oozing mud banks. A battered old trawler on blocks is up for sale. Inland, sunshine falls like rain over grazing horses. At the mouth of the estuary, pounding waves are beating up the ebbing river, like a gang of muggers setting about schoolchildren as they exit the playground.

The modest town of Southwold, with its mastheads over doors and Dutch gables, nestles barely a whisper above the beach, its skyline broken only by a lighthouse and church tower. Below the dunes, sheltering in the trenches, are a line of two-storey clapboard holiday homes with names such as The Ark and The Shed. They lead me to a grassed headland peppered with Georgian and Victorian grand mansions guarded by a cannon pointing seaward. The greensward is known as Gun Hill, a place that has never quite got over the shock of witnessing the Dutch fleet firing on English ships in the bay on 28 May 1672. Around five hundred died on the *Royal James* alone that day, including the 24-stone Earl of Sandwich (it remains unclear who actually won the battle but it did augur Britain's era of supremacy at sea).

Suffolk's coastline is straight and flat with no coves and tight bays, no towering cliffs nor castles on unscalable crags. Like the rest of the towns gracing it, Southwold possesses a mood that's relaxed, gentle and prosperous. George Orwell, a Southwold boy, despaired of its precious- ness and gentility. Today it is a seaside town of vintage cars and vintage wines. I drink a pint of Adnams in the Sole Bay pub and then walk past the Adnams brewery opposite, the Adnams Wine Cellar and Kitchen Store, the Swan and the Crown hotels (both owned by Adnams), and Adnams Estate Agent (where a sign declares that caretakers and cleaners are urgently wanted).

On the northern side of town, I arrive at the new 623ft Southwold Pier, the first pier to be built in the country in 45 years. In 1987 Chris and Helen Iredale bought the stubbed cigarette butt that was all that was left of the original pier after a succession of storms had rendered it unusable. What remained was dismantled. The couple started with a clean slate in

1999 and it opened on 3 July 2001. What they created has majorly broken with the tradition of cheap and nasty tack. True, the original brick building on the promenade houses a small arcade but it's a very discrete affair with only one blood-and-guts machine modestly shielded from sensitive eyes by a curtain. It even has a traditional funfair section of clear-the-cans, darts and hook-a-duck.

The first of the five white-and-cream wooden pavilions is given over to a tea room and bar. This is followed by an exhibition on the history of piers and the advent of seaside holidays (where I learn that mixed bathing was not permitted in the resort until 1902 and even then male and female bathing machines had to be kept a minimum of twenty yards apart and the occupants dressed from neck to knee). Further along the pier an eccentric clock has been built from an old hot-water cylinder and other scrap metal.

But its best feature is undoubtedly the Under-The-Pier Pavilion, whose exhibits – sorry, amusements – should by rights be gracing a museum of contemporary arts somewhere. One item, the £1 Micro Break, provides an armchair rocking gently to Hawaiian music on a requisitioned Sega Space Harrier base in front of which an old-fashioned TV screen promises for just £1 a 'Fast Efficient Holiday – Total relaxation never leaving your chair. No risk deep vein thrombosis. Perfect for busy executives – entire trip only takes three minutes.'

All the amusements seem to gently mock the Londoners who have bought up whatever Adnams didn't want in town. Instant Weight Loss Laboratoire Hunkin, once lubricated by an appropriate coin, provides a freshly cooked grain of corn guaranteed to make you slimmer with its weight-free nutrients (the proof of the weight loss is there in the body-distorting mirror). There's a Gene Forecaster, where for a measly 60p and a lock of your hair as DNA sample, you get a 3D readout of your future rather than the arcane mumblings of some Madame Rosa. My favourite machine, however, is the £2 Bathyscape, Epic Underwater North Sea Adventure in which I'm promised the opportunity to 'Discover Robert Maxwell. Be disgusted by raw sewage. Witness canisters of nuclear waste mating.'

As I emerge from the bathysphere, its inventor, Tim Hunkin, is fixing a glitch in the Expressive Photobooth that is preventing it from blowing air at its occupants to provoke different reactions that are then captured on film. I ask him if he's thinking of opening similar attractions at other resorts.

'Don't think they'd work anywhere else. The humour only works here in Southwold. If it was in Southend, everything would be trashed!'

It's now 8 p.m. Under the pier a group of five kids are swimming in wet suits (I've noticed a distinct increase in wet suits since hitting the more affluent Norfolk and Suffolk beaches) and whooping through the white fizz of surf. People sit and read in their beach huts while the sun gilds the peaks of cloud like dawn creeping over the snow-capped Himalayas.

Back on Gun Hill a family are excitedly unloading their car and dragging stuff into their holiday home. Southwold is a resort for Londoners who have no need of amusements or excitement – they come seeking merely beauty, a beach, the breeze, the marram grass, a few pubs . . . clothes shops selling Ghost and D&G, bistros, a specialist cheese shop, a hair salon, tea rooms, groovy gastro pubs, art galleries, letting agencies, bookshops and an organic food shop.

The next morning I stroll back through the colour-washed town, where all the shops are already doing a brisk trade. In the window of Jenny Jones Estate Agents a beach hut is advertised for £21,500. I pop inside to learn more.

'It's on the north end, which is why it's going so cheap,' Adrian Smith explains. I almost roar with laughter, but manage to control myself. 'Last year we sold one below Gun Hill for twice that.' Again I manage to muzzle myself. Adrian is not shocked by the prices – after all, a two–up, two–down will sell in Southwold for £225,000. He does, however, admit to a momentary sharp intake of breath when a mid-terrace fisherman's cottage sold for £470,000 a month back. 'Mind you, it did have three bedrooms.'

Adrian claims that 90 per cent of all property purchases are by people from London, Essex, Herts or Bucks.

'How much would a Georgian home in the Gun Hill area go for?'

'One million plus.'

I think back to the Grade-II Georgian in Great Yarmouth, ten miles away, that went at auction for £16,000 recently. There are clearly plenty of people with money along this coast. Between Southwold and Aldeburgh, Emma Freud, Clement Freud, Rowan Atkinson, Richard Curtis (of *Blackadder* and *Notting Hill* fame) and Caroline Quentin are just a handful of the celebs who own property.

Sid and I make our way along the shivering sea to Walberswick, which I'd visited twice the year before with my family, lured as much by its ice cream as its fabulous sandy beach. My son Max managed three that hot summer day, in between swimming with the dog and lazing in the dunes.

Walberswick has a couple of pubs, where you wait an hour to get average food, and a sprinkling of teahouse cafés. On the village green today, a troupe of morris dancers who've never grown up are skipping in pinnies, yellow socks and dingle-dangle bells to a squeeze-box player who looks like Rolf Harris. A minor fug settles on me when I discover that the little café beside the green has stopped selling our favourite ice cream. I turn for solace to the downy sand of the tilting beach behind the dunes. Kids are riding waves and dogs zipping about chasing balls, while more sedentary bodies slowly roast and turn behind windbreaks.

From Walberswick the B1125 skips like a morris dancer past the old-fashioned petrol stations, topiary, signs warning of rogue deer and neat village greens that are the emblems of rural Suffolk.

My next port of call is Thorpeness. Constructed by Glencairn Stuart Ogilvie in the early 20th century as a pioneer holiday village, it consists of scattered homes and tennis courts, a cricket green, riding stables and a 65-acre lake themed on the tale of Peter Pan. The owners of the fantasy home known as The House In The Clouds, which is perched on top of a water tower, definitely have the best view of all. But most of the other denizens – many of whose families have been returning for four generations – don't do too badly either, shacked up in mock-Tudor, Jacobean and traditional 18th-century tarred weatherboard just a slingshot from the beach.

Down at the Meare families are hiring boats from a muscular man with close-cropped hair and earrings. Craig Block, sporting faded jeans and a gallery of tattoos, became boatman when his father died of a stroke at the age of 61. 'If someone else had taken the job, Mum would have been kicked out of the boathouse cottage,' he says by way of explaining his serendipitous career. That was thirteen years ago and Craig is still ensconced, though his mother now lives in one of the estate's almshouses.

His only challenge these days comes from 'pissed-up City boys who think it would be fun to take a boat out in the dark after the pub shuts'. Craig gives them time to get out on the lake before he lets his Alsatian out. 'It sounds like the Hound of the Baskervilles and scares the shit out of 'em.' He then shines his high-powered torch on the pirate boat. 'They jump ship, wade out of the Meare and leap over the fence, legging it home. Works a treat every time.'

When Craig was growing up in the village, the school bus used to creak getting all the kids on before ferrying them to the secondary school at Leiston. 'Now I think four get picked up.' Craig claims that only twenty of the town's three hundred homes belong to people who were born into them and still live here all year round.

'You can't go down your local and have a chat because there are no locals. Lights go out in September and don't come back on till Christmas briefly and then Easter. It's a holiday village really.' Craig has forgotten that a holiday village was exactly Ogilvie's original intention.

When I pull into Aldeburgh, the fourth ace in the Suffolk coast pack, it appears to be enjoying the rosiest days it has known. The high street bristles with stylish kitchenware shops, designer bathroom emporiums, art galleries, a theatre/cinema, restaurants and tea houses for its relocated London luvvies. Of course, the modern heyday will be short-lived; mere braggadocio until the roar of the sea muffles it. Behind the chi-chi shops stands the Moot Hall (erected 1520), which three hundred years ago had three streets between it and the North Sea but is now next up on the sea's menu.

The Hall is a gingerbread house of chevron brick and flint, oak beams and leaded windows, topped by a twisting brick chimney. Sitting in an alcove, out of the wind, an elderly couple are warming their bones in the sun.

Doris Ling is one of those rare birds who was actually born here; one of thirteen children shoe-horned into a small fisherman's cottage at the impoverished Slaughden end (now decidedly upmarket).

'When I was a young girl, the shops sold nails, chamberpots and pans. Now it's aromatherapy, art, Indian head massages and car valeting,' Doris drily observes. Her husband, snuggled up alongside her, was born half a dozen miles inland at Snape, 81 years ago. 'Bob's my toy boy, as I'm 84,' she giggles.

Her toy boy points to the pavilion behind us. 'That's where we did our canoodling. Met at a dance and I asked her how old she was and she said she was eighteen so I said I was too. I was fifteen really.' They married a week after Bob became eighteen.

Bob started work at the Snape Maltings brewery in 1938. Once the pair had two children to support, Doris found herself holding down several jobs at once: domestic cleaner, working in the kitchens at the local school and delivering newspapers with Bob on Sundays.

When the railway station closed in 1965 and the brewery went with it, Bob and Doris became roving gravediggers. The pair often dug as many as three graves in a day and there was invariably a lot of travelling between them, criss-crossing Britain's second-largest county.

'We often slept in our Commer van in the actual graveyards.' Doris sighs nostalgically. 'Loved that. Best job we ever did. When people are grieving they don't talk about pillows or curtains. You get the real them before the mask comes back. And we used to make it so nice for them.'

Bob adds the practical details. 'We kept all the grave boards, grass mats, shovel, picks and forks in the van so sometimes you'd get a nasty shock when you rolled over in bed at night.'

'What were the grass mats for?' I ask.

'Once you'd dug the pit six foot six deep and about the same length . . .'

'. . . And don't forget it had to be tapered and shaped to take the coffin,' Doris interrupts. 'Bob was really good at that.'

'. . . well, then you'd put the grave boards round the sides and the grass mats at the bottom to make it nice and neat for the coffin to go in.'

After five years, however, the pair were offered a milk round and Bob, fantasising about 'women in lingerie inviting me into their kitchens', took it. The reality, according to Bob, was 'flannelette jim-jams and no invitations'. His disappointment was compounded by the fact that few of his customers felt the need actually to pay for their milk. The couple jacked it in and temporarily returned to gravedigging before they got jobs back at Snape Maltings, which by then had become a major international concert venue under Benjamin Britten and Peter Pears. 'In one month we went from the bottom of the grave to talking to John Williams and Julian Bream.'

'Bob still returns in the summer three times a week to conduct tours round the backstage,' Doris says. 'It was a really good life but not as good as the graves.'

*

It is early evening by the time I resume my walk through town and stop
off for a pint on the terrace of the Cross Keys, where I eavesdrop on two
South Africans and two Aussies discussing kite surfing and Cambodia. I
then pick up the best haddock yet at Aldeburgh Fish & Chips and eat on
the hoof, strolling beneath a silhouetted roofscape and singed clouds.

Back beside the beach yellow-horned poppies sprout on the shingle
and in equally small clusters the healthy, wealthy teenage sons and
daughters of second-homers are meeting up with their bottles of cider
and roll-ups. Parents, meanwhile, swing wide their french windows to
dine or drink within sniffing distance of the sea. It could be the Continent
if it weren't so English.

Further up the beach ten women in their thirties and early forties sit
behind a redundant windbreak (there isn't a breath tonight) playing an
alphabet game of song lines. The first woman starts by singing 'All you
need is love . . .' The second storms into 'Born to be wiiiild.' 'California
dreaming . . .', 'My, my, my Delilah . . .', 'Evergreen – I can't remember
the words', 'Fa fafa fafa fafa fafa, fa fafa fafa fafa fa . . .', 'Good Golly Miss
Molly' and 'Hi-Ho Silver Lining' follow in quick succession before the
ninth member falters and fails. By now I'm hooked on the game and
almost join in with either The Troggs' 'I Can't Control Myself' or Dr
John's 'Iko Iko'. The gulls too offer suggestions but the woman is already
taking her punishment – a full tumbler of wine down in one. Near by a
father-and-son team are skimming stones, hanging out, chewing the fat.
If I had a spare, very large wad of money, I would join these second-
homers tomorrow.

I head further up the beach, sit on the shingle near the campsite and
scribble a few notes. When you write, you're alone with the illusion that
you're not. Pebbles washed by the waves crackle on the shingle bank like
firecrackers. Waves of oceanic yearning churn inside me – a feeling that
has ebbed and flowed through my life. A desire to be joined up and part
of things, rather than passing through. I think about my journey. Too
many people, too many roads, too many places, an island too dense. I
write it in my notebook and then immediately realise the absurdity of
what I've written as I raise my head and look along the miles of empty
beach. One beach to yourself is surely enough for anybody. We live in
greedy times. One of anything is never enough. Greed in love, greed in
sex, greed in marriage, greed in the number of homes we need, greed in

holidays, in friends, in possessions. Filling up. More bigger snacks now. The question, of course, is are we left feeling satisfied? We can only live under one sky and have one sea to slip into. It seems to me that opening up, trusting and sharing is considerably more difficult than simply collecting. It's something I'm not very good at. Earlier tonight Susanna had rung to tell me how brilliantly Max had done in his school report. I mark my own, 'Must try harder.'

I return to Sid, illuminated by the mushroom lights of the campsite but sitting in the inner gloom of his own inanimate darkness. Tonight, for the first time on the trip, I have been bitten by mossies.

There is something of the Swallows and Amazons about Essex's placenames – Dengie, Brightlingsea, Burnham-on-Crouch – and its rivers and creeks, like Blackwater and Hamford Water. I have skirted the estuaries of the Rivers Orwell and Stour and slipped across a land sieved by dykes and streams (and further irrigated by sprinklers performing the demented water dance of the banshee) when the road peters out at Walton-on-the-Naze.

The small town first grew into a resort in the 1830s when it became known for its sea holly, whose candied roots were sold as an aphrodisiac. Today it is an instantly forgettable place with a phalanx of equally unremarkable bookies, launderettes, discount stores, takeaways, pubs, chemists and burnt-out beach huts.

On its outskirts I bump my way along a dirt track through an industrial estate to a foundry jetty in the back of beyond where I join eleven other passengers on the *Karina* for a trip through the backwaters.

The fishing boat pulls out into a channel beyond which a forest of masts thrusts skyward from an adjacent creek. The 21ft, 28-year-old fibreglass boat has a heavy metal tiller that would spin the boat round and round, spewing its contents into the drink, if it were not being held firmly by skipper Tony Haggis. Tony is a gangly man with cascading tight curls, a tanned face, blue whale T-shirt and Tibetan bracelets. He looks to be in his thirties but is in fact 51.

For 32 years Tony – Walton born and bred – fished the backwaters and North Sea for dogfish, bass and cod before a back injury forced him to take up a gentler mariner's life running boat trips. Three of his four brothers still fish full-time, like their father before them (the only family in Walton still doing it) but Tony is clearly as happy as Larry operating his wildlife boat trips.

'When I was in the sea cadets as a young boy, some dignitary handing out certificates asked me what I wanted to do when I grew up. He was using a microphone at the time and when I replied, 'Bird watching' everybody in the audience laughed. Well, the laugh's on them. I got my wish.'

Tony predicts that out on the backwaters we'll probably see avocets and little terns, possibly marsh harriers and almost certainly seals. At the moment, however, all I can spot are the tall necks of cranes grazing the Essex savannah across the estuary in Felixstowe.

Having lost sight of the jetty, we enter muddied waters that lead to the blazing strand of soft sand at Stone Point. 'We've seven thousand acres of backwater,' Tony tells the group, 'but Stone Point is the only place you're allowed to land on the SSSI nature reserve.' A couple of boats have availed themselves of the opportunity, moored in the channel and rowed ashore. One man is flying a kite while his son builds an elaborate sand fortification.

Rounding a bend we arrive at the north end of Horsey (the largest island) whose owner, Joe Backhouse, breeds racehorses. The water in the channel is so iridescent, it seems to be underlit. We follow the sun across wind-whipped waves up Oakley Creek. Out on the saltings the samphire is ripe for picking and the banks covered in sea lavender and 2ft-tall sea asters. A host of waders are daintily high-stepping the mud banks, while overhead a little egret flits like a wind-blown snowflake. Suddenly a whiskered seal pup pops up next to the boat. Onshore two more seals stretch out, tails pointing heavenward, regulating their body heat. The kids on board go mad.

'Don't point at them or they'll disappear,' Tony warns. 'God knows why they hate pointing fingers, but they do.' Maybe it's a race memory of rifle culls.

As we continue our tour, I discover that fisherman and boat trips are not the only entries on Tony's CV. In the mid-1980s he was the skipper on Radio Caroline's *Ross Revenge*, a 1,000-ton trawler, anchored fifteen miles offshore from Walton. Tony also did stints as a volunteer on Greenpeace's ocean-going tug *Solo* and has spent a good deal of time travelling. Once winter comes and no one wants to come out on the creeks, he takes off for India, Tunisia or Morocco. He claims, however, that he's never happier than when he gets back to the backwaters and Walton.

'The town went to sleep in the seventies and I doubt it will ever wake up. But at least it isn't Frinton.' When Richard Harris was shooting *The Snow Goose* on the backwaters – they thought it looked like Dunkirk, for some reason – one boozy night he came out with the line, 'Harwich for the Continent, Frinton for the incontinent.' Walton's neighbours have never lived it down.

Frinton doesn't look too geriatric as I drive the esplanade that links it to Walton. Tonight its staid and sedated image is being challenged by expensively dressed roaming pubescent teenagers flirting and finding hideaway places to do things they're not meant to.

The town is as far away spiritually from Walton-on-the-Naze as the River Dart is from the River Mersey: a one-off in which Essex's well-heeled inhabit leafy mansions on a grid of avenues leading to Art Deco apartment blocks gracing a broad clifftop grassland called the Greensward. The local militia selflessly battle to maintain the town's elegant and genteel air; to keep things carefully planned and regulated. Recently, however, they have had to concede defeat to a fish and chip shop and a pub that finally obtained permission to open in town. The tone the seniors would rather see followed is that set by First Avenue with its tennis and golf clubs at one end and the cricket club at the other. The current generation rushing to adulthood, however, prefers the chippy and pub: the boys dressed in surfer pants whose backsides thoughtfully sweep the pavements behind them; the girls dressed in long blonde hair and little else.

Frinton's high street retains a feel of the 1950s despite the gourmet foods, tanning studio, nail bar and stylish cafés. As usual, I eschew the trendier restaurants for the local Indian. I then toy with the idea of parking up for the night on the esplanade but know the signs warning against overnighting are serious and that to do so here would be to risk marauding citizenry setting about me with meat cleavers at worst or the constabulary disturbing my sleep at best. Instead I pull into a lay-by off the B1032, halfway to Clacton.

*

Clacton is wiping the sleep from its eyes when I pull in on its seafront. Across the Thames Estuary there is no sign yet of Kent.

The town has none of Frinton's style or pretension. It is garlanded with iron pawn-broker lamp posts and has a necklace of gardens, a long shingle-and-sand beach and a fat, though not overduly long, pier. And that's it. Behind the shorefront ugly shops are hidden like unwanted carbuncles. Clacton is as uninspiring and run-down as Morecambe but, unlike the latter, is not on the cusp of recovery; its only current claim to fame is that it was recently ranked 'Top for totty' by the *Alternative Beach Guide*.

I settle down at a café and watch the early arrivals to the beach. A sprinkling of families are setting up camp while bin men trap rogue ice-cream wrappers between the claws of their mechanical prongs.

Clacton takes its name from a Saxon chieftain. It has existed since 1050 and doesn't look as if it's had a lick of paint since. By the 1980s its traditional holiday-makers had dumped it for Spain, local industry had died and even Butlin's had abandoned it. Today the only sign of new life is the £35 million privately owned Clacton Factory Shopping Village and some light industry on the shoulder of town that's providing employment for the new housing estates accommodating relocating East Enders.

Down on the pier the rides are still sleeping, though a few fishermen have paid £4 for their day permit and are trying their luck dangling lines in their arcane ritual. I notice many of the planks have been replaced. For a moment I wonder whether they're finally making a start. Then I notice Clacton's crown jewels, the Victorian Theatre, still crumbling inside its Tardislike casing (it closed in 1964) at the end of the jetty.

Opposite the pier, on Marine Parade East, stands the dilapidated, once-gracious Royal Hotel, with a couple of grotty bars but otherwise boarded up. Beyond the Royal the town puffs its way up the hill, exhausted and ready for the knacker's yard. Dustcarts rumble through the street. They should sweep the lot away. The pallid faces of the inhabitants remind me of the shock I experienced returning after a year travelling Asia when I encountered the pasty grimness of my race at Victoria station.

Rasputin's Vodka Bar, crackling amusement arcades and karaoke lead me to the closed TIC (it's moved from its prominent easy-to-find position to a Portakabin somewhere in the back of beyond, where it's almost certainly cheaper to operate as no one will find it). At the Castle restaurant seniors can get a Sunday roast any day of the week up to 7.30 p.m. for £3.95. Beyond it a scrum of awfulness hunkers: Woolworth's, Tesco, Coral, McDonald's, Dixons, Argos ('Final Clearance Sale'), Swagman Souvenirs and Gifts ('Closing Down All Items Must Go'), and Thing-Me-Bobs ('No children unless accompanied by an adult'). The Folkestone, Scarborough and Great Yarmouth makeover is not happening here.

I head back to Sid, passing the trembling leaves of the aspen in the Sensory Garden, their white underbellies reputedly shaking with fear for having provided the wood for Christ's cross. To 'tremble like an aspen' was an old saying. I feel pretty much that way having witnessed the horror of Clacton.

The coast road staggers drunkenly out of town. Fifteen minutes later a rabbit, dragging ruined back legs, emerges from a hedge and commits suicide under my juggernaut. I try to avoid it but instantly feel the slight rise and flattening crunch beneath the motorhome, rather like a small burp.

The road narrows on the rural stretches and then fattens for the feeding frenzy of suburbs and commuter villages. In Colchester I enter an insane series of back-to-back roundabouts and, as I do, make up new lyrics to that awful sixties song 'England Swings':

> En-ger-land swings like a hung man do,
> Superstores and roundabouts two by two
> Sliproads and slipknots and bodybags too
> The roads of En-ger-land will strangle you too.

Probably not a hit and I don't really expect a call from the Queen if Andrew Motion pops his laureate clogs. Nevertheless, I can imagine it going down a storm in foreign-language schools. I decide to call it 'Sid's Song' as a homage to my faithful, ever-reliable charabanc.

Sid, unmoved by both the rabbit's demise and my gusty rendition, edges round the next major estuary, the River Colne, before slipping down the B1025 and across a causeway that's still soaking from the last tidal inundation.

The island of Mersea is a weird place. Where the road ends beyond the small town of West Mersea, brent geese zip across big Constable skies. The old staithes of oyster beds rot on the mud flats beside beached boats in a watery jigsaw cut by the River Blackwater and the Strood and Chalcott channels. Even on dry land the experience tends to be somewhat hallucinatory. The finest meal in town (recommended by Rick Stein – he gets everywhere) is to be found in a beaten-up weatherboard shack known as the Company Shed, where the owners provide the local oysters and fresh fish and you bring your own wine.

What little action there is in town is concentrated on the village green where the local museum (shut), a pub, the Art Café, and the squat church of St Peter and St Paul perch. Inside the latter I have another slightly unhinging experience. As I stand admiring the arched and moulded trusses of the 16th-century timber roof in the chancel, I feel someone or something crowding me from above. I slowly raise my eyes and discover Jesus staring down into my eyes from a suspended cross. Despite my evangelical atheism, I give way to an involuntary shiver. On the wall a medallion declares 'Now we know that God heareth not sinners' (John chapter 9, verse 31). Close shave.

As I leave the church, I spot another message ornately written by hand. 'Whosoever thou art dost enter this Parish Church, remember that this is Holy Ground. More than a thousand years have passed since first upon this spot men worshipped God. Beneath these stones rests the dust of some of England's dead. Walk softly. If thou must speak, do so in reverent tones, lest perchance thou disturbest angels praying here . . .'

As I say, weird place this Mersea. Passing decaying 18th-century brick tombs, I head across to the Art Café for lunch, and in doing so almost get run over by an elderly man in a blazer driving a motorised tricycle. The café has been open only six weeks. Inside, a silver-haired man called Simon is selling acrylic paint to a lady while her toddler pulls sketch pads and brushes over the floor. She doesn't bat an eye, but Simon does.

Armed with a chicken, bacon and mayo baguette, I move back outside to a pavement table. Soon the painfully thin Simon emerges with his colleague James to view artwork. It is the fifth batch of canvasses they've had in this morning to look at. Cork Street is probably shaking in its boots.

Simon and James and their two partners own and run the business. Simon is a writer and painter and James is also a painter, though a more successful one. James's wife Maggie runs the food and drink side of the operation and Simon's fiancée, Annette Bell, helps out when she's not running the bookshop up the street.

James Weaver, aged forty, was born on the island and is clearly proud of the fact. 'It's a backwater in all senses,' he tells me. 'At the moment they're reinforcing the causeway but no one wants it done. We like being cut off at high tide. We like the siege mentality.'

As a schoolboy in Colchester, James says he always knew he was home when he crossed the Strood and smelt the ozone. 'It was like an invisible curtain you passed through from the mainland.' His son apparently feels the same way today. 'There's a legend of a Roman legion getting caught out there and you can still hear them howling when the weather's bad.'

James's father, who used to drive the bus to Colchester, continues to cook sprats on a bunsen burner in his shed and wash them down with the local white wine. When he used to drive the bus, if he was late rising, someone else would drive the passengers round to his house for him.

'Everyone knows everyone and it's still a tight community,' according to James. 'We've still got our post office and library; we've got proper shops, a vineyard and not one amusement arcade! It's special.'

I leave Britain's most easterly inhabited island and continue to squiggle my way along the desiccated estuarine coast of sea walls, nature reserves, idiosyncratic seaside resorts, saltings, hummocks of grassland, causeways, piers and expansive esplanades. An out-on-limbs place, an end-of-the-line place, a stitches-that-slip-off-the-needles place.

On the stubbed thumb of the next sea-sculpted outpost, I visit Burnham-on-Crouch. Like Mersea, Walton-on-the-Naze and Frinton, it is a town you have to decide to visit, for it is not somewhere you pass through en route to somewhere else. The pretty high street is a medley of handsome Georgian homes, white weatherboard fishermen's cottages and an eccentric clock tower the pavement has to duck beneath.

The town is home to no less than four sailing clubs. The Royal Corinthian Yacht Club (RCYC), the Royal Burnham Yacht Club and the Crouch Yacht Club were originally 'gentlemen's' clubs that would not countenance commoners in the boat-building professions as members. So in 1930 the Burnham Sailing Club (BSC) was founded to cater for the builders, riggers and sail-makers who liked to race on early closing Wednesday afternoons. It took until the 1970s before the Joint Clubs Committee admitted the grubby BSC and allowed its members to compete in the annual Burnham Week regatta.

The present club house of the venerable RCYC (founded in 1872) opened in 1931 with a radical new policy that actually permitted female membership. Only a secretary inhabits the large white building on the banks of the River Crouch today. I fire off a couple of questions about the club but unfortunately she knows nothing so she makes a call and then, returning the phone to its cradle, smiles and tells me, 'Our ex-commodore – and the first female one at that – says she'll be down in five minutes. She only lives round the corner and she's always happy to talk about the club.'

While I wait I wander the ground-floor bar area with its half-barrel chairs, Thames Estuary table charts, and broad glass frontage on to the river. Out on the narrow estuary, halyards strum tunelessly but reasonably contentedly. A shag sits sentry on the jetty, staring across to the far oyster beds. I strum my own fingers and wander some more. A sign on the club noticeboard advertises the sale of the *Corinthia* for £1,200. There are pictures of the previous four club houses, and the evolution of the current Grade II-listed home. There are paintings of yachts in storms, a list of previous commodores, and photographs of a recent cadets' award ceremony. After ten minutes I hear the door open and the patter of delicate feet unlikely to belong to an obese pink-gin-guzzling retired admiral.

The gamine Wendy Eagling has short hair and is dressed in a striped sweater, culottes, sandals and a welcoming smile. 'It's very quiet today,' she announces after shaking my hand, 'but if you were here in a month you wouldn't be able to move – the last week of August is when we have our big regatta.'

Burnham Week concludes the season's racing calendar. In the old days members would set off for the first regatta along the south coast and work their way through Cowes and the rest before returning to Burnham. It still marks the end of the main sailing season but most members now have smaller boats and transport them on trailers by road for the weekend regattas.

Wendy, a former schoolteacher, signals for me to join her at a table overlooking the pitching boats. I do as I'm bid and simultaneously ask if Burnham Week is the only time the club gets busy.

'God no. It's busy every weekend and on our regular Wednesday night sailing evening. It's just changed a lot, that's all.'

'In what way?'

'I'd say that today it's actually closer to the original philosophy of a truly amateur boating club – that's why they called it Corinthian. In the 19th century sailing was very much a rich man's sport and most owners paid crews to do the sailing for them, but our club was formed by men who wanted to helm themselves. Today the big difference is that our membership comes from all walks, not just the privileged classes. And of course we have children and women – heaven forbid! It's far more family oriented and less formal. The old members would turn in their graves if they saw the chaos on a Sunday!'

They'd probably have a heart attack too seeing a woman as commodore. When Wendy joined in 1963, lunch was still served in the dining room and it was all very pukka and formal. She admits to having been totally in awe of elected flag officers. To mark their status the officers have special flags, which tell their position in the pecking order. 'You can spot the difference easily because the rear commodore's flag has two balls on the lower edge, the vice-commodore has one ball and the commodore has no balls at all, which in my case was most apt and everyone enjoyed telling me so.' Nowadays, she claims, there is absolutely no pomp attached to any of the posts.

I notice Wendy is constantly glancing out to the river, clearly keen to get a boat out and enjoy the fine weather and stiff breeze.

'Is it a difficult river to sail?' I ask.

'Unforgiving. That's the word. Very strong tidal conditions and tricky until you know its moods – that's why we get the kids to do all their training on inland gravel pits before we let them out on it. It's a rite of passage when they get out on the Crouch.'

Wendy has another appointment in Frinton but walks me round the boatyard before heading off. She points out the club's signature boats, known as Dragons and based on an original 1928 design by Johan Anker, a Norwegian naval architect. 'They have a considerable pedigree and are much coveted by members.' Her finger then pans twenty degrees to a couple of sleek white racing yachts. 'Hand-built wooden jobs but unfortunately they cost around £40,000 so you need pots of money to afford them.'

And with that, Wendy's off, leaving me to return to the pedestrianised quayside and the collisions of jetties, alleys, squares, canted boats, cranes, homes and two girls beside the war memorial trying to master the hip-swinging agility required to make hula hoops defy gravity. The last time I saw anyone with a hula hoop was my own knee-high children failing abysmally in our old Cricklewood garden. An old barge is for sale and I make a note of the number but never ring. A path leads me past the Star Inn behind the quay wall and in quick succession a lawnmower shop, a Thai restaurant, the Cabin Dairy Tea Rooms, a bicycle shop, Dengie Shellfish, and Cine Rio (a 1931 classic Art Deco cinema). Burnham-on-Crouch is as good at what it does as Clacton is bad.

I am keen to visit Foulness, to sample the indescribable loathsomeness promised by its name. Unfortunately I make two discoveries, which erase it from my itinerary: first, the derivation relates to a promontory of birds rather than purgatory; second, it's owned by the MOD and closed to the public.

And so I arrive at my final port of call, praying that Southend will continue the uplift of West Mersea and Burnham after the nadir of Clacton. Southend and Clacton are, in fact, very similar in terms of history and eclipse but while the latter continues to freefall, the former appears to be on the up. It is around 8 p.m. when I drive along the front that links the resort to Shoeburyness. Families are scrambling out of inflatables and younger kids chasing gulls. On the grassy foreshore a football coaching session is in progress and up ahead fairylights are chasing each other around Southend's seafront attractions.

In the revitalised funkier part of town round Market Place, the indefatigable stylists in Grateful Heads are sculpting preposterous hairstyles and at neighbouring café terraces the town's more stylish denizens are drinking and eating alfresco. Two hundred yards away the still resplendent Regency terrace of guesthouses and hotels on Royal Terrace looks longingly to sea just as Emma Hamilton once did seeking her Horatio. Beneath the belvedere hunkers the fairground, the skinny pier and the racetrack of multi-coloured neon.

Southend looks the part right down to the couples snogging and pressing their bodies into each other on the prom as if trying to get out the other side. Two girls blow on chips and gingerly pop them in their mouths before huffing and puffing and hopping from high heel to high heel in the process, almost tumbling in their ultra-tight micro skirts. Outside the restored red-domed Kursaal, hair-gelled boys await their dates. A succession of motorbikes and the spinning wheels of car cowboys cruise the electric avenue. I head back to Sid, parked on the prom, and turn the lights out for the last time.

At 2 a.m. something wakes me and I pull back the curtains and peer out. Along the seafront neon is still rushing excitedly out of the amusement arcades, spraying coloured light like plumes of rain from car tyres.

The next morning I wake to a Southend drenched in real rain. By the time I get down to the longest pier in the world, the rain has stopped and the sun is trying to find a way through the curtaining clouds. A gloomy day has been a rarity over the past two months but is perhaps appropriate today as I bring my own curtain down.

For eight weeks I've woken mostly to sunshine and the sound of lapping waves. The waves greet me again today as I set out on a final 1.3 miles to add to the 2,800 I've already travelled, tracking England's coast. Under a white sky, buffeted by a blustery wind, I walk the soaked planks and think of England. What on earth made someone build a pier more than a mile long out into the Thames Estuary? Englishness. I leave the fairground's contortions of twisting blue coaster tracks behind and walk until I can walk no more. Where the pier finally ends, with consummate timing, the sun breaks through and there, almost within touching distance across the refulgent estuary, stand Sheerness's cranes pecking over the start of my journey.

Addendum

For further information on the Swift range of motorhomes, log on to www.swiftmotorhomes.co.uk, email enquiry@swiftleisure.co.uk or telephone 01482 847332.

Further information on the coast is available on www.visitengland.com or by ringing the brochure line on 0845 456 3456.

For help on overnight sites, contact British Holiday & Home Parks Association on www.ukparks.com, email enquiries@bhhpa.org.uk or telephone 01452 526911.

Bibliography

AA Book of the Seaside. Drive Publications, 1972.

Bennett, Peter. *A Century of Fun*. Blackpool Pleasure Beach, 1996.

Cosgrove, Denis and Daniels, Stephen (eds). *The Iconography of Landscape*. Cambridge University Press, 2002.

Dickens, Charles. *Great Expectations*. Penguin Popular Classics, 1994.

Dickens, Charles. *Little Dorrit*. Penguin Classics, 1998.

Fortey, Richard. *The Hidden Landscape*. Pimlico, 1993.

Fowles, John. *The French Lieutenant's Woman*. Vintage, 1996.

Gale, Alison. *Britain's Historic Coast*. Tempus, 2000.

Greene, Graham. *Brighton Rock*. Vintage Classics, 2002.

Greenpeace. *Coastline: Britain's Threatened Heritage*. Kingfisher Books, 1987.

Haggard, Rider. *Rural England. Vol. 1*. Longman, 1902.

Hoskins, W G. *The Making of the English Landscape*. Penguin, 1985.

Jarman, Derek. *Derek Jarman's Garden*. Text by Philippa Lewis, photographs Hulton Getty Collection. Thames & Hudson, 1995.

Pynchon, Thomas. *Mason & Dixon*. Vintage, 1998.

Reader's Digest. *Illustrated Guide to Britain's Coast*. Reader's Digest, 1996.

Richardson, Nigel. *Breakfast in Brighton*. Victor Gollancz, 1998.

Robinson, Cedric. *Forty Years on Morecambe Bay*. Great Northern Books, 2003.

Rose, June. *Marie Stopes and the Sexual Revolution*. Faber & Faber, 1993.

Small, Ken. *The Forgotten Dead*. Bloomsbury, 1989.

Recollections from the Past: British Coastal Life – a Photographic Record. Parkgate Books, 1997.

Varlow, Sally. *A Reader's Guide to Writer's Britain*. English Tourist Board, 1996.

Williams, Derek. *Romans & Barbarians*. St Martin's Press, 1996.

Index

283